# Reflections on the Puritan Revolution

*Books by A. L. Rowse*

Milton the Puritan

*Elizabethan*

The England of Elizabeth I
The Expansion of Elizabethan England
The Elizabethan Renaissance: (1) The Life of the Society;
  (2) The Cultural Achievement
Christopher Marlowe
Ralegh and the Throckmortons
Sir Richard Grenville of the *Revenge*
The Elizabethans and America
Simon Forman: Sex and Society in Shakespeare's Age

*Shakespeare*

Shakespeare the Man
Shakespeare's Sonnets: a modern edition,
  with Introduction and prose versions
Prefaces to Shakespeare's Plays
The Poems of Shakespeare's Dark Lady: edited
  with Introduction
Shakespeare's Self-Portrait
Shakespeare's Characters: a Complete Guide

*Modern*

Memories of Men and Women
Glimpses of the Great
Froude the Historian
Matthew Arnold: Poet and Prophet
Jonathan Swift: Major Prophet
The Early Churchills
The Later Churchills

A Life: Collected Poems

# Reflections on
# the Puritan Revolution

A. L. ROWSE

*The Rabble now such Freedom
did enjoy
As winds at sea, that use it to
destroy.*

*Dryden*

METHUEN

First published in Great Britain 1986
by Methuen London Ltd
11 New Fetter Lane, London EC4P 4EE

Copyright © 1986 A.L. Rowse

The extracts from 'Little Gidding'
from *Four Quartets* by T.S. Eliot
are reproduced by kind permission
of Faber and Faber Ltd.

Printed in Great Britain

British Library Cataloguing in Publication Data

Rowse, A.L.
  Reflections on the Puritan Revolution.
  1. Arts — Political aspects — England
  — History — 17th century    2. Arts, English
  3. Great Britain — Politics and
  government — 1642-1660
  I. Title
  700'.942      NXS43

  ISBN 0-413-40880-9

# To Roy Strong

*Historian of Art*

# Contents

|  |  | *Page* |
|---|---|---|
|  | Preface |  |
|  | Revolution | I |
| I | The Attack on the Cathedrals | 5 |
| II | Colleges, Chapels, Parish Churches | 41 |
| III | Palaces, Castles, Mansions | 66 |
| IV | Works of Art | 87 |
| V | Music and Theatre | 115 |
| VI | Poets and Persons | 151 |
| VII | Ideology | 194 |
| VIII | The Ruined Age | 226 |
|  | Appendix on 'The Puritan Revolution' | 251 |
|  | Index | 255 |

# Preface

For many years I have had it in mind to write this book, as no one else has thought of tackling the subject. Since the Second German War we have had a spate of books on our own Civil War of the 17th century, and its causes – though hardly any on its consequences; and also on the variegated kaleidoscope of sects it threw up. We have been given too many books on the nonsense they thought – Ranters, Diggers, Muggletonians, and such – but nothing on the artistic damage the Puritan Revolution wrought.

Few historians have much visual sense. As I have gone around the country over the years I have kept a weather-eye open for the damage done in cathedrals and churches, the losses in the arts which this country suffered – as all countries do – in time of revolution. Particularly when, in the case of the Puritans, these arose from their iconoclastic convictions, the propaganda they had carried on since the Reformation (with the damage, quite sufficient in itself, that *that* had done. Perhaps someone now will treat that subject in turn.)

I have profited from many of these (rather redundant) books, not only for information but for amusement – the study of history provides one with fun, as well as with lessons to be drawn from it. Perhaps I may mention my debt to the works of my old friend, Christopher Hill – a leader in this field – if not wholly by way of reaction from his school of thought.

A.L.R.

# Revolution

Revolutions often do as much damage as, if not more than, anything they achieve; but it does not seem to have occurred to historians to explore the losses, particularly in culture and civilisation, or even good men's lives lost. It is not enough to regard this question from the point of view of any prejudice we may entertain, however reasonable, but from that of intellectually defensible principle.

Two principles then dominate this study. For the first we have a lead from an eminent scientist. Sir Peter Medawar writes:

> Human beings owe their biological supremacy to the possession of a form of inheritance quite unlike that of other animals. In this form of heredity information is transmitted from one generation to the next through non-genetic channels – by word of mouth, by example and by other forms of indoctrination: in general, by the entire apparatus of culture.

This is why the destructivism of revolution is so harmful, whether Russian or Chinese, the French Revolution or the Puritan in 17th-century England. Kill off the élites – and you are left with people of lesser experience and (usually) lower intelligence. The effects are only too obvious with the Russian and Chinese Revolutions – the difficulty of getting people able enough to run their economies efficiently or successfully. Take the appalling incompetence with which Stalin's Russia, with its enormously superior size and resources, faced Hitler's onslaught in 1941 which enabled German forces practically to reach Moscow and Leningrad. Stalin had killed by far the ablest of Russian commanders in Tukhachevsky (he was an aristocrat) and slaughtered practically the whole officer class in the Army – to make way for Stalin's favourite, the totally incompetent Voroshilov.

[1]

Similarly, with the 'liquefaction of the kulaks' – the virtual extermination of the most enterprising peasants, those with most initiative – Soviet Russia has never been able to get its agriculture on to a satisfactory basis. Contrast the efficiency of American and Canadian agriculture! Communist China faces similar difficulties in getting its industrialisation under way, having massacred its intelligent upper classes in millions.

We do not need to analyse the matter here – the fact is only too obvious. In human society *example* is exceedingly important – the sociologist Tarde had highlighted the power of 'social imitation': from higher to lower standards, superior classes to inferior, the permeation of better downwards, etc. This is one reason, the operation of incentive another, why vertically organised societies are more efficient in operation than horizontal ones. (One cannot get a wall of equal-sized pebbles to stand up.) One sees the effects in all the equalising societies of today: the deterioration of standards, the slackness, the sheer inefficiency – quite apart from what they look like, their squalor, the picture they present to civilised observers.

For the second principle to keep in mind is an aesthetic one. Mankind is redeemed from the slime by works of art and intellect: by music and painting, sculpture and architecture, drama and opera, by works of scientific thought and the analysis of nature and the universe (rather than nonsense-propositions about them). We remember 5th-century Athens for its achievement in the arts, not for its sanitation; the Elizabethan Age for the Shakespearean drama, not for the housing conditions of the people – who simply recur, and are unmemorable.

Thus it is a duty to condemn hostility to the arts and sciences wherever it occurs in human history or whatever form it takes. Maurice Bowra used to describe Calvin as 'an enemy of mankind' – which in a way he was. It is significant that – even apart from the painters, musicians and poets, in massive majority – the scientific minds of the Civil War period were not on the side of the Puritans, with their useless obsession with theology. The great physiologist of the age, Sir William Harvey, discoverer of the circulation of the blood, was a Royalist – though at Edgehill, while the fighting fools killed each other, he sheltered under a hedge reading a book. Sir Christopher Wren, nephew of Bishop Wren – who was imprisoned in the Tower through the whole period of the Puritan ascendancy – described the odious Prynne, who ran Archbishop Laud to death for his good works, as having the 'countenance of a witch'. The most original composer of the day, William Lawes (brother of Henry), was killed at Chester on the King's side, still quite young – no knowing what more he might have accomplished: to the grief of the King, with his cultivated mind. The most incisive philosophic intellect of the time, Thomas Hobbes, left the country to its distractions from the Puritan Revolution.

The Czech artist, Wenceslas Hollar, told John Aubrey that 'when he first came into England – which was a serene time of peace – the people, both poor and rich, did look cheerfully. But at his return he found the countenances of the people all changed – melancholy, spiteful, as if bewitched.' As they all had been – an observant artist would be one to notice such things.

The ordinary, unvisual historian would not. Today our bookshelves are loaded down with the argumentations of academics about the causes of the Civil War, hair-splitting about the various brands of nonsense people thought – Levellers, Diggers, Ranters, Muggletonians (the last of these fools died only in 1979!), Fifth Monarchy men, Millenarians, Anabaptists, Quakers, Soul-sleepers, *ad nauseam*. Most of what most people suppose themselves to think at any time is nonsense – only the thinking of the elect is of any value or permanence: the works of men's hands, their arts and crafts, are more worthy of respect and study than ordinary folks' thinking.

These are neglected by the academic descendants of those who were 'with it' in the efflorescence of the Puritan Revolution – naturally enough, for they have little visual or aesthetic sense. Nor had Victorian historians much. Their mentor, the voluminous Gardiner, for instance, a descendant of Oliver Cromwell – one may range all over his pages without descrying any appreciation of the aesthetic losses from the Puritan Revolution. Naturally too with a Scotch Philistine like Carlyle, with his hero-worship of Cromwell. (What did he construct? What has he left?)

All this is in sharp contrast to Clarendon, who left us an

incomparable gallery of portraits in his History of the Great Rebellion – like the pictures he collected in his grand house, itself a fine work of architecture, for *he* was a man of taste. Taste is more of a distinguishing mark of the elect than even intellectual distinction.

The taste, the artistic achievement, of the Caroline period is highly appreciated by *conoscenti* today. On the other hand, the losses, the deliberate spoliation wrought have not been studied, nor are they properly appreciated – and these even apart from the destruction that inevitably accompanies war.

Kenneth Clark had it in mind to write a study of Iconoclasm – a pity he did not live to fulfil his intention. What distinguishes Iconoclasm, properly speaking, is that it is the consequence of people's fanaticism, their ideological intention. The destruction is deliberate. We shall try to keep this in mind in our study, though it is not always possible to distinguish the strands. Mere Envy is a powerful operative force in revolutions – as in history in general, and revolution gives it its head.

The scholarly antiquarian, Sir William Dugdale, points out in his *Short View of the Late Troubles in England* that 'all rebellions did ever begin with the fairest pretences for reforming somewhat amiss in the government', especially when advanced under the guise of religion, 'the gilded bait usually held forth to allure the vulgar by those whose ends and designs were nothing else than to get into power.' Dugdale saw the signs of what was coming, after three generations of incessant Puritan propaganda against the Church and the establishment. It is touching to find him, along with another scholar – all the antiquarians were Royalists, except Selden, and he was a sceptic of both sides – setting out on a tour of cathedrals and churches to collect inscriptions and historical information on monuments, brasses, painted windows before they should be destroyed.

Thousands were, in the event. The story has never been properly told; nor what England lost by it.

# I

# The Attack on the Cathedrals

It is well known that the Scotch fanatics precipitated the Puritan Revolution with their defeat of the King on the Borders in 1639-40 – though with the Puritan gift for semantics, it was put across as the Bishops' War. It portended the defeat of Charles I and prefigured what would happen in England under Puritan rule.

On the King's visit to his native country for his coronation, Archbishop Laud had been appalled by the ruin of the Scottish cathedrals – St Andrew's had been one of the largest in the whole island.[1] Passing ruined Dunblane, Laud said – 'Reformation! No – Deformation.' A contemporary student of the destruction tells us:

> the sobering fact remains that the furnishings of churches in carved wood and stone, in painting, embroidery and metalwork, represented almost the entire cultural heritage and achievement of the nation. The wilful destruction of all this by misguided men was a national calamity of the first magnitude, the effects of which on native industry and craftsmanship must have been far-reaching. The thoroughness with which all accessories of Scottish medieval church worship were wiped out is unparalleled in Europe. The Reformation in Germany or the French Revolution in France never achieved such a complete annihilation of the past.[2]

The destruction continued into the 17th century – the lovely Anglo-Saxon Rood at Ruthwell was destroyed in 1642, as also was Elphinstone's tomb which had survived in St Andrew's. In

---

[1] The cultivated King wished to restore St Andrew's.
[2] D. McRoberts, in *Essays on the Scottish Reformation, 1513-1625*, 415 foll.

1640 the minister and local lairds broke up the rood-screen, with its Crucifixion with painted stars of gold, for firewood. In 1640 and 1642 devotees of the Covenant destroyed the tombs and woodwork of Aberdeen Cathedral – its polychrome Madonna is now in Brussels. No pre-Reformation brasses remain in Scotland; all the magnificent tombs of the kings in Scone abbey, comparable to those at Westminster, were destroyed. Only a few handfuls of medieval stained glass remain.

All tabernacles and altarpieces with painted panels, poly-chrome statues, carved and gilded, went – a few reliquaries overseas. There was further destruction of manuscripts, archives, books – Scottish libraries had been richer than hitherto realised. James IV's Book of Hours is now in Vienna; the 12th-century Psalter of Couper Angus abbey reached the Vatican. Medieval illuminated manuscripts, service books, antiphon-aries for the music of the Church all burnt as popish trash.

This provides a fine blue-print for what was to happen in England. During the Reformation in England comparable destruction took place – abbeys thrown down, 'the bare ruined choirs' that Shakespeare regretted as he went about the countryside. Of their contents whole boatloads went to the Continent: plate, manuscripts, statues, ivories and alabasters, vestments, books. Indefensible as this was, the offsets were these. Henry VIII used some of the proceeds, particularly the lead, slates and stone, to build a girdle of forts to protect the South Coast; while the Tudor period saw an immense alternative in the creation of secular buildings, palaces, mansions, country houses all over the land.

The declared aim of the Puritans in all their propaganda was to 'complete the Reformation', in other words, to go further in destruction. One sees this consistently carried out, from their propaganda against the institutions and services of the Church, in their actions when they got the chance. Resolutions were sent up and even an ordinance made, though not carried out, for the destruction of cathedrals. Their contents were fair game; stained glass, 'superstitious' images, monuments, tombs, brasses, fonts, carved woodwork, organs – these things were contrary to their convictions, and therefore the object of deliberate attack.

These Philistines had no conception of Dean Donne's point,

Churches are best for Prayer that have least light.

Or that of another poet, on scorned Church Windows:

> Even by vulgar eyes, each pane presents
> Whole chapters with both comment and contents,
> The cloudy mysteries of the Gospel here
> Transparent as the crystal do appear.
> 'Tis not to see things darkly through a glass,
> Here you may see our Saviour face to face.
> Let the deaf come hither; no matter though
> Faith's sense be lost, we a new way can show:
> Here we can teach them to believe by the eye –
> These silenced ministers do edify.

In short, where the Puritans were determined on 'completing' the Reformation, Laud was bent on repairing some of the damage done by it, so far as he could. Hence the conflict: the issue was as simple as that.

The monastic cathedral of Durham suffered heavily at the Reformation, as we know from the complete account of its Rites before the suppression of the cathedral monastery which has survived. A zealous Protestant bishop, one Pilkington, deserves discredit for destroying the stained glass depicting scenes in the life of St Cuthbert that decorated the cloister. Under the Laudian impulse for reparation, and the inspiration of his ideal, 'the beauty of holiness', something was done to recover ground. A marble altar was set up, with cherubim; three organs were installed, the greater over the choir entrance, smaller ones on either side of the choir. Ritual proper to a cathedral, copes and candles about the altar on Candlemas day, were restored by the Laudian Dean, John Cosin – to the fury of an inveterate Puritanical prebendary, one Smart.

It may be imagined what the Scotch Covenanting soldiery did when they occupied Durham. On Midsummer's Day 1641 they went for the great organ, tore out the keys, and destroyed the ancient font – in accordance with Puritan convictions as to church music and baptism with the sign of the cross. As the war deepened and worsened the cathedral was used to house Scotch prisoners after Dunbar. They completely destroyed the wood-work, organ cases, seats, carved stalls, wainscot, burning it for firewood. When Cosin returned at the Restoration as bishop, an enormous amount of reparation awaited him, not only in cathedral and neighbouring Castle, but at Auckland Castle and throughout his diocese. Hence it is that a pride of Durham now is the splendid Restoration woodwork throughout, not only in the cathedral, but the grand staircase in the Castle, the restoration of Auckland, the hall formed into a chapel, etc. All the cathedral plate had to be renewed – as in all the cathedrals at the Restoration. This is to say nothing of his generous public works, the founding of almshouses and of a public library.

At the western end of the Border Carlisle suffered much worse, permanent damage from which the cathedral has never recovered. Of the original eight bays of the Norman nave only a stump of two of them remains: all the rest was pulled down by the Scotch garrison between 1645 and 1652, along with the cloisters, chapter house, part of the deanery and prebendal buildings. They intended to pull down the whole cathedral as useless, leaving only a parish church, St Cuthbert's, for the ministrations they favoured – endless sermonising and tedious extempore prayer, with psalm-singing. For fourteen years the precincts lay in ruins, the floor of the cathedral open to the sects that proliferated. The charters of the Chapter were sold to provide a tailor with measures.

From other Border churches the Scots carried off furnishings, books, registers. The bishop's residence, Rose Castle, somewhat damaged, became the headquarters of a Parliamentary general; the brass lectern was embezzled and other furnishings made away with, as the churches were plundered of plate and linen throughout the diocese. A heavy burden of restoration awaited Bishop Rainbow, a devoted prelate, from 1664, but it was too big a task for an impoverished see to rebuild the nave of the cathedral. It is somewhat surprising that this was not done in the heyday of Victorian prosperity – after all, Cornwall built Truro cathedral through decades of impoverishment from the collapse of tin-mining and the emigration of a quarter of its population. Today, with the wasteful extravagance of a demotic society on trivial objects, it is unlikely that the nave of Carlisle cathedral will ever be rebuilt.

At York it has always been held that only the authority of Fairfax, the Parliamentarian commander-in-chief, a patriotic Yorkshireman and an aristocrat, minimised the damage and protected the rich heritage of stained glass in the churches. All the same, the churches of St Olave, St Maurice, St Denis, St Sampson and St Cuthbert were damaged; St Nicholas and St Lawrence were virtually destroyed, the former remained in ruins, the latter rebuilt after the Restoration.

In the Minster, by order of the mayor, plate and brass furnishings, canopies over the chantry altars, vestments and copes were sold. The vast church was disfurnished for its proper ritual, two Presbyterian preachers appointed instead, and two for the city. From 1660 the Minster was slowly refurnished and rehabilitated; in 1662 the great organ, lectern, etc, set up again. The splendid medieval woodwork of the choir survived - to be destroyed early in the 19th century by another religious lunatic, who set fire to the Minster because he disapproved of its choral services.

As bishop of London for five years, from 1628 to 1633, Laud had worked tirelessly to prop up Old St Paul's, the fabric of which was tottering. Early in Elizabeth I's reign the spire had fallen, damaging the church below. It was the tallest in the country, over 500 feet high, much taller than Wren's dome, and Old St Paul's was a good deal larger, one of the grandest edifices in Europe. But it was in a decayed state. Laud, with characteristic energy and devotion, raised large sums for repair, which was being carried on to the outbreak of the Revolution.

The greatest architect of the time, and one of the most original geniuses in the history of English art, Inigo Jones, was called in. The central tower was settling and needed shoring up. The originator of pure Renaissance classicism with his famous works - the Banqueting House in Whitehall, the Queen's House at Greenwich, St Paul's, Covent Garden - he introduced Tuscan columns within, and renewed the stonework of the long nave in classic style. To the west end he added the immense portico which was the grandest monument of its kind north of the Alps -

[9]

evidently competing with St Peter's at Rome. Laud intended this exterior area to clear out the merchandising and secular chaffering which disgraced the interior. All this was anathema to the Puritans: the classic style was Popish, only rebarbative Gothick would pass muster – and, come to think of it, Laud's enemy, the odious Prynne, to judge from Aubrey's description of him, was much of a Gothick gargoyle himself, 'of a saturnine complexion', he says.

On taking up his grievous burden Laud was faced with one of the many libels that were the bane of his life. A notice was fixed on his door at St Paul's: 'Laud, look to thyself. Be assured thy life is sought, as thou art the fountain of all wickedness. Repent thee thy monstrous sins before thou art taken out of the world.' And so on. The poor man could never cope with the mounting tide of misrepresentation and vilification against him, a devoted servant of Church and State. It must be admitted that he was not good at putting his own case or explaining himself; a scholarly man of eminent ability, a benefactor unparalleled on his own age, the best Chancellor the university of Oxford has ever had, he was a reserved man, withdrawn into the recess of his own secret life, his religion. Because of the purity of his own motives, of which he was well aware, he did not defend or explain himself; he did not consider it necessary, it should have been self-evident. But it never is, to ordinary humans. The result is that, though he had disciples, he had hardly any friends – except Strafford, another misunderstood man with a touch of greatness, treated with equally barbarous injustice. (The younger Henry Vane, Milton's hero, perjured himself to bring Strafford to the block, since no evidence of 'treason' could be found against him, any more than against Laud. Such are the ways of revolution.) Traduced all his life, Laud has received scant justice, and no understanding, from historians.

He was already an elderly man when he took up the burden of the Primacy – it was now too late, and one has the impression of an old man in a hurry. For some twenty years Archbishop Abbot, who should never have been appointed, had let things slide and, sympathetic to Puritans, had let them get ahead, after his predecessor Bancroft had reduced them to order. Laud was in the proper succession of Bancroft, and Whitgift before him, whose duty it was to maintain order and uniformity in the Church, the necessary decency and discipline against the disorder which the proliferation of sects inculcated. Purely intellectually, Laud was far more open-minded and tolerant than Puritans were, with their fixation on Old Testament savagery, their Bible mania, their nonsense about Predestination and Eternal Punishment. Laud was a believer in free will, an ecumenical spirit who wished for the reunion of Christendom, and refused to subscribe to the evil Puritan habit of describing Rome as the Whore of Babylon and the Pope as Anti-Christ. He was a civilised man, no Roman but a firm Anglican. One sees something of his reserved personality in Van Dyke's marvellous portrait of him: the self-contained little busy-body, the touch of irascibility, the competence, the man of integrity, somewhat constipated: no easy flow between him and others.

On succeeding to Lambeth – praying privately, 'though unworthy, Lord, make me able' – he found all in disorder and neglect. In the chapel the windows were 'defaced, demolished in such sort that nought but a few broken imperfect fragments of them remained, pieced up with white incoherent glass . . . . Altogether unrepaired, unfurbished, utterly neglected. It grieved his very soul to see it, so as he could not resort unto it to worship God with any comfort.' Initially he set to work with his chaplain to piece together the fragments, and make out the story 'as well as we could by the remains that were unbroken'.

Gradually he got things into order, calling in expert glaziers to reglaze windows in the Hall, then in the chapel. The central pane in the east window depicted the Crucifixion; behind the altar a painted arras had the Last Supper for subject. These things were venomously pressed against him as popish by Prynne at the Archbishop's trial. Even Prynne gave evidence of the restored radiance of the windows, in his inadvertent phrase, 'their fresh lively colours'.

Laud was a man of taste – he is given no credit for this by the insensitive who overlook the beauty of his Canterbury quadrangle, with the bronze statues of Charles I and Henrietta Maria, at St John's College, Oxford. And it seems to be unknown that this solitary man – like his predecessor, Bancroft – was a lover of music. I found from his will that Bancroft, regarded as an austere man, solaced himself by playing the viol: he was a good friend of the royal musician, Alphonse Lanier, husband of Emilia, Shakespeare's Dark Lady. In Laud's will he left to his attendant 'my harp, my chest of viols, and the harpsichord that is at Lambeth'. To repair the organ in the chapel he called in Robert Dallam, of the famous family of organ-makers who enriched the Caroline cathedrals with organs that were all religiously dismantled or smashed during the Commonwealth. This organ Laud bequeathed to his successor for the benefit of the see 'for ever': it was destroyed along with the rest of Laud's work, and not only that but Archbishop Parker's tomb was broken open and rifled, the lead of the coffin sold, his bones thrown into an outhouse. Characteristic revolutionary behaviour.

Meanwhile, across the water at Westminster, the revolution gathered impetus. The King, threatened by organised mobs brought down from the City (compare the use of the mob in the French Revolution), made two fatal mistakes. He permitted the execution of his leading minister, Strafford, and he signed away his prerogative of summoning Parliament, which now assumed control of events. Laud was taken into custody, thence to the Tower. 'As I went to my barge hundreds of my poor neighbours stood at the gates and prayed for my safety and return to my House, for which I bless God and them.' Neither prayers nor blessings were of the slightest use.

Revolutions are made by determined minorities. Puritanism was always a minority cult, contrary to the sense of the nation; even Gardiner admits that 'the House of Commons was more Puritan than the nation'. In spite of their armed might, their victories in the field, the energy of their propaganda and preaching, they became the minority of a minority. They could never command a consensus, any more than Laud could, though he was in keeping with traditional ways. He was in fact a traditionalist, and thought of himself as such, not an innovator, as contemporary historians describe him. (They would prefer the slackness and neglect of Abbot's long and nerveless régime: that was in keeping with the brief rule of Grindal, whom Elizabeth I cashiered; not with the rule of Whitgift and Bancroft, which had kept order in the nursery.)

In 1642 Parliament gave the lead to iconoclasm with its Ordinance 'for pulling down all monuments of superstition and idolatry'. A Commission, headed by the godly Sir Robert Harley (he got £4000 a year as Master of the Mint), was 'to take into their custody the copes in the cathedrals of Westminster, St Paul's and Lambeth, and give order that they be burnt, the gold separated from the gilt by fire, and converted to the relief of the poor in Ireland'. Iconoclasm was already rife about the country, now it was given authority and direction from above, the revolutionary epicycle at Westminster.

Later that year special attention was directed to St Paul's. It was ordered that the Committee for taking away superstitious ornaments 'do open Paul's Church' – though they regularly referred to themselves as the Saints, they objected to the traditional use of the word for saints of the Church, as for observing saints' days, feasts, Christmas etc, – 'and that they shall have power to remove out of the said Church all such matters as are justly offensive to godly men'. In Puritan semantics they were always the 'godly'; those who did not subscribe to their nonsense were the 'carnal'. How nauseating to persons of taste and refinement! – one sympathises with cultivated persons like the King and Archbishop for what they had to put up with.

Now the good work could go forward with a will and encouragement from the revolutionaries. Famous St Paul's Cross, 'which had been for many ages the most solemn place in this nation for the greatest divines and most eminent scholars to preach at, was pulled down to the ground'. So also the most prominent cross in the City, the beautiful medieval Cheapside Cross. This was in accordance with Puritan convictions: they hated the symbol of the Cross, whether in stained glass, pictures, carved wood or stone. All over England they were defaced or thrown down. In hundreds of churchyards one sees the remains, the bases and steps, often the shafts remaining, but rarely the sculpted heads. The beautiful 13th-century Eleanor crosses Edward I erected in memory of his wife, like that which existed at Charing Cross (the Victorians replaced it with one less good) almost all disappeared. That at Dunstable was shortly to disappear – I remember seeing only one beautiful example still remaining, in the village of Geddington in Northamptonshire.

In the City the large sum of £17,000, funds collected for the repair of St Paul's, was seized, and the vast structure of scaffolding around the central tower sold for nearly £2000 to pay a regiment. On the removal of scaffolding part of the south transept with its roof fell in. The grand portico was let out for shops and cluttered up with staircases to chambers above; the statues of the two Kings above were thrown down and smashed to pieces. The nave, Dugdale observed with bitterness of heart, was used for cavalry barracks and stables, pavements trampled to bits, tombs rifled and defaced. Many were the noteworthy tombs damaged, the grandest that of John of Gaunt.

A part of the east end was walled in for the ministrations and congregations of Cornelius Burgess. This enterprising man was a most effective propagandist. Disappointed of preferment, he exerted himself to organise petitions, collect signatures and lead mobs down to Westminster to bring pressure on the King and add the weight of the populace, with whom he was a powerful voice, to urge on further measures. He advocated the suppression of Deans and Chapters, though he did not favour alienating their properties from public uses for 'any private person's benefit'. Leading his rabble to the doors of the Parliament House, he would say to his friend, Colonel Venn (later regicide): 'These are my bandogs: I can set them on, and I can take them off.'

Venn fomented the mob in Cheapside with: 'You must go to the Parliament with your swords, for the party which is best for the commonwealth is like to be over-voted.' Venn was made Governor of Windsor Castle, while the King was still alive, and got £4000 for his expenses out of papist and delinquent lands. His spiritual director was Christopher Love, chaplain to his regiment, whom Cromwell had executed later as trouble-maker. Which they all were: Venn was lucky to die before the Restoration, for as a regicide, who had taken part in the 'judicial' murder of the King, he would have paid the penalty. As it was, he left a considerable estate in several counties.

Parliament well rewarded its faithful preachers for their services. Where a poor vicar might receive £20 or £40 per annum for year-long services in a parish, Burgess was awarded

£400 a year for his pulpit oratory, and the deanery of St Paul's to live in. He did so well financially that he was able to advance £3500 to Parliament to fight their war. With his good business sense he invested in the purchase of confiscated episcopal lands – by 1659 worth some £12,000. A further chance came in 1650, when he was made Lecturer in Wells cathedral. He stripped lead from the roofs to rebuild the deanery for himself and let out the gatehouses to the Close as cottages. Here, an orthodox Puritan, he objected to sharing the cathedral with an Independent congregation. The citizens showed what they thought by walking noisily up and down the cloisters all sermon time, so that the constables had to be called in. A large number of his popular sermons were published – the presses groaned under the burden of the theological trash produced at the time – under such edifying titles as 'The Necessity and Benefit of Washing the Heart', 'The Vanity and Mischief of the Thoughts of an Heart Unwashed', or 'Prudent Silence', which he would have done better to keep. At the Restoration he was made to disgorge his ill-gotten gains.

Fulham, the country residence of the bishops of London, came into the possession of a silk merchant, and – like everything else episcopal – needed much reparation by 1660. An important factor that is overlooked is that, with the confiscation of Church property, the lands of bishops, deans and chapters, the upkeep of their cathedrals went unprovided for and they all suffered severely from neglect, even apart from deliberate damage. This is vividly brought home by Wren's report on the work necessary to make Old St Paul's safe, before the Fire consumed it.

Westminster Abbey suffered severely. Henry VII's Chapel was equipped with splendid painted windows comparable to those of King's College Chapel, Cambridge, and by the same makers. These were destroyed – think of the loss! Torrigiano's altarpiece was wrenched out, as was the high altar in the sanctuary, where the exquisite medieval pavement was mutilated and the tapestries around the choir thrown out. The Chapel of the Pyx was broken into to get at the Regalia – the Parliamentarian poet Wither (not a very good one) paraded round in crown and sceptre, the soldiers quartered in the abbey capering in surplices, burning altar rails and smashing the organ. Later, the medieval regalia – crown, orb, sceptre, vessels, plate – were broken up and destroyed; for the coronation of Charles II everything had to be made anew, less well.

Seating arrangements were re-fashioned to face the dominating pulpit where Puritan bores performed: in place of the impersonal ritual of the Church, the exhibitionism of the preacher's personality. Hugh Peters, not really the bad man he has been made out to be, was yet a popular mountebank in the pulpit. On occasion he would fall silent for a space, lean down his head upon the cushion, and after a while rise up exalted as if he had received a revelation. He was always a good turn. We can hardly think so of the Sabbath exercises in the Abbey, as reported by the Scotch humbug Baillie – I merely follow the lead of their fellow Puritan, Milton:

> Because you have thrown off your prelate lord,
> And with stiff vows renounced his liturgy
> To seize the widowed whore, Plurality,
> From them whose sin ye envied, not abhorred:
> Dare ye for this adjure the civil sword
> To force our consciences that Christ set free,
> And ride us with a classic hierarchy
> Taught ye by mere A.S. and Rutherford? ...
> By shallow Edwards and Scotch what d'ye call ...
> *New Presbyter* is but *Old Priest* writ large.

Milton meant by 'classic hierarchy' the organisation into Presbyterian *classes* which prevailed in Scotland and which the Scotch sought to impose on England, along with the humbug of their Solemn League and Covenant. This was clean contrary to the natural instinct and sense of the English, and never took on: Pym bought it in order to purchase a Scottish army to help to beat the King.

Meanwhile the Abbey became the *locale* for the Westminster Assembly of Divines, gathered to compile a Directory for Public Worship (with Francis Rouse's appalling doggerel for the Psalms), to take the place of the Prayer Book liturgy and Calvinise the Church of England. During the Interregnum one could attend, if one wished, such entertainments in the Abbey as

Baillie describes. Stephen Marshall would pray 'two large hours'. Then Mr Arrowsmith preached an hour, and a psalm was sung; followed by Mr Vines who prayed for nearly two hours, and Mr Palmer preached an hour. Mr Seaman prayed near two hours, another psalm; after that Scotch Henderson preached. Dr Twisse finished up, as he had begun, with a short prayer. 'Thus spending', Baillie concluded, 'nine to five very graciously'. Eight hours of it! – one wonders what they all did about the needs of nature.

This was the kind of thing that took the place of the divine music of the Church – of Tallis and Byrd, Weelkes, Orlando Gibbons, Tompkins – which those Philistines detested. They particularly disliked the beautiful effects of antiphony (as in Monteverdi's Vespers): they called it 'tossing the ball from one side to the other, nothing but roaring boys and squeaking organ pipes, and the cathedral catches of Morley, and I know not what trash'.

They preferred such types as Stephen Marshall. He was famous for his sermon, 'Curse ye Meroz', which he had preached at least sixty times. A witness said that 'this cursing sermon ushered in, as well as promoted, the late bloody civil wars'. A son of a lower-class glover, he was a typical Emmanuel product, a Puritan of no particular education, but an effective propagandist. He had once approached Buckingham for preferment, but disappointment 'made him turn schismatic'; his son-in-law said that 'if they had made his father a bishop before he was too far engaged, it might have prevented the war'.

Under the patronage of the Parliamentarian Rich, earl of Warwick, Marshall had been reported to Laud, 'he governeth the consciences of all the rich Puritans in those parts [Essex], and is grown very rich'. Like Burgess, Marshall took a leading part in organising petitions against the bishops and the liturgy – it was said that he doctored the signatures and arranged different documents to appear as if they came from 700 people, when only 80 had signed. This movement generated a demand for the abolition of episcopacy, which few really favoured. At Edgehill Marshall went from regiment to regiment praying fervently to encourage to slaughter, and was frequently called on to preach to what remained of the House of Commons at St Margaret's

[17]

Westminster on their solemn fast-days. The House had chosen
to resort thither, because they would not accept 'the copes and
wafers' at the Abbey.

Marshall received his reward: he was made one of the seven
morning lecturers at St Margaret's preaching daily in rotation,
at a salary of £300 a year each. He was a swarthy, broad-
shouldered man, of a shackling gait, rather uncouth, who rolled
his eyes holily in the approved manner; I do not know if he had
the nasal twang affected by Puritans, which nauseated civilised
persons. Dorothy Osborne heard him:

> God forgive me, I was as near laughing yesterday where I should
> not. He is so famed that I expected rare things from him. And
> what do you think he told us? Why, that if there were no kings, no
> queens, no lords, no ladies, no gentlemen nor gentlewomen in
> the world 'twould be no loss at all to God Almighty. This we had
> over some forty times . . . . He stood stoutly for Tithes, though in
> my opinion few deserved them less than he, and it may be he
> would be better without them.

This, however, was far from their intention: they saw to it that
they did well out of it, as Milton, disillusioned by them, later
saw. And Dryden too:

> Pretending Public Good, to serve their own.
> Others thought Kings an useless heavy load . . .
> With them joined all th' Haranguers of the Throng
> That thought to get Preferment by the Tongue . . .
> Resumed their Cant, and with a Zealous Cry
> Pursued their old beloved Theocracy:
> Where Sanhedrin and Priest enslaved the nation
> And justified their Spoils by Inspiration.

It must have been insupportable to live through it (as the poets,
elect spirits, ultimately found with the Russian Revolution).

This was the man, along with another humbug, whom
Parliament placed insultingly upon the King to attend him in
confinement at Holdenby. Naturally, the cultivated monarch
never attended his two-hour long sermons; at dinner, Marshall

invoked a blessing at inordinate length, of which the King took no notice, and said a brief grace himself. The uncouth Saint, with his lower-class manners, did not neglect the pleasures of the table, however. An unfriendly observer watched him once at a wedding-feast, 'having eaten a little more than his share of a jole of salmon and afterwards taken in a full quart of sack for digestion, most devoutly cried, "Blessed be God! how good the Creatures are being used with moderation!" One recognises the typical cant. This was the man Parliament sent to trouble Laud in his last days in the Tower and attend him on the scaffold. The Archbishop ignored him.

There is no complete survey of the destruction wrought in the cathedrals, much less of the aesthetic losses from the Puritan Revolution and Civil War as a whole; one can piece together the story only bit by bit, fragmentarily. However, in the case of Peterborough we are fortunate to have an eyewitness account of the damage done.[1] This was one of the half-dozen sees erected by Henry VIII out of former monasteries; a dozen were intended but not carried out, owing to the enormous expense of his third French war. Otherwise we should have such a splendid fane as Bury St Edmunds saved for a diocese of Suffolk; besides other fine churches like Reading abbey, Osney at Oxford, Leicester, Shrewsbury, perhaps Glastonbury, Plympton or Tavistock, possibly St Germans or Bodmin for little Cornwall.

Symon Gunton was born and lived most of his life at Peterborough, where as a boy he often transcribed monuments for Dugdale (as did Sanderson at Lincoln). Many of the abbey records were kept in the chapter-house, which was destroyed. One important volume was saved by the Chanter, who hid it under his seat in the choir: the history of the Abbey by Hugh Candidus and Robert of Swaffham. When all the stalls were pulled down in April 1643 the Chanter offered the soldier who found it ten shillings for it. One notes the touching fidelity – and also by what a thread precious things were lost, or saved.

On the way to the siege of Crowland, where also much damage was done, Cromwell's horsemen, under his son, broke

<hr />

[1]Symon Gunton: *The History of the Church of Peterburgh*, 1686.

open the locked doors of the cathedral and threw down the pair of organs, broke and trampled them 'with such a strange furious and frantic zeal as cannot be well conceived but by those that saw it'. They disapproved of church music – here was an end-result of their long propaganda against it. So too with other targets of their dislike. They tore up the prayer-books in the choir, ripped the Apocrypha out of the Bible (Popish!), broke down stalls, seats, wainscot panelling. The big brass candel-abrum and lectern they sold for the brass. A protester was silenced: 'See how these poor people are concerned to see their *idols* pulled down.' Liturgical ornaments had been described as such for the past three generations by Puritan propaganda, and at last they had their way.

The chief glory of the church had escaped the Reformation, the reredos with lofty spires reaching almost to the roof: this was pulled down by ropes. Over it was a painted Christ in glory, which was shot at and defaced. What fun these brutes had! One is reminded of the baroque portal of St Mary's at Oxford, where a soldier shot off the head of the Virgin – if one looks closely one can see that it has been repaired. Very often there was so much to do in defacing monuments and figures that the miscreants had to content themselves by taking off the heads.

Altar, furniture and communion rails were broken down and smashed as everywhere. Actually, in most of the cathedrals the high altar had retained its traditional position. Laud had ordered its railing in, not only for sanctity but decency: frequently the communion table was a depository for hats and garments, and dogs prowled the sanctuary. All offensive to Laud's spirit of order – and thus ubiquitous target for Puritan venom, with which they were well supplied.

A few months later a further visitation of musters broke open the vestry and took altar frontals of crimson satin, vestments etc. From Katherine of Aragon's tomb they took the herse and black velvet pall, and displaced the gravestone; from Mary Queen of Scots' former grave they tore down the arms and scutcheons. Bishop Dove had a remarkable recent monument (was it by Nicholas Stone?), an effigy on black marble, four classic columns, his library of books about him: this was destroyed with other works in the north aisle. So too the painted windows: 'they thought they saw Popery in every picture and painted piece of glass'. Sculptures, alabasters and brass inscriptions were torn away, none left. Sir Humphry Orme had built his tomb while still alive; though a secular monument, the vandals were provoked by the inscription in which the words 'Altar' and 'Sacrifice' appeared. Some soldiers carried effigies to the market place, some in surplices, others tooting on organ pipes. One sees the philistinism of the common man, and what happens when the ideological nonsense preached by intellectuals, of inferior calibre, reaches down to the idiot people. At Yaxley, not far away, that June soldiers 'break open the church doors, piss in the font and then baptize a horse and a mare, signing them with the sign of the cross'.

In the chapter-house they ransacked the records, tore up parchments and broke the seals. To a gentleman who remonstrated with them: 'We are pulling and tearing the Pope's Bulls in pieces.' They enjoyed a fortnight of destruction here. A prime glory of Peterborough was the cloister, where the windows were 'most famed of all for their great art and pleasing variety': on one side Old Testament scenes, another the New Testament, a third the founders and benefactors of the church, a fourth, the kings of England. All destroyed.

The east window in the Lady Chapel was considered the fairest – it depicted Julian the Apostate's story: Gunton gives us the verse inscriptions under the windows, pages of them, all he could do. The tapestry hangings of the choir were taken away; the Abbot's chair beside the altar beaten down – then, some years later, in 1651 a private person had the base levelled as 'not a thorough reformation'. One sees the consistency of Puritan conviction, their manic beliefs.

Next a Public Order had the cloisters pulled down, the older chapter-house, the bishop's hall with its chapel at one end – here there had been three 'stately seats', carved, painted and gilded – and the Green Chamber. The materials were sold off, but the ship carrying them to Holland was lost at sea – hence total loss. Oliver St John saved the Minster from demolition by securing it for a parish church, since the town's church was decayed. But the town found the upkeep expensive – naturally since the endowment had been confiscated – and pulled down the Lady

Chapel, selling the materials. They used the painted roof to wall the choir and keep out draughts (except those from the pulpit); for the Committee of Plundered Ministers sent down a preacher at £160 a year to preach to them. The purchasers of the bishop's palace demolished the chapel, the font of which had been broken in the visitation of 1643.

What a scene it must have presented – heart-breaking to those who cared for such things or had any taste. Above all to John Cosin, the Dean, who had done his best to bring things together; after twenty years in exile he returned briefly as Dean to begin the work of repair, then move on to Durham where there was still more to do. For this kind of thing was going on all over England. Some cathedrals suffered much worse – Lichfield, for instance, which endured three sieges and where the destruction was far greater. Most of what one sees there today is Victorian restoration.

In the case of Norwich we have a rarity – the reaction of good Bishop Hall, as he sat shut up in his palace listening to the hammering and sawing being carried on next door in his cathedral. He describes it in his *Hard Measure*; for Hall was a distinguished writer, the first to write English Satires after the classical model. In point of fact, the Caroline bishops – like the Restoration ones, after their trials were over – were rather an eminent lot, more so than the Elizabethan bishops on the whole.

Hall was a moderate, not a High Churchman, and had tried to mitigate Calvinist venom at the Synod of Dort. There the extreme Calvinists had triumphed, and proceeded to persecute and imprison Grotius, one of the cardinal intellects of the century, comparable to Erasmus, for his moderation and tolerance. (He had a narrow escape from their vengeance.) At Dort Hall learned his lesson: he returned to find England 'begin to sicken of the same disease'. Indeed it provided the ideology of the Puritan Revolution. Hall preached constantly for moderation and good will; he argued for omitting the accretions and errors of Rome without denying its catholicity. This gave great offence to the Puritans. No Arminian, Hall made a strong case for the liturgy as impersonal, and for episcopacy on practical grounds as the most convenient traditional way of church government. This was proved true for England by the experience of the revolutionary upheaval, which could find no permanent base for consensus or government. Before the end Cromwell's own brother-in-law, the eminent scientist John Wilkins, told him that religion could not be run in England without bishops, and himself consented to become one at the Restoration.

As bishop of Exeter Hall had no trouble in his diocese and in 1641 was translated, a moderate, to difficult Norwich as a conciliatory gesture. It did no good – one can never appease extremists (nothing could appease Lenin or Robespierre, or Hitler, except *power*: that is what they are all after, the Puritans no less, as Dugdale saw. Hobbes, who had a fine disillusioned view of human nature, thought Laud a fool to make the effort he did. He was certainly naif.)

At the beginning of the Revolution the sheriff and aldermen of puritanical Norwich searched the Bishop's chapel for superstitious pictures. Hall tried to minimise their defacing by taking out heads himself. Nothing would do.

> Lord, what work was here! What clattering of glasses! What beating down of walls! What tearing up of monuments! What pulling down of seats! What wresting out of iron and brass from the windows and graves! What defacing of arms! What demolishing of curious [elaborate] stonework! ... What tooting and piping on the destroyed organ pipes! And what a hideous triumph on the market day before all the county, when in a kind of sacrilegious profession all the organ pipes, vestments, copes and surplices, together with the leaden cross which had been newly sawn down from the Green Yard pulpit, and the service books and singing books were carried to the fire in the public market place.

And so on. It reads like the burning of books which used to amuse Nazi Germans in the 1930s.

We see that the damage at Norwich took much the same form as at Peterborough, or for that matter in all the cathedrals – the Puritan targets were the same, in accordance with their beliefs. The eastern counties, with Essex, were the hot-bed of

Puritanism, i.e. the dioceses of Norwich and Ely, where Bishop Wren wrestled with such difficulties. Essex fell to Laud, when bishop of London; try as hard as he might, encouraged by the King, he could not keep order in the nursery – his efforts as such have been labelled 'persecution' ever since. The Puritans he had to deal with were intolerant – one can see the 'toleration' they inflicted when they got their way in New England – intolerable and totally irrepressible. When some of the stiff-necked left for Massachusetts – to persecute the Quakers over there and drive the inspired Anne Hutchinson and her family into the wilderness to be massacred by Indians – the King minuted on Laud's report, 'a good riddance'. One cannot but agree.

As early as New Year 1643 Oliver Cromwell took it upon himself to suspend the choir services at Ely, 'so unedifying and offensive'. And, later, 'I heed God's House as much as any man [typically plausible beginning]; but vanities and trumpery give no honour to God, nor idols serve him, neither do painted windows make man more pious.' One recognises the cant; I fear Carlyle's Hero was no aesthete. In bleak East Anglia they had more people with them. The nasty Puritans of Great Yarmouth petitioned to have Norwich cathedral pulled down – they hated cathedrals as such. The bailiffs and aldermen besought Parliament 'to grant us such part of the lead and other useful materials of that vast and altogether useless cathedral, towards building of a workhouse and repairing our piers, or otherwise as you shall think fit'. Think of it! – today still the jewel of East Anglia. During the Revolution it was the townsfolk here who tried to wreck it, as they practically did the Bishop's palace and chapel – the latter having to be rebuilt at the Restoration.

In 1644, when the tide of war turned in their favour with Marston Moor and Cromwell's New Model Army, inspired by his fanaticism, Norwich expelled friendly Bishop Hall and his family. He took refuge at the Dolphin Inn (which still remains at Higham), where he gave himself up to devotional works, without resentment or complaint, a model of Christian charity – as few Puritans were.

At Ely the Lady Chapel is famed for its marvellous medieval sculpture – but all the heads of the figures were religiously knocked off and the acres of painted windows put out. Before that the visual effect must have been incomparably richer – just what those pure souls hated – where today all is bland and white. After their victory it was actually discussed whether to demolish the whole building. Victorious Parliament ordered a committee 'to consider of and examine the structure ... in relation to the ruinous condition of the same; and what other churches there are in the same [the Isle of Ely] for the people to meet together in, for the hearing of the Word of God and communicating in the Ordinances of God, and to bring in an Ordinance for making sale of the materials of the said cathedral.' These destructive ordinances did not take effect – too expensive to pull down such structures, they were left for neglect to do the work, until the Restoration restored them. But Ordinances! One is reminded of Karl Marx on the slogan, 'Liberty, Equality, Fraternity': 'Why don't they say what they really mean, "Infantry, Cavalry, Artillery"?' For Parliament's Ordinance we might substitute what was really effective: their Ordnance.

Lincoln as a whole suffered much worse than Norwich; since it was twice besieged, the Royalists contributed to the destruction. This was inevitable in the course of war, and so is hardly my subject. When Manchester and Cromwell stormed the city, 'pillage of the upper town was given to the troops' – by the rules of war; when the Royalists returned the compliment with their siege, they fired the Bishop's palace as part of the operations.

Sir Frank Hill sums up these amenities for us.[1]

> The damage cannot be calculated. The injury to timber buildings must have been very great, and there were losses due to plunder by troops of first one side and then the other ... St Nicholas and St Peter in Eastgate were destroyed in 1643; St Swithin was burnt on 5 May 1644, and it seems that St Bartholomew was burnt on the same day. After the Restoration the churches of St Michael, St Mary Magdalen, St Paul and probably others were either roofless or their roofs were in need of

[1]J.W.F. Hill, *Tudor and Stuart Lincoln*, 162 foll.

repair. St Botolph and the tower and nave of St Benedict had fallen.

The Minster suffered severely. Windows were broken, brasses torn up, monuments and statues mutilated or destroyed, and barge-loads of metal removed.

An officer with a couple of soldiers locked themselves in for two days, and wrenched out scores of medieval brasses. One can appreciate the loss when one thinks of the splendid specimens of the art that remain in remote villages in East Anglia, like Felbrigg.

Their love for books was equal – all the service-books, music, muniments dispersed or torn up. Robert Sanderson's large collections for the history of Lincolnshire disappeared; 'hence the Winchelsea Book of Monuments is the only evidence of so many of the memorials in the Minster which perished'. However, Parliament compensated religiously by allotting £300 a year for two Puritan bores to preach – two 'suitable ministers' to be selected by the Assembly of Divines.

What is significant historically to notice is that these actions precisely fulfilled the propaganda that had been going on for so long and which Laud had been totally unable to quench, let alone put his own side of the case. It was a Lincolnshire member who urged the Long Parliament

> to lay the Axe to the root, to unloose the long and deep Fangs of Superstition and Popery .... I shall humbly move that the groves and high place of Idolatry [note the Old Testament jargon] may be removed and pulled down, and then God's wrath against England will be appeased .... [Religion] will never be safe nor well at quiet until these heavy drossy cannons with all their base metal be melted and dissolved. Let us then dismount them and destroy them, which is my humble motion.

This was a Puritan gentleman speaking. Apart from the personal venom, these gentry were after the property and possessions of the Church. The secular gentry had been enormously enriched by the Dissolution of the monasteries: they wanted the Reformation 'completed'. It was made a charge against Laud that he had had a churchman, Bishop Juxon, appointed Lord Treasurer. Naturally, for secular peers were out for the rewards of high office for themselves: the Paulets, Cecils, Howards, Sackvilles had made immense fortunes out of the state. Celibate churchmen like Laud and Juxon had no families to provide for, and dedicated all their revenues to public purposes and cared for the poor.[1] No wonder aristocrats looked down on Laud as a lower-class man, resented his precedence as Archbishop; and when he publicly reproved their selfishness, protested at 'being choked by a pair of lawn-sleeves'.

At Lincoln the glorious rose-window, with its rich glow of colour, was the only complete one left. One sometimes finds this the case – with the great west window at Peterborough, for instance; too high for the poor fellows to reach. Since the cloisters were half-ruined, at the Restoration Dean Honywood called in the Royalist Wren to design the beautiful Library over one wing. Books and gifts began to flow in; already in 1660 the splendid large candelabra from a [Royalist] M.P.

At Lichfield, after three sieges, devastation was complete. Even before the war there were pointers as to what might happen. An aristocratic creature, Lady Eleanor Davies, with the wife of the town clerk, expressed their disapproval of the altar by pouring tar all over it and smearing the hangings. Later, a group from the town dragged the altar into the nave and broke down the communion rails. The first siege of the cathedral was directed by the fanatical Lord Brooke. He was a close friend of the ambitious intriguer, Lord Saye, and together with him founded Sayebrook in Connecticut. Lord Brooke was directing close fire on the cathedral, upon St Chad's day, its patron saint, when a bullet got him in the eye. Since before the war he had expressed a wish to live to see the day when not one stone of Old St Paul's should be left upon another, one can hardly regard his death as a loss to the arts.

Dugdale describes the soldiery stabling their horses in the nave, 'they kept courts of guard in the cross-aisles [transepts], broke up the pavement, polluted the choir with their

---

[1] Juxon left St John's College, Oxford, £7000.

excrements, every day hunted a cat with hounds throughout the church'. Ordinary humans enjoy themselves according to their tastes. 'They brought a calf in wrapped in linen, carried it to the font, sprinkled it with water and gave it a name in scorn of that holy sacrament.'

In 1646 the central spire collapsed into the choir. In 1649 the Parliamentary Commissioners reported that much of the roofing had gone, the lead and iron taken away; the library was a wreck, the gate-house in ruins, eight houses in the Close destroyed, the Bishop's palace badly damaged. Two years later Parliament ordered the lead to be stripped off the rest of the roof: this with other materials raised £1200, which mostly went into private pockets. 'A Presbyterian pewterer who was the chief officer for demolishing of that cathedral' destroyed the Jesus bell; some were broken, others taken away. The communion plate and linen had been carried off by the Parliamentarian commander after the second siege. Books and manuscripts destroyed or scattered. The chronicle history of the cathedral painted on folding wooden screens in the south transept was destroyed by 'our good bailey, Sir John Gell', a brash Derbyshire commander.

One sees the consequences of the convictions of such fanatics as Lord Brooke: he would not have minded them. At the Restoration Bishop Hacket, 1661–70, had to face an immense task of rebuilding, the Bishop's palace not rebuilt until 1687. It was enough to make Dr Johnson, a Lichfield man, a life-long Tory, with a hatred of Scots, Presbyterians, Dissenters, sectarians of all sorts.

What of the western cathedrals?

Trouble had already declared itself at Worcester in Bishop Thornborough's time, a typical childish row between mayor and citizens and the cathedral clergy over the placing of the pulpit. The politic bishop wrote to Laud to let the 'fools' have their way, and this he amicably did. The King himself expressed his view, peaceably enough, to Thornborough's successor: 'a principal cause of rebellion hath been the great increase of Brownists, Anabaptists, and other sectaries mistaken and mispersuaded in their religion'.

The Catholic antiquary, Habington, describes the stained glass of the cathedral as complete before the war – afterwards all destroyed. Early on, Essex's troops damaged altar, furnishings, service books in the familiar manner. One trooper mounted a ladder to get at the organ, fell and broke his neck: no loss. Grievous damage was done by removing lead and timber from the roofs. Altogether, from the east transept, prebend's house, dean's hall, dorter, Queen's chamber, the large sum of £8204 was raised; there were 2140 yards of water pipes, conduits and lead cisterns. The removals left the church bare of fittings, but one still sees Bishop Thornborough's monument, with its classic columns and astrological symbols, erect in the nave, restored today in its colours, but with the marks of its defacing ineradicable.[1] One Birch bought the bell-tower, on the north side of the choir, pulled it down and realised £1200 from the lead and oak. A couple of London speculators bought the cloister for the lead and wood. Citizens helped soldiers to destroy St Oswald's hospital; in 1647 the spire of adjoining St Michael's was pulled down. All as usual. In September 1660 the restored liturgy provoked a demonstration of loyalty, an immense concourse of gentry and citizens. They had learned their lesson – though £10,000 would not repair the damage. Under the restored bishops conformity was a necessary condition of preferment. Quite right.

In Herefordshire the opposite number to Sir Robert Harley, who did so much damage to Westminster Abbey, was the Royalist Viscount Scudamore. Son of the Scudamour who appears in Spenser's *Faery Queene*, he was a friend of Laud, who co-opted him in his plans for restoring St Paul's. Scudamore shared Laud's constructive ideas, and helped him in his unsurpassed work of collecting manuscripts for the Bodleian Library. He repaired and put the roof on beautiful Abbey Dore and equipped it with the admirable Caroline woodwork we see there today. Moreover he endowed it, and restored the alienated tithes to several churches, which his ancestor had received under Henry VIII. He gave employment to the poor

[1]cf. my *Simon Forman: Sex and Society in Shakespeare's Age*, 160.

and provided for the aged; he kept Christmas festivities, which Puritans sourly disapproved, with open house.

All this was much to Laud's heart – as was a similar piece of good work at Cartmel priory in Lancashire, where the roof was put back and the church once more filled with good woodwork. Or at Thorney abbey in Cambridgeshire, where the nave was re-roofed for a parish church. Laud's mind, we see, was essentially constructive.

In 1643 Waller captured Scudamore at Hereford, and his goods were seized. However, his cheerfulness in prison was that of other Cavaliers expressed by their poets:

> Although rebellion do my body bind
> My King alone can captivate my mind.

It had been a sore surprise to Parliament, which had won the game politically by 1641, that the name of King could raise an army for him at all.

Before the war Hereford had five parish churches; two of them, St Martin and St Owen, were destroyed in the siege of 1645. At the beginning, Dean Croft, of good Herefordshire family, had dared to preach against the soldiery invading his cathedral, when they levelled their muskets at him. They had their way, however, with nearly all the tombs of ecclesiastics, knocking their heads off wherever fancy took them, in nave and transepts. All the brasses were broken. The Chapter House, 'of uncommon architectural interest', according to an authority today, with very early fan-vaulting, was stripped of its lead and fell into ruin. However, Harley, who undertook the job of alienating the lands intended for the upkeep of the cathedral, provided generously for its spiritual needs: he ordained six ministers for Hereford, three for the cathedral at £150 a year, with the Deanery to live in, and three for the city. The number was never made fully up; perhaps they were unwanted.

Gloucester cathedral had a narrow escape: its destruction was planned, but in 1657 – when the high tide of fanaticism was receding – it was handed over to the mayor and citizens. It suffered the usual losses, and, like all the cathedrals, needed complete re-equipment at the Restoration: chalices and patens, credence paten, flagons for wine at communion, altar candlesticks and furniture, alms dish. It got, and has kept, them all, along with a new organ by Thomas Harris, with a fine case of 1665.

Remote St David's did not escape. The lead was stripped from the Lady Chapel; this was the time when the roofs of the eastern aisles and chapels fell in – to be gradually restored in the past century. All the painted glass was destroyed, and the Elizabethan organ which had been installed in 1581. A sea captain from Milford Haven brought away a cope, two crosses and 'other relics of Rome', which he thought worth a journey to London to exhibit.

Pursuing our way west, we have seen the egregious Burgess profitably installed at Wells, making hay while the sun shone. (Was he, one wonders, an ancestor of our own revolutionary, Guy Burgess?) Pevsner regards Wells as 'the most memorable of all bishop's palaces in England. It combines high architectural interest with exquisite beauty of setting. The hall is in ruins. If it were complete, it would be one of the most inspiring of the century' – the glorious XIIIth, apogee of the Early English style.

We learn from a contemporary that on 7 April 1643 Parliamentary soldiery

> broke down divers pictures and crucifixes in the church and Our Lady chapel. Likewise they did plunder the Bishop's palace and broke all such monuments and pictures as they espied, either of religion, antiquity, or the kings of England, and made havoc or sold for little or nothing the household stuff. On Wednesday 10 May, being Ascension, Mr Alexander Popham's soldiers, he being a colonel for the Parliament, after dinner rushed into the church, broke down the windows, organs, fonts, seats in the choir and the bishop's seat, besides many other villainies.

On the return of Royalist forces, a local Puritan luminary was forced at the sword's point to eat his words and acknowledge that it was wrong to deface churches and images, condemn the Prayer Book and resist the King. He was made to preach sermons to this effect – good for him.

*Mercurius Rusticus* gives us a detailed account of the profanation of Exeter cathedral.

> Over the communion table in fair letters of gold was written the holy and blessed name of Jesus: this they expunged as superstitious. On each side of the Commandments the pictures of Moses and Aaron were drawn in full: these they deface, they tear the books of Common Prayer to pieces and burn them at the altar. They broke and defaced the glass windows, and left all those ancient monuments, being painted glass and containing matter of story only a miserable spectacle. They struck off the heads of all the statues on all the monuments: especially they deface the bishops' tombs, leaving one without a head, another without a nose, another without a hand, and another without an arm. They brake down the organs and, taking two or three hundred pipes with them, went up and down the streets piping with them.[1]

And so it goes on at length.

We can hardly expect contemporary journalism to get all the details right, so we may rely on a modern authority to sum up.[2] The cathedral was divided in two by a brick wall on the choir screen, for a convenient barrier between the whining sectaries: the chancel went to the Independents, the nave to the Presbyterians. Clarendon said that they might well be left to convert each other, but in fact they quarrelled throughout the Revolution they had made. As Sir Jacob Astley said, after the triumph of their Army in the field: 'You have now done your work, and may go to play – unless you will fall out among yourselves.' This is precisely what happened. The simple truth is that it was impossible to run the country on their basis. Like other revolutions, theirs ended in a military dictatorship.

The Lady Chapel was used for storage; the cloisters demolished for a serge-market, only one wing of them reconstructed by the Victorians. The Treasurer's house became a workhouse and a house of correction for vagrants – Puritans

---

[1]Reproduced in *The English Revolution* III, vol. 4, 299 foll.
[2]R.J.E. Boggis, *History of the Diocese of Exeter*, 410 foll.

were quite as much in favour of discipline as Laud, only he was consistently sympathetic on the Privy Council to the case of the poor. The 15th-century hall of the Vicars Choral became a wool-hall (destroyed by the barbarians in our late war). Of the seventeen parish churches thirteen were sold by an order of 1656, leaving only four – each with its prating minister, two for the poor echoing cathedral.

This was the pattern that was followed at all the cathedrals, with variations. At Salisbury the chapter-house was badly damaged, the glass so much that only fragments remain – replaced by dull glass, inoffensive to Philistines. John Aubrey tells us that Bishop Davenant had hung the choir with purple velvet, 'which was plundered in the sacrilegious times'. And so with other depredations upon the furniture, equipment and ornaments.

Under Laud's pressure the Cathedral had only recently been re-equipped, after a report that 'there are no copes in our church; most of them were sold away about 66 years since, and the rest turned into pulpit cloths and cushions ... and there is a great defect of ornaments about the altar'.[1] This was remedied at considerable expense. Then came the war, when there was fighting in the Close. In 1645 the Prayer Book was suppressed, then Church property confiscated. The Corporation bought the canons' houses for their Puritan ministers in the city, with one Mr Faithful Tate for the cathedral. The Bishop's palace suffered as usual: the hall (required for hospitality) pulled down, the rest converted to an inn and tenements for handicraftsmen.

'In 1653 Dutch prisoners were kept in the cloisters, where they damaged the pillars, and in the Library, where they broke the windows.' Secretly members of the Hyde (Clarendon's) family employed workmen to repair the cathedral: 'They who employ us will pay us; trouble not yourselves to inquire who they are ... they desire not to have their names known.' Thus was the light of civilisation kept going – as Clarendon himself kept the hope of better days going in exile abroad. When they eventually came,

---

[1]D.H. Robertson, *Sarum Close*, 194 foll.

it was to a scene of desolation that the restored clergy returned. Only three of them had survived the Commonwealth .... The task of restoring order was soon begun: the Chancellor undertook the business of sorting the cathedral muniments; extensive repairs were put in hand at the School. The whole of the musical establishment had to be reconstructed. The organ was re-installed, Bishop Duppa subscribing £100 towards the cost, and during the next few years considerable sums were spent in 'pricking' music for the choir. Although a choir of sorts sang at Bishop Henchman's enthronement on 12 December 1660, a complete new choir was not appointed until 16 September 1661.

At Winchester, Norman Sykes tells us, in December 1642 the Parliamentary soldiers

rode up through the body of the church and choir until they came to the altar. They rudely plucked down the table and broke the rail, they threw down the organ, they broke the curiously carved work. From thence they turned to the monuments of the dead; some they utterly demolished, others they defaced. Having wreaked their fury on the beautiful chantries, they flung down several of the mortuary chests and scattered the bones all over the pavement.

In 1651 a Committee of Parliament ordered all cathedral churches, where there was other accommodation, to be surveyed, pulled down and sold for the use of the poor. However, Winchester folk petitioned against this barbarism, and the gem of their city was spared.

Even so, much had been destroyed beyond reparation. The 14th-century series of carvings beneath the canopies of the choir stalls, representing sixty-two biblical episodes, were ruthlessly hacked away. Similarly many of the chantries were defaced and their delicate figures despoiled, while the treasures of the Library, both manuscripts and printed books, were scattered to the winds.

[34]

The devoted Chapter Clerk recovered a number of documents. But later, in 1649, the deanery and prebendal houses were stripped of lead and given over to supporters of Parliament.

*Mercurius Rusticus* adds details germane to our theme. The windows in Bishop Fox's chapel were smashed, 'not because they had any pictures in them, of Patriarch, Prophet, Apostle or Saint, but because they were of painted, coloured glass. Queen Mary's chapel, so called because in it she was married to King Philip of Spain: here they brake the communion table in pieces, and the velvet chair whereon she sat when she was married.' A splendid recent monument was to Lord Treasurer Portland, 'but being of brass their violence made small impression on it; therefore they turn to his father's monument, which being of stone was more obnoxious to their fury'.[1]

Inigo Jones had constructed a rare work of recent art in a classic choir-screen, with life-size bronze statues of James I and Charles I (were they by Le Sueur?). 'They break off the swords from the sides of both the statues, they break the cross from off the globe in the hand of our gracious sovereign now living, and with their swords hacked and hewed the crown on the head of it.' The remains of this fine work of Caroline art – which Puritans detested more even than medieval Gothic – found a home in a Museum at Cambridge.

It is astonishing to think what a treasure-house England was before the spoliation of the Civil War. As again, after the recovery and accumulations of the centuries since, to the comparable spoliation, destruction and dispersals of our time.

In Chichester the now familiar routine was followed. *Mercurius Rusticus* reports that on Innocents' Day 1642 Waller's troops entered the cathedral.[2] 'They seize upon the vestments and ornaments together with the consecrated plate: they left not so much as a cushion for the pulpit nor a chalice for the blessed sacrament. The commanders, having executed the covetous part of sacrilege, they leave the despoiling and destructive part to be finished by the common soldiers.' They followed the usual

---

[1] *The English Revolution* III, vol. IV, 289 foll.
[2] *The English Revolution* III, vol. IV, 283 foll.

inspiration of their kind, smashing the organ with their pole-axes, 'Hark, hark, how the organs go.' They broke down altar, the pictures about it, rails, and desecrated the sanctuary; then came the turn of service-books, gowns, surplices. More particularly, here they went for the series illustrating the history of the church's foundation, in one transept portraits of the kings, in the other of the bishops. 'One of those miscreants picked out the eyes of King Edward VI's picture, saying that, "All this mischief came from him, when he established the Book of Common Prayer." ' The miscreant was only expressing the convictions with which he had been indoctrinated – Puritan ideology.

At the House of Chaplains today, in the carved panel over the doorway, one sees the heads of the figures kneeling to the Virgin Mary religiously knocked off. By 1658, with the neglect consequent upon the confiscation of properties to maintain it, the north-west tower, engraved by Hollar, was ruinous. In the city St Sepulchre, a round church, a rarity, was destroyed in 1642.

The doings at Rochester were much the same: I forbear to repeat the routine, but merely add that here the arras hangings of the choir were torn in pieces, and upon the south gate the statue of Christ was shot to bits. And exceptionally, for once a colonel with his officers called a halt. The cathedral was so impaired by neglect that by the time of the Restoration part of it fell in. The new bishop was a rich man, who out of his private fortune had contributed £8000 to the relief of the clergy thrown out of their livings. Now he devoted himself to the repairs of the cathedral, and endowing Bromley College for their widows in distress.

We may end with Canterbury, cradle of English Christianity. Here the city was plagued by a nasty fanatic, one Culmer, whose conscience forbade him to read the Book of Sports, which enjoined reasonable relaxation after church on Sundays for parishioners working all the rest of the week. Culmer pursued the gentleman who had reported his refusal with false accusations against him to the Privy Council. For this he was committed to the Fleet, and henceforth became a vindictive enemy of Laud, who described him as 'an ignorant person and, with his ignorance, one of the most daring schismatics in all that country'. The Archbishop was right as usual, though he did not know how destructive Culmer would become. His story reveals much of the motivation behind those individuals regarded, absurdly, as victims of Laud's 'persecution'.

In Kent Parliament was in the ascendant, and in 1643 this fellow was presented to the good living of Chartham, where he immediately became unpopular. The parish of Harbledown said that they didn't care what minister they had, so long as it was not 'Blue Dick': refusing to wear a parson's regular black gown, he wore a blue one, just to be different. Any local lies in the district for years were known as 'Culmer's News'. He had got his father to hand over considerable property to him, and then left him in want. In 1644 he published his *Cathedral News*, with scurrilous stories about Archbishop and Chapter; a reposte to him exposed his covetousness.

Naturally, such a candidate would be chosen as a commissioner to demolish superstitious monuments. He took charge of the good work in the cathedral – we have a rare illustration of the miscreants at it, with an immensely tall ladder to get at the carvings and sculptures high up – one of the workers, happy to say, fell and was killed. We have a survey from the antiquary Somner to tell us the state of the great church by the time of the happy Restoration.

> The windows, famous both for strength and beauty, so generally battered and broken down as it lay exposed to the injury of all weathers; the whole roof with that of the steeples, the chapter-houses and cloister extremely impaired and ruined, both in the timber work and lead; the water tables, pipes and much other of the lead in almost all places cut off . . . the choir stripped and robbed of her goodly hangings, her organ and organ loft.

We interrupt the tale to observe that the tapestries from Canterbury are now in the cathedral at Aix-en-Provence.

> The communion table [stripped] of the best of her furniture and ornaments, with the rail before it and screen of tabernacle work [i.e. reredos], richly overlaid with gold behind it; many of the

goodly monuments of the dead shamefully abused, defaced, rifled and plundered of their brasses, iron-gates and bars; the common Dorter (affording good housing for many members of our Church) with the Dean's private chapel and a goodly library over it, quite demolished, the books and other furniture sold away; our houses, with those of our six preachers and petty-canons much impaired ... our very common seal, our registers and other books, together with our records and evidences seized, many of them irrecoverably lost; the Church's guardians, her fair and strong gates turned off the hooks and burned.

When Culmer led his posse in with Parliament's authority for the work, he needed soldiers to escort him; and the citizens set on him when he left. But the work was done. A good deal of the splendid glass survived, as we can see – out of reach; but nearly all the brasses were got at, only the indents left. The fine Laudian font of 1639, of classic black and white marble, was battered down – to be re-assembled at the Restoration. The grand wooden doors now at Christ Church gate were presented then by Archbishop Juxon.

As for Culmer, for his services he was presented by Parliament to the living of Minster in 1644. His former parishioners arranged a bevy of loose women to meet him on his penetration to read himself in: they had locked the church against him, so that he had to smash a window – he was used to that – to penetrate. After that they beat him up. When he required a servant from the parish he was refused any but an illegitimate female; when he fixed ladders to take down the cross from the spire, the people taunted him as the chief cross in the parish. He replied by breaking the stained-glass windows. The parish petitioned again and again against him, and at last refused to pay tithes to support him: he was offered his arrears to go away. When arrested in London, asked why he had destroyed the figure of Christ in windows, not the Devil, he had his answer pert. He replied that Parliament's orders were to take down Christ, not the Devil.

Described as 'odious for his zeal and fury', he had had his innings with the Revolution, and at the Restoration he was one of the 'Ejected'. He was of the stuff of which those martyrs were made, who scuffled out of the Church rather than conform in 1662. I dare say that Archbishop Sheldon – who had helped to keep Anglicanism together through all the miseries of the Revolution – was not sorry to see them go, since Laud had never been able to keep them within.

Enough of their works. Discouraging as it is to live in the squalid, shiftless society of their descendants today, it must have been agonising for persons of taste and culture to live through the havoc those miscreants made during their Revolution – as for artists of genius, Shostakovitch, Solzhenytsin, Pasternak, Akhmatova, Mandelstam, to live through that in Russia.

Why their hatred for works of art and culture?

In addition to the ideological impulse towards iconoclasm, destruction in accordance with beliefs and convictions, however absurd, there is specifically this, which no one dares mention. Nothing brings home to the inferior their inferiority so much as matters of taste and artistic discrimination. I have noticed that psychological phenomenon again and again: the inferior resent intellectual superiority – they call it arrogance, not knowing the precise meaning or application of the word – but not so acutely as they do superior aesthetic standards. For those bring home to them their congenital commonness – the bureaucratic Zhdanovs of the world; for the world of art is a paradise into which they can never penetrate. But they *can* destroy.

It is left to the poets to keep the standards of artistic creativeness – what distinguishes man from the animals and brought him out of the slime – alive in bad times. As a poet wrote during the Puritan Revolution, 'In Defence of the decent Ornaments of Christ Church, Oxon, occasioned by a Banbury brother, who called them Idolatries':

> You that profane our windows with a tongue
> Set like some clock on purpose to go wrong,
> Who when you were at service sighed, because
> You heard the Organ's music, not the Daws,
> Pitying our solemn state, shaking the head
> To see no ruins from the floor to the lead:
> To whose pure nose our Cedar gave offence,

Crying it smelt of Papists' frankincense;
Who, walking on our Marbles, scoffing said
'Whose bodies are under Tombstones laid?'

Counting our Tapers works of darkness, and
Choosing to see Priests in blue-aprons stand
Rather than rich Copes which show the art
Of Sisera's prey Embroidered in each part.
(Our decent Copes only distinction keep
That you may know the Shepherd from the Sheep.)
Thinking our very Bibles too profane
Cause you ne'er bought such Covers in Duck Lane,
Loathing all decency, as if you'd have
Altars as foul and homely as the grave.

Had you one spark of reason, you would find
Yourselves like Idols to have eyes yet blind.
'Tis only some base niggard Heresy
To think Religion loves deformity.

That about sums it up.

# II

# Colleges, Chapels, Parish Churches

Hardly less important than the cathedrals, as repositories of the nation's artistic treasures, were the collegiate churches, the colleges of Oxford and Cambridge, the greater parish churches, and even more the royal chapels. Somerset House was the Queen's residence, and Henrietta Maria was a Catholic. She was no friend of Archbishop Laud, who had indeed converted more individuals from Rome than any other bishop and held others from going over. She was a marked liability with her continual proselytising in the Court circle: like her son, James II later, she hadn't the sense to see how stupid that was in a madly Protestant country. She had no effect on Charles I this way, who was intellectually firm about Anglicanism, founded on the philosophic Richard Hooker. When the Scotch Presbyterian Henderson wrestled with the King for his soul, he was dumbfounded to find that Charles was so well able to defend his position intellectually; Henderson could not cope with it, and was unnerved to find that someone could think differently from himself.

The mob threatened Somerset House, with its household of Capuchin Friars, as early as 1640. In 1643 Parliament saw to their expulsion, a committee was to destroy the idolatrous monuments and 'other superstitious Pictures and Matters' in the chapel; special attention was directed to the quantities of crucifixes, beads, images and pictures of the Friars. In March the chapel was 'licentiously rifled', altars smashed, images broken, ornaments and books burnt. The fact that such objects are venerated by one set of fools is no reason for their destruction by another. We should value them as works of art, the admirable works of men's hands. The altarpiece was by one of the greatest painters there ever have been, Rubens, a personal acquaintance of the cultivated King and Queen. It was thrown into the Thames – think of it, the idiots!

At Whitehall the egregious Harley was in charge of the destruction in the King's Chapel, 'as in all other places of the King's Houses and Chapels': superstitious pictures, monuments, ornaments, and 'all copes, surplices, and other superstitious utensils'. A few years later to the Whitehall Committee was referred the possible sale of tapestries and hangings, particularly where the subjects were 'superstitious', to raise money for the soldiery quartered there. The famous organ case, with its scroll-work, is now in Stanford church, Northamptonshire.

The interesting thing about Harley is that he was a bookish man, interested in collecting books and objects, where his religious views were not affected. This pinpoints our theme: iconoclasm is primarily the product of ideological conviction. Sensible people do not go in for it, civilised sceptics not at all. At his castle of Brampton Bryan he had a valuable library: all destroyed when the place was stormed by the Royalists, as was his birthplace, Wigmore Castle. His losses from his beliefs were enormous, estimated at nearly £13,000. But he built a new church at Brampton Bryan to replace that burnt in the siege: a simple preaching-box, nave and chancel all one, such as his soul could approve. How much more preferable Scudamore's Abbey Dore! Harley was a religious light to all his neighbourhood, maintaining preachers to prate in his three churches. 'He wept much when his servants suffered him to sleep on the Lord's day later than he used, although he had not rested all that night.' The losses to the country for which he was responsible should have kept him awake at night: they were irreparable.

*Mercurius Aulicus* reported his doings pretty faithfully. Besides altar and rails, painted glass windows in the Chapel, in the King's Gallery 'he reformed of all such pictures as displeased his eye ... and so went on, according to the principles of Reformation, till there was nothing left that was rich or glorious'.[1] St George's Chapel, Windsor was a bigger affair – in the next century it was often referred to as a 'cathedral' – and was packed with treasures. Charles I had equipped it with a specially rich service of plate, designed by the leading foreign

[1] *The English Revolution*, III, vol. 3, 132.

goldsmith, Vianen. After Edgehill Colonel Venn appeared to garrison the Castle and all the plate was looted. Here the pillage was on a magnificent scale: Edward IV's coat of mail with its rubies and other gems, all the enamels from Wolsey's unfinished tomb, which Henry VIII had intended for himself. Before the high altar were four splendid bronze candlesticks – now in the church of St Bavon in Ghent. In our time George V and Queen Mary replaced two with replicas. By 1647 the equestrian bronze statue of St George was seized upon for melting down, along with other broken brass and metal, to raise money to prosecute the war. Henry III's fine Purbeck font was broken in accordance with their convictions.

Dean Wren, Sir Christopher's father, tried to save some of the books in his custody, and managed to retrieve a few volumes of records. As usual organs and painted windows were smashed, the big cross in the town destroyed. The organ had been made by the celebrated Ralph Dallam, who made a number of fine organs to serve cultivated Caroline taste – the case ultimately fetched up at St Peter's church, St Albans, which also has a complete altar service with which it had to be re-equipped at the Restoration.

Le Sueur's fine equestrian statue which we see at the head of Whitehall today was not 'miraculously' preserved, it was faithfully hidden throughout the bad times, or that would have gone too. The Parliamentarian poet, Wither, celebrated the spoliation – if he had had more aesthetic sense he would have been a better poet:

> We have seen the pride of kings,
> With those much desirèd things,
> Whence their vain ambition springs,
> Scorned, despised, and set at nought.
> We their *silk*, their *pearls*, their *gold*.
> And their precious *gems* behold
> Scattered, pawned, bought and sold
> And to shame their glory brought.

The shame was theirs who wrought it.

Later, several of the royal residences were sold – and so came to ruin: Nonsuch, Oatlands, Theobalds, Holdenby. Windsor escaped this fate by only one vote – a useful receptacle for prisoners. In 1651 many of the tapestries, hangings, pieces of furniture were removed; in the ransacking a splendid jewel came to light, worth the enormous sum then of £6000: sold by order of Parliament.

Bath Abbey was as yet unfinished; the nave and south transept had been roofed by the Jacobean Bishop Montagu only in 1612–16. The splendidly carved west door had been given by Sir Henry Montagu in 1617. We see the impulse towards reparation and recovery from the bleak days of the Elizabethan age, so far as churches were concerned. Above that doorway the main west window has many defaced figures of angels around the statue of Christ; and all the stained glass has gone, giving a blank lightness in place of the enrichment and colour so regular a Perpendicular church with big windows demands.

At Ripon Minster most of the medieval glass went; a few fragments are collected in only one window in the nave. Some of its monuments were smashed when the town was occupied in 1643. The Caroline monument to Hugh Ripley, of 1637, was defaced – to be re-erected in the next century. Owing to the confiscation of its properties there was no money for its upkeep. So in 1660 the spire of the central tower fell, wrecking woodwork in the choir, and in 1664 the twin spires of the west front had to be removed, leaving that fine church with a more stolid appearance than the original design.

Southwell Minster was another dependency of the arch-bishopric of York. The canons' stalls and archbishop's throne went, but a local squire stopped the idiots from pulling down the choir-screen. In addition to the usual depredations it suffered a loss of its records. The White Book escaped somehow, for it was in the custody of the Chapter, not of the Archbishop, whose palace was ransacked, the library lost; occupied by contending armies, plundered by both.

Oxford was occupied by the King throughout the first war, until 1646, and so did not suffer so badly as Cambridge, which fell in the Puritan-infected area of East Anglia. Oxford's chief loss was practically the whole of its medieval plate. All the colleges, except two, faithfully contributed their plate to be melted down – think of the loss! We can appreciate that the more when we look at the magnificent medieval pieces which the two exceptions, New College and Corpus Christi, retained. Adventitious losses occurred, like one of the Elizabethan engraved brasses by the remarkable craftsman Richard Haydock,[1] at New College, where it was a casualty from the arms storage in the cloister. At the surrender the aristocrat, Fairfax, mounted a guard to protect the Bodleian Library, otherwise it would have suffered from the characteristic attentions of *hoi polloi*.

Of course the proper equipment of college chapels was dismantled and they were left bare. At the Restoration the chapel at All Souls needed restoring and was given a painted ceiling by the English artist, Streeter. He also covered the vast canvas ceiling of the Sheldonian Theatre, Wren's first building: a munificent gift from Archbishop Sheldon, who had been ejected by Parliament as Warden of All Souls, and spent the appalling years intervening in the wilderness. These works of art may be regarded as Royalist demonstrations of the country's return to sanity.

Out at Cuddesdon there was devastation. The Laudian Bishop Bancroft built the see a residence there, between 1632 and 1641, with a chapel: Laud had encouraged the good work and inspected its progress on his visit in 1636. In 1644 it was scorched as a precaution in that border country, against the Parliamentarian forces, and by 1652 destroyed. Parliament sold it up – the lands, remains of the palace and chapel: all had to be rebuilt by Bishop Fell at a cost of £2000 in 1679.

We are fortunate to have an account of the unfortunate doings at Cambridge, because William Dowsing left his record of them. This nasty type has always had a bad name for his destructive activities, but we must remember that he was given the job by the Parliamentarian commander, Manchester, and many counties would have had their Dowsings, only too willing to destroy what they could not appreciate.

Peterhouse, under Cosin as Master, had followed Laud's lead in beautifying churches and ritual, in accordance with his ideal

[1] For him v. my *Elizabethan Renaissance, The Cultural Achievement*, 177-9.

of 'the beauty of holiness'. Peterhouse figured in the charges against him by Prynne, who ran him to death. 'There was a glorious new altar set up and mounted on steps ... basins, candlesticks, tapers standing on it, and a great crucifix hanging over it, and on the altar a pot, which they usually called the incense pot.'[1] This might be regarded as utilitarian, when one reflects what ordinary people smelt like in the seventeenth century.

Dowsing was at Peterhouse just before Christmas 1643 – which Puritans did not otherwise celebrate. 'We pulled down two mighty great angels with wings, and divers other angels; and the four Evangelists and Peter with his Keys over the chapel door. And about 100 cherubims and angels, and divers superstitious letters in gold, and six angels in the windows.' Dowsing was apt to exaggerate numbers, I suspect, to show his masters what a good workman he was. I suggest that a hundred is a round estimate, and refers to the small carved corbels in the roof – such as are a glory of East Anglian churches, where they have survived.

The east end was of course *gleichgestaltet*. The fine east window, depicting Christ's Passion, was restored later, Cosin having taken the precaution of hiding it. Next door, at St Mary the Less: 'We brake down 60 superstitious pictures, some Popes, and some crucifixes, with God the Father sitting in a chair and holding a globe.' Again, we must remember that when Dowsing mentions improbably large numbers, he is referring not to whole windows, but to offending pieces in them.

At King's the Latin accounts of the college show that it had been made to take down its organ, and subsequently the case; while taking away the steps of the sanctuary meant considerable expenditure on 400 paving tiles. Later, there was work on the rood-loft, for woodwork broken at the time of the Parliamentary Commission. Dowsing, on Innocents' day 1643: 'Steps to be taken and 1000 superstitious pictures, the ladder of Christ and thieves to go [i.e. one section], many crosses, Jesus writ on them.'[2] He was given a tip of 6s. 8d.: was this to go away? It has

[1] J.W. Clark, *The Architectural History of the University of Cambridge*, I. 46 foll.
[2] Clark, I. 511.

been said that those glorious windows were spared, because the Provost knew Oliver Cromwell – after all, he was a Cambridge man. In our time the Leftist descendants of the Dowsings of the 17th century have levelled the steps to the dais in hall, in accordance with their ideology – the illusion of equality.

Dowsing celebrated New Year 1644 at Christ's; 'we pulled down divers pictures and angels, and the steps D. Bambridge have [sic] promised to take them down'.[1] This was the chapel as Milton knew it. The organ escaped destruction, though damaged, for later it was patched up and in 1658 put in the Parlour; in 1660 restored to the chapel. We recall the young Milton there:

> But let my due feet never fail
> To walk the studious Cloisters pale,
> And love the high embowèd Roof
> With antique Pillars massy proof,
> And storied Windows richly dight
> Casting a dim religious light.
>
> There let the pealing Organ blow
> To the full voiced Choir below,
> In Service high and Anthems clear,
> As may with sweetness, through mine ear,
> Dissolve me into extasies
> And bring all Heaven before mine eyes.

What caused him to change? The young Milton was an idealist, who did not know the facts of life before his miserable marriage; and, like such gifted young people, he had a vision of reforming the world. So he threw in his lot with the reformers, sharing their fatuous Millenarian expectations of a new Heaven and a new Earth.[2] The idealist became, as happens in revolutions, an idealogue – to be disillusioned later. Out of his disillusionment came his *Paradise Lost*, inner consolation for defeat; and last, his

---

[1] Clark, II, 207.
[2] cf. Sir Christopher Hill, *The Experience of Defeat*, c. III.

autobiographical fabric of wish-fulfilment, blind like Samson Agonistes.[1]

At Jesus College, under the Laudian impulse – Cambridge has a splendid Van Dyke of the Archbishop, with characteristic anxious expression – a costly new Dallam organ had been installed in that beautiful medieval chapel. It had to be taken down, and was concealed for better times, when the sanctuary and altar had to be properly re-equipped, a new floor laid, new hangings etc. Dowsing: 'We digged up the steps, and broke down of superstitious Saints and Angels 120 at least.'[2] Magdalene College: 'We brake down about 40 superstitious pictures; Joseph and Mary stood to be espoused in the windows.'[3] The Restoration saw repairs, the Master himself giving a new organ. Queens': 'We beat down 110 superstitious pictures, besides Cherubims and Engravings; none of the Fellows would put on their hats in all the time they were in the chapel. We digged up the steps for three hours, and brake down 10 or 12 Apostles and Saints within the hall.'[4] The college gives account of the repairs later, apparently by private munificence; but we must remember how much that was shattered beyond repair could not be replaced.

At Trinity in 1636 the Senior Bursar was entrusted with 'the beautifying of the chapel and the decent adorning of the communion table'.[5] A new pavement, partly of marble, was laid down, walls wainscoted and decorated with gilt, new altar frontals and hangings. The organ was repaired, painted and gilded. Dowsing: 'We had four Cherims, and steps levelled.' The College was forced to 'reform' its chapel, take down the organ, whiten over figures; payments made to 'masons, bricklayers, carpenters, and upholsterers, for removing the hangings and rails'.

We may see the reaction to this miscreant's doings from an eye-witness, a Cambridge don. Dowsing 'goes about the country like a Bedlam breaking glass windows, having battered and

[1]cf. my *Milton the Puritan: Portrait of a Mind*, cc. X, XI.
[2]Clark, II. 143.
[3]Clark, II. 375.
[4]Clark, II. 39.
[5]Clark, II. 575 foll.

beaten down all our painted glass, not only in our chapel but (contrary to Order) in our public Schools [the Old Schools at Cambridge], halls, libraries and chambers, mistaking perhaps the liberal Arts for Saints'. This reflects a cultivated person's scorn for Dowsing's lack of cultivation – to judge from the 'Lating' [sic] of which be boasted.

As against all this damage, Cambridge did not suffer so severely from the loss of medieval plate as Oxford did. At the outbreak of war Cromwell signalised himself by preventing the carriage of plate to the King at Oxford; hence more has been preserved by the Cambridge colleges, and for that at least we may be grateful.

It is impossible to do justice to the vast subject of the devastation in parish churches – especially of stained glass, sculpture in wood and stone, monuments and brasses – throughout the length and breadth of the land: from the splendid churches of the East Riding of Yorkshire and Lincolnshire, to the smaller churches of Sussex, to the magnificent fanes of the Fenland to remote Cornwall. There the little church of Mevagissey had its two church bells sold to a Quaker pewterer of St Austell, Lawrence Growden; who invested handsomely in Pennsylvania, and whose ultimate heiress, Grace Growden, married the Loyalist, Joseph Galloway. This sale was commemorated in Cornish folklore, going back to those bad times:

> Ye men of Port-hilly,
> O weren't you silly people
> To sell your bells
> For money to pull down your steeple?

The steeple never has been replaced.

Or take St Agnes on the north coast of Cornwall. The 18th-century antiquary, Thomas Tonkin, tells us: 'in the windows of this church was formerly painted the history of the life and martyrdom of St Agnes; which being broken in the time of the Grand Rebellion, there is nothing now left but a small piece in one of the south windows, in which the heads of some figures are still to be seen'. Altogether, little medieval glass is left in Cornwall now.

If we wish to see the ideal of a Laudian church unspoiled, we should pay a pilgrimage to Leeds, to see St John's church, Briggate. Even the pedestrian Pevsner waxes enthusiastic about it:

> ...the only church at Leeds of more than local interest, built in 1632-4, and there are few large churches of that date in England. The interior is delightfully complete in its original form. How grateful we must be for this! – original screen across nave and aisles, very sumptuous with tapering pillars or balusters; pulpit with tester equally sumptuous; benches nearly complete; three small brass chandeliers in front of the altar; Royal arms of wood, carved, originally above the rood screen; plate, two cups of 1634. Monument to John Harrison, cloth merchant and founder of the church, 1656.

He must have protected the creation he had reason to be proud of, through the bad times.

Or we may still see similar interiors with their splendid Caroline woodwork, rood-screen and all – rare as they are – at Leighton Bromswold in Bedfordshire, or Croscombe in Somerset. If we wish to see an example of the Puritan ideal of worship, we have an example at Taynton in Gloucestershire: the church, destroyed in 1643, was new-ordered by Parliament – a plain hall orientated North and South, not East and West. The Restoration put in altar and font. In contrast we have a beautiful church at Staunton Harold in Leicestershire, built as a challenge to the Puritan régime in 1653: sumptuous woodwork, rood-screen, stalls, wrought iron and velvet. Over the door we read the inscription: 'When all things sacred throughout the nation were either demolished or profaned, Sir Robert Shirley, Baronet, founded this church, whose singular praise it is to have done the best things in the worst of times.' For this challenge he was sent to the Tower.

Apart from religious prejudice, we all know which is to be preferred as art. Beyond that, the preaching-boxes are without the sense of mystery essential to religion; and this without prejudice to dogma, in which it is unnecessary to believe.

The little community of Nicholas Ferrar at Little Gidding in Bedfordshire (that other Bedfordshire Saint, John Bunyan, has received more than his due from everybody) represented Laud's ideal in being.[1] In consequence it was continually libelled by Puritan propaganda, and attacked in pamphlets as 'the Arminian Nunnery'. It was not: it was a family community, devoted to good works, neighbourly charity, medicine and surgery as needed, with a school. The community lived by regular rule, but also accomplished artistic work in fine needlework and embroidery, printing books and providing them with fine bindings.

Ferrar had bought the neglected estate, with its derelict church which had become a haybarn. He restored it, put in organs in house and church (they were cultivated people, devoted to music), in the church a cedar-wood altar, woodwork, tapestries, carpets. Spies were sent down to see what was going on; great offence was taken to the inscription, IHS – *Jesus Hominum Salvator* – that of the Jesuits, they ignorantly called it. Bishop Williams, no friend of Laud, advised them to take it down because of 'the folly and madness of the people'. QED.

The community produced a magnificent Concordance of the Four Evangelists, in English, Latin, French, and Italian, which they brought up to Laud for presentation to young Prince Charles.[2] The Archbishop was a connoisseur, and himself acquired a splendid bible, with the Five Wounds of Christ richly embroidered on the cover. Next day, Maundy Thursday, Laud took them across to that other connoisseur, the King, who was similarly impressed with the workmanship.

There can be few specimens of Little Gidding printing and binding in existence, for shortly the place was attacked and ransacked; papers destroyed, organs burnt, plate and furniture carried away, the west front of the little church damaged beyond repair – to be rebuilt in the next century. The silver claws of the lectern were wrenched off, though that is the only thing that remains: a grand 15th-century eagle, like that at Urbino, with moulded stem and lions at base.

[1] cf. A.L. Maycock, *Nicholas Ferrar of Little Gidding.*
[2] cf. D. Gardiner, *The Story of Lambeth Palace*, 138–9.

[51]

Little Gidding has inspired a poem by Eliot, in our time:

> you leave the rough road
> And turn behind the pig-sty to the dull façade
> And the tombstone. And what you thought you came for
> Is only a shell ... You are here to kneel
> Where prayer has been valid ...
>
> If I think of a king at nightfall,
> Of three men, and more, on the scaffold
> And a few who died forgotten ...
> These men, and those who opposed them
> And those whom they opposed
> Accept the constitution of silence
> And are folded in a single party.
> The Dead, the memorable Dead.

Has any such poem, or work of art, been inspired by Puritanism in our time?

We may see something of the desirable impulse the reforming Laud gave, in the case of a remote Dorset parish, Hardy's Puddletown. At the Reformation the church had been robbed of a rich collection of vestments and plate. The moment Laud (belatedly) became archbishop to take up the long-neglected work of reparation, his sensible Visitation Articles directed communion tables to be placed at the east end, with a decent rail 'to prevent it from being thrust and tumbled by the crowd'. Communicants were to kneel at the rail 'for convenience and comeliness', *not* for altar-worship. Laud was not a Papist. Next year his instructions were carried out: St Mary's Puddletown was to have new seats throughout, pulpit, chancel screen, communion table, 'a new cover for the font that is all in decay'. In 1635 a west gallery was erected, with the Royal arms; in 1638 the vicar bequeathed a chalice.

Dowsing left a disgraceful record of his work throughout Suffolk; with so many churches, it is impossible to go into it in detail.[1] Let us select only a few. Ipswich had a dozen churches.

---

[1] *The Journal of William Dowsing*, ed. C.H.E. White.

At Peter's was on the porch the Crown of Thorns, the Sponge and Nails, and the Trinity in stone; and the rails were there, which I gave order to break in pieces. Mary Elms: There was four iron crosses on the steeple, which they promised to take down that day or the next. Nicholas: We brake 6 superstitious pictures and took up 2 brass of *ora pro nobis*, and gave order for another *cujus anima* [sic] *propitietur Deus*. Matthew's: We brake down 35 superstitious pictures, 3 angels with stars on their breasts, and crosses. Mary's at the Tower: We took up 6 brass inscriptions with *ora pro nobis*, and *cujus animae propitietur Deus*, and *Pray for the soul* in English. I gave order to take down 5 iron crosses, and one of wood on the steeple. Margaret's: There was 12 Apostles in stone taken down, which a godly man, a churchwarden, promised to do. Clement's: They four days before had beaten up divers inscriptions.

Enough, though not the whole. This accounts for the fact that today the fine fabrics of Ipswich churches are bleak in their interiors. We note that frequently enough Dowsing left orders for things to be destroyed: if some have survived, it may be oversight, or his orders were not carried out. The editor of this volume supplies us with Notes as to what was lost from the churches, particularly from the splendid roofs with numerous winged angels that are such a feature in East Anglia – such as have survived.

Sometimes others had been at work before Dowsing arrived. 'At Haverhill we broke down about an hundred superstitious Pictures, and seven Friars hugging a Nun; and the Picture of God and Christ, and divers others very superstitious. And 200 had been broken down before I came. And we beat down a great stoning cross on the top of the church'. Only very occasionally did anyone dare to resist. 'At Cornard Magna: I took up 2 inscriptions *Pray for our souls*, and gave order to take down a cross on the steeple, and to level the steps. John Pain, churchwarden, for not paying and doing his duty as enjoined by the Ordinance, I charged the constable to carry him before the Earl of Manchester.' Evidently not a godly man. We have a long account of the destruction at Ufford – 30 superstitious pictures and 37 more to be broken down, 'and some of them we brake now'; 12 cherubims on the roof of the chancel. 'We brake down the organ cases, and gave them to the poor. There is a glorious cover over the font, like a Pope's triple crown, with a pelican on top all gilt over with gold.' But – 'we were kept out of the church above 2 hours, and neither churchwardens that were enjoined these things three months before had not done them in May. And I sent one of them to see it done, and they would not let him have the key. And now neither the churchwardens, nor the constable, and the sexton, would not let us have the key in 2 hours' time.' New churchwardens were intruded. Dowsing was grieved when a townsman said that 'I sent men to rifle the church'; and the old churchwarden said, 'I went about to pull down the church, and had carried away part.'

Thus we could accompany this creature on his work, and giving orders for others to carry out more, all round Suffolk. We refrain – too sickening.


The spirit thus revealed is in marked contrast with that which inspired Caroline worship – George Herbert, for example, on 'The Church Floor':

Mark you the floor? that square and speckled stone
    Which looks so firm and strong,

                        Is *Patience*;

And th'other, black and grave, wherewith each one
    Is checkered all along,

                        *Humility*;

The gentle rising, which on either hand
    Leads to the Choir above,

                        Is *Confidence*;

But the sweet cement, which in one sure band
    Ties the whole frame, is *Love*

                        And *Charity*.


Had the Puritans much Humility? we may ask. No more than Lenin. These qualities of Humility and Charity, so evident in the poet Herbert, are not evident in the poet Milton.

Herbert on 'The Church Windows':

[54]

But when thou dost anneal in glass thy story
  Making thy life to shine within
The holy Preachers – then the light and glory
  More reverend grows, and more doth win,
  Which else shows waterish, bleak and thin.
Doctrine and life, colours and light, in one
  When they combine and mingle, bring
A strong regard and awe; but speech alone
  Doth vanish like a flaring thing,
  And in the ear, not conscience, ring.

The pulpit oratory of the Puritans, which spilled over into hundreds of publications at the time, has certainly vanished; the glorious windows that have survived their vandalism speak to us still, in 'colours and light'.

George Herbert was in the habit of walking across the meadows from his church at Bemerton to hear and take part in the music of the cathedral at Salisbury. The Recorder of the city was a Puritan lawyer, Henry Sherfield. A vestryman at St Edmund's objected to some people bowing to God the Father in a painted window, in red and blue cloak measuring sun and moon with compasses (it must have been charming). In 1630 Sherfield got the vestry to agree to destroy it. The bishop, John Davenant, a civilised person, forbade this. So Sherfield broke the window himself. For this Star Chamber fined him £500, and Laud made him apologise to the Bishop.

The fact that some people bowed to a painted image is no reason for destroying something beautiful; but this was what Puritans meant by 'completing' the Reformation. Their Revolution gave them their chance.

The poet Strode describes the function of painted glass in instructing those who could not read, as we see from his poem on the splendid windows of Fairford church, which fortunately survived:

Those images so faithfully
Report true feature to the eye
As you may think each picture was
Some visage in a looking glass . . .

But these have holy physnomy:
Each pane instructs the laity
With silent eloquence; for here
Devotion leads the eye, not ear,
To note the catechising paint,
Whose easy phrase doth so acquaint
Our sense with Gospel that the Creed
In such a hand the weak may read:
Such types even yet of virtue be,
And Christ as in a glass we see.

Bishop Davenant, like Hall – both moderates – had been at the Synod of Dort in 1618, where Davenant argued for universal redemption against the Calvinist doctrine of redemption only of the Elect, i.e. themselves. The conviction that they were the redeemed and others eternally damned gave them the assurance with which they attacked more tolerant and civilised persons. It reminds one of Lenin's insistence on his narrow doctrines as orthodoxy, and any deviation as heretical. As bishop, Davenant issued a declaration against preaching on these nonsensical propositions, over which people were at each other's throats. Himself preached on 'God's Love for Man' and disputed any 'absolute decree for their damnation'. This was contrary to uncivilised Calvinist orthodoxy.

Naturally, any gaiety in the Christian life was repugnant to these people – hysteria, or excitement (they regularly called it 'inspiration'), and play-acting with such as Hugh Peters (their opponents diagnosed it as hypocrisy, which it was in the literal sense of the word). Like George Herbert, Herrick would walk to his cathedral for services and to hear the music – from Dean Prior into Exeter:

### To Music, to becalm his Fever

Charm me asleep, and melt me so
With thy delicious numbers;
That being ravished, hence I go
Away in easy slumbers...

Fall on me like a silent dew,
Or like those maiden showers
Which, by the peep of day, do strew
A Baptism o'er the flowers.

Herrick too kept the proper feasts and saints' days of the Church:

## Ceremonies for Candlemas Eve

Down with the rosemary and bays,
Down with the mistletoe;
Instead of holly now upraise
The greener box for show.

The holly hitherto did sway –
Let box now domineer,
Until the dancing Easter day,
Or Easter's eve appear.

Herrick also was given to good works: he was not obsessed by Justification by Faith alone. In his Devonshire vicarage,

Lord, Thou hast given me a cell
Wherein to dwell,
A little house, whose humble roof
Is weather-proof . . .
Low is my porch, as is my fate,
Both void of state;
And yet the threshold of my door
Is worn by the poor . . .

Even a bishop, like Bishop Corbet of Oxford, could enjoy the folklore of the countryside, in his 'Farewell rewards and fairies' (which so enchanted Kipling):

Lament, lament, old Abbeys,
The Fairies lost command;
They did but change priests' babies,

[57]

But some have changed your land:
And all your children stoln from thence
Are now grown Puritans,
Who live as changelings ever since
For love of your demesnes.

Since it is impossible to do justice to the destruction in parish churches all over the land – some nine thousand of them – let us look briefly at a couple of summaries from different areas.

In Hertfordshire a score of churches had their communion rails pulled up, those at Bocking burnt before the Captain's lodging[1] – and we must remember the excellence of Caroline craftsmanship. At Hingham parish zealots did the job of destruction themselves. They had encouragement from the pulpit, where a Puritan, in a long extemporary prayer before a longer sermon, prayed, 'We have offended Thee in wearing the surplice, in signing with the Cross and using the ring of marriage.' Such was the cant. Puritan semantics were no less distasteful: they regularly referred to themselves as 'the Saints' and 'the godly', loyalists were 'malignants', 'delinquents', and 'carnally minded'. We hear of the 'malignant queans' of Grantham, i.e. loyalist women folk. The Royalist defence of Crowland was inspired by 'a Baalam's priest in the town, a right son of Belial; who brought the Crowlanders to church and read certain collects out of his idol service-book by way of thanksgiving for their good success, as they impiously called it'. The reality behind the cant was expressed by *The Soldier's Pocket Bible*, edited by the Puritan Calamy, encouraging 'to fight the Lord's battles, both before the fight, in the fight, and after the fight'.

We can accompany an antiquarian-minded Royalist captain, Richard Symonds, around the country, who in the intervals of serving in the field took time off to record antiquities, inscriptions, objects of beauty and historic interest, at risk not only from the accidents of war but from the attentions of fanatics and fools.[2] 'Buckingham church: never were any windows more

[1]cf. A. Kingston, *East Anglia and the Great Civil War.*
[2]Richard Symonds, *Diary . . .* , ed. C.E. Long. Camden Society.

broken, in May 1644, by the rebels of Northampton' – the church so damaged as to need rebuilding in the next century. At Hillesden, where the fine Elizabethan house was besieged and burnt, the splendid church next door was much damaged – one still sees the bullet-marks when one goes there.[1] It is bereft of all its medieval windows; effigies were broken, altar-tomb in chancel destroyed.

Essex's army on its way west in 1643 destroyed the crosses in town-places they passed through, as at Abingdon. Banbury lost all its three crosses – the High Cross of which is remembered in traditional folklore, 'Ride a-cock horse, to Banbury Cross' – for the town was a hot-bed of Puritanism. Two of these had been defaced already, and the third was attacked before the Civil War.[2] When the shaft fell and the cross was smashed in small pieces, a townsman crowed, 'God be thanked, the God Dagon is fallen to the ground.' (Bible-mania again.) Laud ordered it to be replaced: the town would not carry it out. Bishop Corbet:

> The crosses also, like old stumps of trees,
> Or stools for horsemen that have feeble knees,
> Carry no heads above ground.

As I pass through the town of Faringdon I always note that the spire on the church is missing – local tradition says, as usual, by Cromwell. (He gets the blame for more ills than he was responsible for, though he wrought many.) Marching through Devon in 1644 Essex's army took the communion cup from Newton St Cyres, and rifled the poor-box; at Whitstone they stole the fine funeral pall of black velvet. Taunton had had a splendid new organ, costing some £200, installed just before the outbreak of revolution; so too South Petherton, and Kingsbury where was a new pair of organs in the chancel. All were wrecked. One sees what a period of reparation and beautifying of churches Laud's era had been.

John Aubrey tells us that at Westport at Malmesbury,

---

[1] v. 'Hillesden in Buckinghamshire', in my *Times, Persons, Places*.
[2] P. Harvey and B.S. Trinder, 'New Light on Banbury's Crosses', *Banbury Historical Society*, 1967.

here was, before the late wars, a very pretty church consisting of three aisles, with a fair spire-steeple with fine tuneable bells: which, when the town was taken by Sir W. Waller was converted into ordnance, and the church pulled down to the ground. The steeple was higher than that now standing in the borough, which much added to the prospect. The windows were well painted, and in them were inscriptions that declared much antiquity.[1]

In Cornwall, St Issey rectory had belonged to the Dean and Chapter of Exeter – consequently confiscated. During the Commonwealth the recipients of the tithes spent nothing on maintenance, so by 1662 the chancel and vicarage were ruinous, the font wrecked, by 1684 the tower in ruins. Similarly at Goran the vicarage house was ruinous, Tonkin tells us, 'let down by sequestrators in the late rebellious times', the church windows broken. This kind of thing must have been widespread: we must wait for local historians to collect the information from their counties. All the trees between Carn Brea and the sea were cut down in the war – still mostly bare heathland today. We must remember in the deplorable account the devastation of the timber resources of the country, as well as the loss of horses – the Royal Stud, for example, was dismantled and dispersed. No wonder the country's blood-stock needed reviving by the importation of such famous stallions as the Godolphin Arabian (which has *his* monument at Gogmagog, near Cambridge).

Cornwall retained most of the brasses in its churches; since it was a poor county it had not a large collection.[2] Puritan counties lost a much higher proportion.[3] In Huntingdonshire, Cromwell's home county, only 9 medieval brasses remain, to 48 indents, i.e. the impression left in the stone where the brasses had been ripped up – 'slave to mortal rage', in Shakespeare's phrase, who as a conservative, cultivated man disapproved of such vandalism. (Did Milton?) In West Sussex, dominated by Parliament, 52 medieval brasses remain as against 87 lost; in East Sussex, which was more Royalist, 54 as against 40

[1]John Aubrey, *Brief Lives*, ed. A. Clark, I. 326.
[2]cf. E.H.W. Dunkin, *The Monumental Brasses of Cornwall*.
[3]J. Bertram, *Lost Brasses*.

destroyed. In Bedfordshire, surprisingly, almost a half remain – 101 as against 109 lost; in Somerset 38 compared with 48 indents. Peterborough lost 22, Winchester 23, and Lincoln a vastly greater number, apparently all.

In remote and Royalist Cornwall conformity with Puritan ideals was rather belated. It was not until 1647 that the organ and altar rails were taken away from the parish church at St Ives.[1] Before the war there had been a regular organist. A good many parish churches must have had small organs. Puritans seem to have had a crazy objection to the organ in itself – almost the first thing they made for when they attacked cathedral or church.

As the Complaint from Cambridge summed up later, these people 'widowed the arts and drove the Muses from their ancient habitations'.

We can see something of the kind of thing that happened in the parishes from the centre, at Westminster.

The living of St Martin's-in the-Fields was the first in England to be sequestrated. On 1 December 1642 the vicar was extruded, and one Dr Wincop 'appointed Lecturer to preach every Lord's Day in the forenoon', by the House of Commons. He held office till the Restoration, but nothing was done for the fabric .... In 1645 Parliament ruled that anyone possessing a Book of Common Prayer was made liable to a heavy fine or to imprisonment up to one year.[2]

This was inoperable, like their barbarous imposition of the death penalty for adultery.

In 1647 the pleasant Spring Gardens, thrown open to the public by Charles I and much used for walking in on Sundays were closed on that day, since every form of enjoyment was treated as a desecration of the Sabbath. A parishioner of St Martin's, Dr White, was fined for having company in his own house on a Sabbath day. Even the inn sign of the Golden Cross at Charing

[1]J.H. Matthews, *A History of ... St Ives*, etc, 220.
[2]K. A. Esdaile, *St Martin in the Fields*, 72-3.

Cross was removed as Popish; and the use of the Prayer Book, even for family prayers, led to arrest, fine or imprisonment. The State Papers, like the parish records of St Martin's themselves, are full of such petty tyrannies ... soldiers were authorised to enter any house and take such proceedings as they thought fit. At St Margaret's, Westminster, the churchwardens were fined and imprisoned in 1653 for holding a service on Christmas Day, and adorning the church.

It was, in fact, a sour régime imposed upon, and against, the natural spirit and gaiety of the English people. However, cheerfulness would keep breaking in. It was unthinkable that this state of things would go on for long – it was prolonged, as Cowley saw, by Cromwell's military dictatorship. When one reads the correspondence between Sir Justinian Isham and extruded Bishop Duppa one notes a real sense of persecution, of latent threat and fear.

It is no part of my design to write the story of the clergy extruded from their parishes, though this was on such an enormous scale that it amounted in itself to a revolution in the Church, apart from the dislocation and disarray of the services, and the unpopularity of the intruders – often a haphazard, job lot. On a conservative estimate some 3000 to 3500 clergy were ejected, out of about 8600 livings, i.e. more than a third.[1] The proportion varied in different areas: in Puritan East Anglia some 44 per cent, in Royalist Dorset under 30 per cent. All over the country it meant a tremendous upheaval and much suffering. Parliament did not wish to have clergy starving, and allotted one-fifth of the value of a living to maintain the extruded clergyman's wife and children. But often these livings had been exiguous in themselves – another matter which Laud had ardently desired to reform; and often enough the fifth was hard to come by or in default. In Cornwall such payments varied from a mere £3 to £24 at most. If the clergyman was a celibate priest, with no wife or children to support – though he might have parents or other family to maintain – he got nothing.

[1] cf. G.B. Tatham, *The Puritans in Power*, esp. cc. 3 and 6, from which quotations come.

The extrusion of the local cleric whom the parish was used to was usually unpopular, and in some cases led to a riot, and reinstatement. The evidence shows that those who took up the complaints encouraged by Parliament against 'scandalous' or 'delinquent' ministers were always a minority in the parish – usually no more than nine or ten, i.e. the Puritan minority. Parliament recognised the fact unwillingly in a typically humbugging statement urging people to bring forward complaints:

> Because it is found by sad experience that parishioners are not forward to complain of their ministers, although they be very scandalous, but – having this price and power in their hands, yet want hearts [!] to make use thereof, too many being enemies to that blessed reformation so much by the Parliament desired, and loth to come under a powerful ministry. And some, sparing their ministers because such ministers, to gain the good opinions of their people, do spare them in their tithes, and therefore are esteemed quiet men or the like .... You are therefore required to call unto you some well-affected men within every hundred ... to further the public reformation ... and encouraged by you to inquire after the doctrines, lives and conversations of all ministers and schoolmasters, and to give you information both what can be deposed, and who can depose the same.

This revealing declaration reinforces several of our themes. First, under the Puritan semantics, notice the nasty spirit, quite in accordance with revolutions, encouraging to spy and report on their neighbours – in which decent English folk are reproved for being backward. The partisanship may be taken for granted: it is the 'well-affected' who are to do the mean business. Secondly, the evidence shows that it was always *political* unsatisfactoriness that counted most in throwing the clergy out, not only when obvious Royalists in their sympathies but even in cases where they tried to be 'neuters'. This was perhaps to be expected, but it corroborates the point that this was a revolution. Less to be expected was the fact that leading Puritan families, the gentry, did not appear on these commissions: they were staffed from the lower orders. This highlights once more a main theme of this book – the class element in the Puritan Revolution.

This is brought home also in the imprisonment some of the clergy suffered. Lambeth and bishops' town houses in London were used as prisons for them. In 1645 ruthless overcrowding at Lambeth brought on gaol-fever, from which there was 'an appalling mortality'. White Kennet, a careful scholar, tells us that most of these had been brought up from the Royalist West, of whom nearly a hundred disappeared. At one point, in the scare of the King's approach to London in 1643, prisoners were transferred temporarily to two hulks in the Thames.

One of the prisoners singled out for this treatment was a chaplain of Laud's, and Master of Jesus College, Cambridge. From Ely House he wrote in October 1643 that he had already spent '19 weeks in the Tower, 30 weeks in Lord Petre's house [since he was a Catholic, his house was used as a prison], 10 days in the ship, and 7 weeks here in Ely House', i.e. Bishop Wren's. To add insult to injury he had to pay for his keep. On board ship they had had to lie the first night on the bare deck without cover; when it rained they were never dry; when it was fair weather they sweltered, 'there being of us in that one small Ipswich coal ship, so low-built too that we could not walk nor stand upright in it, within one or two of threescore: whereof 6 knights, and 8 doctors of divinity, and divers gentlemen of very good worth'.

Once more one sees the class element. At the beginning the Revolution was made by one half of the governing class against the other half; as it progressed it became the Revolution of a very small minority, upheld by the Army, against the bulk of the country, perhaps nine-tenths of it. Of the Church, the whole governing element – bishops, deans and chapters – was cut off, their endowments confiscated; at the universities, most of the Heads of Houses. This Sterne survived to see a better day. After the Restoration he became archbishop of York, and, even better, he was great-grandfather of the clerical novelist, author of *Tristram Shandy*.

Many of the extruded clergy suffered want, whether at home or in exile. The Dean of Bristol's little maid was seen 'in the market selling of rosemary and bays to buy bread'; Dean Cosin in Paris was 'exceeding poor and necessitous, even to the want of necessities for his health'. Only in a very few cases was a Royalist cleric done to death. That of Dr Raleigh, Dean of Wells, was notorious, for he was the nephew of Sir Walter Raleigh.[1] A person of marked ability, he was one of the Great Tew circle, a friend of Falkland and Chillingworth, and of the King's eminent chaplain, Dr Hammond. He was in and out of prison several years, at one time in his own Deanery, turned into a gaol; then in the county gaol at Ilchester and elsewhere. Meanwhile, his wife, thrown out of his rectory at Chedzoy, lay a couple of nights in the cornfields, till she could seek refuge with the Dean's father, Sir Carew Raleigh. The Dean was returned to his Deanery, to the charge of a shoemaker, who, upon some altercation, stabbed him in the back – a wound from which, after lingering some weeks, the Dean died.

There were a very few other examples of this extreme inhumanity; perhaps we may put them down to the accidents of war.

---

[1] J. Walker, *The Sufferings of the Clergy*, ed. of 1862, 289 foll.; G.B. Tatham, *Dr John Walker* and 'The Sufferings of the Clergy', 166, 216.

# III

# Palaces, Castles, Mansions

Royal palaces and residences, bishops' palaces and castles, castles in general, mansions and country houses may be said to have suffered even worse than cathedrals and churches, for where these rose again, many of those other edifices disappeared totally. Monarchs with their dependent Court needed a number of palaces, if only for sanitary reasons: after a couple of months' residence by several hundred people the place needed a thorough cleansing, so the Court moved on. The Crown's residences were mostly along, or not far from, the banks of the Thames, for it was easier to move up and down by barge – as the Valois kings and their Court moved up and down the châteaux of the Loire. As for hygiene, it was said of 17th-century Versailles that it could be smelt three miles away; and even the Compiègne of Napoleon III had only one bathroom.

Whitehall was the least disturbed of the royal palaces – except for the chapel – for it came to house the Puritan government and bureaucracy; such as Hugh Peters, the Cromwellian 'archbishop', as they called him had his rooms there. Hampton Court was saved as a country residence for 'his Highness', the Protector – as head of the state he had to have a certain style, and anyway he was an aristocrat; he liked music, of a sedate kind. Windsor Castle became a prison.

Somerset House, the Queen's residence, suffered severely – not only the chapel which had been mauled, the works of art within, the statues and fountains from the terraces. At the Restoration all was to do again, as described in Cowley's poem, 'On the Queen's Repairing Somerset House':

> Nothing remained to adorn this Princely place
> Which covetous hands could take, or rude deface.
> In all my rooms and galleries I found

[66]

The richest figures torn, and all around
Dismembered statues of great heroes lay –
Such Naseby's field seemed on the fatal day.
And me, when nought for robbery was left,
They starved to death: the gasping walls were cleft,
The pillars sunk, the roofs above me wept,
No sign of spring or joy my garden kept:
Nothing was seen which could content the eye
Till dead the impious Tyrant here did lie.

(Cromwell's body lay in state there in 1658.)

The pity of this was all the greater because the Caroline period marked a brief and brilliant apogee of the arts in England. An authority tells us,

> Charles I was the most enthusiastic and discerning patron of the arts to grace the English throne and he assembled a collection of pictures and works of art unequalled in the history of English taste. His accession in 1625 was an event of cardinal importance for the arts in England; the activities of the Whitehall group (the small circle of collectors, patrons, and amateurs of which the King was the heart) were a new and integral part of the life of the Court. That life was set against, and inevitably coloured by, the magnificent possessions with which Charles filled his palaces.[1]

Even the supercilious Lucy Hutchinson, wife of the regicide Colonel, allowed in her Memoirs that

> King Charles was temperate, chaste, and serious. Men of learning and ingenuity in all arts were in esteem and received encouragement from the King, who was a most excellent judge and a great lover of paintings, carvings, gravings, and many other ingenuities, less offensive than the bawdy and profane abusive wit which was the only exercise of the other Court.

We may regard the Court of Charles II as a natural reaction against the rule of the Saints, while wars deteriorate standards.

[1] M. Whinney and O. Millar, *English Art, 1625–1714*, i. (*Oxford History of English Art*).

We must not underestimate the Elizabethan architectural heritage the Stuarts succeeded to, or the distinctive style the Elizabethans achieved in their palaces and mansions, great and small. An authority speaks of it as 'a style to a considerable extent independent of, and even hostile to the classical architecture of the Continent: it drew its strength as much from native Gothic roots.'[1] He pays tribute to the 'novelty, daring and unity of the architecture as a whole that emerged in the last twenty years of the reign and ran on well into the 17th century: an architecture which would have been impossible if England had been exposed to the full blast of the Renaissance, and which is one of the curiosities and the triumphs of European art.'

If we wish to see an Elizabethan palace on the grandest scale, such as has survived, we should study Burghley House near Stamford, in which the inspiration, the ambition and fantasy, of the age are expressed. The great Lord Burghley built an equally grand palace for the junior branch of his family at Theobalds in Hertfordshire. It was enormous, with its courts, four square towers and turrets, its splendid chambers with their decorative plaster work and frescoed walls, busts of Roman emperors in the garden-house. For the palace was surrounded by gardens and canals, where the great man could be at leisure from the press of business in the garden with a book. The house was on such a scale, he declared, precisely to entertain the Queen and Court, which meant at least a couple of hundred people, including attendants.

When James I saw it, he fell for it and persuaded Burghley's son, Robert Cecil, to exchange it for Hatfield, where he built his own palace. Since Theobalds came to the crown it was a victim of the Civil War and lapse of the monarchy. Nothing whatever remains of it, except a few humps and tumps. Think what the country lost with such a masterpiece of Elizabethan art and craftsmanship!

The same thing happened to Holdenby in Northamptonshire. This was built by Sir Christopher Hatton on quite as grand a scale, for the same declared purpose to entertain the Queen on her summer progresses, 'for whom we both mean to exceed our

---

[1]M. Girouard, *Robert Smythson and the Architecture of the Elizabethan Era*, 15, 32.

purses in these'.[1] (Hatton did, Burghley did not.) That both were connoisseurs, critically conscious of their work, is evident from Burghley's appraisal to Hatton: he admired 'the great magnificence in the front or front pieces of the house, and so every part answerable to the other. I found no one thing of greater grace than your stately ascent from your hall to your Great Chamber, and your Chamber answerable with largeness and lightsomeness.' (Compare today the lovely Presence Chamber at Hardwick.)

James I bought Holdenby (which had bankrupted Hatton); Charles I was confined there, in his own house, after his defeat in the war. In 1651 an Army captain bought it and demolished the palace for its materials. Nothing of it remains, except for the materials the captain used to build his own small house on the site. What would one not give to have seen those vanished palaces! Burghley also built a smaller mansion nearer London, at Wimbledon. This was bought from his grandson by Queen Henrietta Maria for a suburban residence – hence another casualty of the war.

Greenwich Palace had been a favourite with Elizabeth I – she had been born there; it became a biscuit-factory and receptacle for prisoners, and deteriorated so much that it was gradually rebuilt after the Restoration. Of Richmond Palace, where she died, John Aubrey gives us an engraving, with its fantasy of a skyline with gathered turrets: 'a splendid and magnificent House, which was after the most exquisite architecture of that age, sc. as Henry VII's Chapel at Westminster. 'Twas pity it was spoiled in times of usurpation; it is since a little repaired.'[2]

On the other side of the Thames was Henry VIII's fantasy, Nonsuch Palace, with its extraordinary plasterwork and stucco decoration all over, its turrets and elaborate finials. One sees something of the impression it gave from 'Nonsuch' chests, with its outline in poker-work or sculpted wood. Elizabeth I bought it back for the crown from Lord Lumley. Aubrey tells us that it was largely destroyed in the late civil wars, so that by his time

[1] cf. my *The Elizabethan Renaissance. The Cultural Achievement*, 139, 140.
[2] John Aubrey, *The National History and Antiquities of . . . Surrey*, (ed. 1975), I. 158.

'there remains hardly one stone upon another'.[1] Charles II gave what was left of it to his Villiers mistress, the beautiful Castlemaine, who sold it for the materials. Fragments of its splendid Holbeinesque decoration spun off to houses round about – at Loseley Place, for example – where one can see bits and pieces, and regret the artistic loss.

Similarly with Oatlands, near Weybridge, much favoured by Elizabeth I for its good air. Aubrey says that it

> was a very fair building and, when in its glory, much resorted to by the Royal family, nobility and gentry during the summer season. Here was a fair park well stored with deer, but disparked by the late Usurpers. Here remains still (1673) a large brick wall, which once encompassed ten acres. Of the chief pile there are but small vestigia .... In this palace was born Henry Stuart, Duke of Gloucester, fourth son of King Charles the Martyr, and baptized here, 22 July 1640, and died at Whitehall on 13 September 1660.[2]

A brick gate was the only remnant, the site of the courtyard occupied by mean, insignificant houses.

So too with the castles belonging to the Crown in various parts of the country. Queen Elizabeth generously gave Kenilworth to Leicester: 'of the ruinous castles of England undoubtedly one of the grandest', says Pevsner. 'It has superb Norman, 14th century, and Elizabethan work; where one sees all three together and all three in the strong yet mellow red of their sandstone, the view could not be bettered.' Like Burghley and Hatton, Leicester had built the grand Elizabethan apartments for the reception of the Queen in 1575. After his (illegitimate) son left the country, Charles I bought it back for the Crown; hence it was not spared, unlike that of the Parliamentarian Brookes at Warwick. Temporarily it was granted to some Army officers; the splendid Norman keep was slighted in 1649, and the demolished fabric sold for its materials.

Pontefract Castle on its rock, in the West Riding of Yorkshire,

---

[1]Ibid, II. 123.    [2]Ibid, III. 107.

was the Windsor of the North: a spectacular structure, a *ceinture* of fourteen towers and a vast keep. It underwent several sieges in the war; the fine church of All Saints, too close to the Castle, was ruined and only partially repaired in the 19th century; the Castle itself slighted in 1649. A few ruins remain as ornament for a popular recreation ground (a narrow escape for Windsor!).

In Cornwall the centre of administration of the Royal Duchy was Lostwithiel, where a line of buildings ran – as their remains still do – along the river Fowey. These were medieval: Shire court, exchequer hall and gaol. They were damaged by Essex's army in the campaign of 1644, and the Stannary records – of the mining jurisdiction in Cornwall and Devon, a large source of income – were said to have been destroyed then. Certainly they have totally disappeared.

Of episcopal palaces and castles more were repaired, restored or totally rebuilt, since they were needed for the residence of the Restoration bishops. Aubrey tells us what happened to Lambeth Palace:

> divided into several tenements, of whom Thomas Scot, one of the Regicides, and one Harding were two possessors. The stately hall was demolished, the High Commission Court [by which Laud had tried in vain to keep order in the nursery] was made a dancing-school, the gate-house and Lollards' Tower [precursors of the Puritans] in 1646 a prison for the faithful but unhappy Royalists. The chapel was divided into two rooms, that towards the east was made a dining-room and floored with boards after the pavement had been taken up. After the Restoration Archbishop Juxon repaired the whole house and rebuilt the hall in the ancient form. Nor could all the persuasions of men versed in architecture, and his friends, induce him to rebuild it in the modern way.[1]

In the chapel Archbishop Parker's body was interred and rested quietly there till disturbed by Scot, who dug up the corpse, which was enclosed in a leaden coffin. The wretch found

[1] Ibid. V. 273-5.

'the body as fresh as if lately dead, and then tumbled it into a hole near an outhouse where poultry was kept, and sold the coffin to a plumber.' Dugdale learned later what had happened, and got Archbishop Sancroft to re-bury the remains by the altar 'under a monument erected by himself (removed in 1648) opposite to that part of this chapel where he used to pray'.

Croydon was the country residence of the archbishops. There Queen Elizabeth's favourite prelate, Archbishop Whitgift, had built almshouses for twenty-eight people under a Warden, also a free school and endowed it. He resorted a good deal to his residence next the church, where 'in the Rebellion one Bleese was hired for half-a-crown per day to break the painted glass windows, which were formerly fine'.[1] Laud had made many improvements there, putting in stalls, altar rails and a gallery; but at the Restoration the dilapidations were such that £1400 would hardly cover them.

So we could tour round the country with our eyes open to the damage, some of it still visible, from the war and neglect due to the confiscation of Church lands which had gone to the upkeep of the bishops' residences. At Durham the Castle needed heavy repairs at the Restoration; so too Auckland Castle, which the odious Haselrig, who had made a good thing out of the Revolution, had invested in. Farnham Castle was a chief residence of the bishops of Winchester. Here the keep was slighted and remains a ruin; heavy repairs were necessary, £10,000 on the great hall alone in the 1670s. At Winchester Wolvesey Palace fell into ruin, so that Bishop Morley built himself a convenient (and pretty) late-Caroline house nearby. The castle at Bishop's Waltham remained a complete ruin, as one sees today.

We have seen that at Lincoln the bishop's palace was fired in the siege. At Buckden in Huntingdonshire the bishops had a castle conveniently halfway between Lincoln and London: now a ruin, but some part of it may have been fitted up for the excellent Robert Sanderson, Dugdale's friend, who died there only a couple of years after the happy Restoration. Eccleshall Castle, the country residence of the see of Lichfield and

[1] Ibid, II. 30, 32.

Coventry, was slighted after the war; a Restoration bishop built himself a house within the enclosure. Residences for the sees of York at Southwell, of Lichfield and Norwich, and for the archbishop at Canterbury needed complete rebuilding. Few escaped damage or depredation.

A grievous artistic loss to the country among secular houses was Basing, near Basingstoke, for it was a veritable palace – in fact two. Within the circuit of its walls, earthworks, gatehouse and moat, were two mansions: the Elizabethan New House built by the Tudor Lord Treasurer, and beyond that the medieval castle, the Old House. The whole place was a vast complex, with, it was said, a dozen courts. With its numerous towers and turrets it must have had a skyline rather like Nonsuch. Here too there were Renaissance medallions of terracotta, and, within, decorative plaster work by the French masons who had worked at Longleat.[1] It had a great hall, with a huge hexagonal kitchen to provide for an immense household. It had been made into a fortress, a storehouse of armaments – but that is not our subject; what is, is that it was a treasure-house of art objects, pictures, tapestries, furnishings. For the Paulets, a Catholic family, were persons of taste.

Basing had withstood several attacks and sieges; its endurance, holding up forces for the last campaign in the West, angered the Parliamentarians. The capture of Winchester Castle, large portions of which were blown up, enabled Cromwell to concentrate on Basing, which was stormed and fired, with much loss of life. Hugh Peters, Cromwell's Army chaplain, reported: 'The Old House had stood two or three hundred years. A nest of idolatry, the New House, surpassing that in beauty and stateliness, and either of them fit to make an Emperor's Court. In truth the House stood in its full pride.'[2] We have an inadequate sketch of it, with its four towers, the tall stately gatehouse, and inner keep-like mass of building.

Determining to storm it, Cromwell spent some time of the

[1] *V.C.H., Hampshire*, IV. 115 foll.
[2] G.N. Godwin, *The Civil War in Hampshire (1642–45) and the Story of Basing House*, 350 foll.

night before in prayer: 'Not unto us, O Lord, but unto thy Name give the glory; for thy mercy and thy truth's sake. Wherefore should the Heathen say, Where is now their God? Our God is in the Heavens. Their idols are silver and gold, the work of men's hands', etc. This kind of thing greatly impressed the naif (and Philistine) Carlyle; it appeals less to more sceptical minds in an age that has seen too much destruction. Inspired by their Bible-mania, little mercy was shown. 'This made our men far more resolute, who cried out "Down with the Papists!", and by this means there were few of them left who were not put to the sword.'

Among those who were brought out, along with the Marquis – and four priests, of whom two were 'for the gallows' – were four artists. Inigo Jones, the most original (and originating) aesthetic mind of the age, was brought out in a blanket, his clothes having been plundered off him. He may have been employed on works within, for it seems that the house displayed some of his favourite Tuscan columns. He survived his hideous experience six years longer, but no more work came from his genius in such conditions. Wenceslas Hollar was also within, and came out with Sir Robert Peake and William Faithorne.

Peake was the son of James I's Serjeant Painter, of whom Faithorne was a pupil. The younger Peake was a print-seller and publisher of engravings, patron of younger artists, who had been knighted by the King at Oxford. Faithorne became the most celebrated and prolific engraver of the age, to whom we owe a whole gallery of portraits of its figures – comparable to Clarendon's pen-portraits in his History of the Rebellion. As Flatman wrote:

> A *Faithorne Sculpsit* is a charm can save
> From dull oblivion, and a gaping grave.

Even while in prison, he executed a famous engraving of Buckingham. Not one of these artists would take the oath to the revolutionary (and Philistine) régime: the younger three all passed into exile. The one 'mercy' we discern in the surrender of Basing was that these valuable lives were saved.

The plunder was on an enormous scale. Peake was said to have had £500 worth of plate in his chamber; one of Cromwell's godly troopers, of his New Model Army, 'first laid his hands on a bag of £300 in gold, a good purchase for one'. Another got 'a box of jewels, rings, and bracelets, and a box of graven brass plates', upon which Faithorne had been working. The vast house had been richly furnished, one bed alone, velvets and silks, gold and silver thread, had cost £1300. Apart from the stores of food and wine, 'numerous crucifixes, Popish pictures and books, six copes' and other vestments; 'beds, clothes and goods which filled 1000 chests, trunks and boxes' were estimated to be worth £8000, the Marquis's cabinet and jewels £50,000. 'One soldier found £300 in a hole, and another had 120 pieces of gold for his share. Not able to keep his own counsel, it grew to be common pillage among the rest, and his comrades pillaged him by piecemeal to an half-crown coin.' We observe ordinary common fools at play.

'Plunder in abundance, both plate, hangings and other goods sold exceedingly cheap; the noise whereof caused one hundred hackney horse this morning to be hired in London for brokers to go purchase upon, if the fair be not past.' Hugh Peters was given the profitable job of carrying the good news to Parliament.

> In all these great buildings there was not one iron bar left in all the windows (save only what were on fire) before night. And the last work of all was the lead. By Wednesday morning they had hardly left one gutter about the house; and what the soldiers left the fire took on, leaving nothing but bare walls and chimneys in less than twenty hours.

The parish church next door was badly damaged. At the Restoration a report said that the church was demolished, certainly roofless, 'the seats and pulpit burned, the bells and other ornaments thereof plundered and taken away'. The parishioners had raised over £300 for repairs, but now another £1500 would be needed. The church was patched up with brick: when one goes there today one still sees the marks of gunfire and shot; but of the palace of the Paulets few remains, only lumps and mounds under the grass. The family never came back: they could not have afforded to rebuild on such a scale – and perhaps they hadn't the heart.

Raglan Castle was the last to hold out for the King, and, though the ruins remain, the loss of its contents is hardly less lamentable. The Marquis of Worcester was even richer than Winchester, and also a Catholic. He was an ingenious man, interested in inventions and the possibilities of water-power. He had a remarkable library, which was totally destroyed. He was a man of taste, as one can discern even from the ruins: classic caryatids, remains of a fountain in the Fountain Court, and along the terrace a recently constructed series of large niches for life-size statues. All the lead was sold, staircases, woodwork, furniture removed and scattered – great spoil made; the keep was slighted. The family never came back to it; at the Restoration they moved to Badminton, where in the family apartments one sees a sitting-room of complete Jacobean panelling from Raglan. During the siege the tower of the church was destroyed for military reasons; much deliberate damage was done: in their chapel the tombs of recent Somersets were rifled, the multilated effigies tumbled on the floor. We must remember that, owing to the Reformation prohibition of images, English sculpture had been largely reduced to secular figures on tombs.

However, Hugh Peters did well out of it: he was granted £200 a year out of the Marquis's confiscated estates.

Symonds reports, while in this area, that news came of the firing of Bridgwater, 'most of the town was burnt, except some houses near the castle . . . . The castle of Abergavenny burnt, viz the habitable part; the garrison drawn out and quitted. About this time the garrison of Kilpeck Castle in Herefordshire slighted'[1] – when one goes there today, nothing but grass-grown moats. We learn from him too that Steppleton Castle in Herefordshire was strong, but because there was no water near it was pulled down by Ludlow's governor, lest the enemy might make use of it. Defaced. 'Croft House defaced by Ludlow's men [i.e. from the Castle there]. Mr William Lyttelton's house defaced, lest the enemy should make use of them.' Interestingly, Symonds reports that in those backward areas the crosses had remained untouched, sometimes two or three in a parish – doubtful how many survived the Puritan Revolution intact.

[1] *Diary*, 203, 210, 212.

Bridgwater was not the only town to be largely fired, Bridgnorth and Chester suffered worse. At Bridgnorth only one half-timbered house escaped the fire; the church of St Leonard's which Leland reported to be 'of great beauty', was heavily damaged and was rebuilt in poorer style. It has the sword of Colonel Francis Billingsley, killed in the churchyard on 31 March 1646. The old town hall was burnt during the siege.

For Chester we have an account of the losses, town, castle, and cathedral Close.[1] The city suffered a long and severe siege at the hands of Sir William Brereton, the redoubtable Parliamentarian commander in those parts, the North-West.[2] We may omit the destruction of townspeople's houses with what they contained of value.

> Without the Bars, the chapel of Spital [Boughton], with all the houses and gardens there. Without the North gate, Mr Dutton's Jolly's Hall, all burned and consumed to the ground, with the chapel of Little St John. Besides the Halls of several gentlemen in the city and near to it, as Batch Hall, Mr Edward Whitby's the Recorder. Blacon Hall, Sir Randall Crewe's: Overleigh Hall, Mr Ellis; Flookersbrooke Hall, Mr Shingleton's in lease ... Bretton Hall, Mr Ravenscroft's plundered and burnt little after the Parliament party first going into Wales ... Hoole Hall, Mr Bunbury's, The Water Tower at Dee Bridge, shot down in time of siege. The Nuns' within the city, Sir William Brereton's plundered and plucked down at the first beginning of the wars because he was of the Parliament Party against King and city.

Most of the gentry and nobility in the West and North-West, and in Midland Nottinghamshire, as Mrs Hutchinson allows, were on the King's side; Brereton was a notable exception. 'Lord Cholmondeley's house in St John's churchyard, plucked down and burnt by the Parliament Party. Mr William Gamull's house near the New Gate, with the new gate-house which was his; Mr

---

[1] R.H. Morris, *The Siege of Chester, 1643–1646*, 203 foll.
[2] The commander on the Royalist side was Lord Byron, whose house Newstead Abbey was plundered by Parliamentarians from Nottingham. For Byron, Brereton and the siege, v. my *The Byrons and Trevanions*, c. IV.

John Werden's house near unto it .... The destroying of the
Bishop's palace ... and the ruin of the great church.'

The sufferings of Chester in the last prolonged siege were such
that, shortly after, there was an outbreak of plague that carried
off over 2000 people. After the war the castles in this area were
all slighted and left in ruins: Beeston of the Cholmondeleys,
Eastwood old hall, and beautiful Wingfield Manor of the
Talbots, where Mary Queen of Scots was confined for a time.
When one goes there one sees the fine ashlar stone of the ruins
looking as freshly cut as if yesterday. That fine house should
have survived. Denbigh – where Elizabeth I's Leicester had
built both at castle and church – was also slighted.

We come south to lovely rose-red Goodrich in its strategic
situation overlooking the Wye: a noble ruin, but one would
prefer to see it intact. Here the vicar, Jonathan Swift's
grandfather, was a devoted Royalist, who advanced all he
possessed to the King's cause. For his pains Parliamentarian
troops plundered his property to the value of £300. The
tradition there is that, when ejected, he went on administering
the sacrament from the silver chalice of his church.

Colchester suffered as badly as Chester, in the Second Civil
War when Sir Charles Lucas and Sir George Lisle seized the
Castle for the now imprisoned King, and held out during a
twelve-week's siege.[1] A forlorn hope, but immense damage was
done: 200 houses in the town destroyed – more important, the
Grimston's mansion and St John's house gutted, the grand
church of St Botolph's priory battered into ruin, with the
remains of the fine Romanesque front we see today. St Mary-at-
the-Walls was so nearly demolished, it had to be rebuilt.

All to no point on either side. Colchester, in bleak East
Anglia, had been a Puritan town: Evelyn described it as 'a
ragged factious town, and now swarming with sectaries'. Before
the war Colchester, like Ipswich, had refused the appointment
of properly licensed preachers from the beneficed clergy, in
favour of their own Puritan 'lecturers' – such a headache to
Laud; they objected to removing the communion tables to the
east end of their churches, and they sacked the house and chapel

---

[1]G. Martin, *The Story of Colchester.*

of the Lucases. In the upshot the Presbyterians, with their town-preacher, were completely disillusioned – they always were a stiff-necked crew – and were outed by the Independents. Revolutionaries are always vulnerable to those on the Left of themselves: when a young Quaker came to spread his ill-seen doctrines, he was imprisoned and succumbed to ill-treatment in the Castle – what was left of it, a gaol. Then plague came to fill the cup of their misfortunes: it halved the population, some 4000 died.

Perhaps that at least taught them that there were greater ills in life than having the communion table moved to the east end of the churches – where they all are now, even in their own Dissenting chapels. To what point all the fuss?

To the Royalists Lisle and Lucas, who were shot to death in cold blood after their surrender, were heroes. Henry King who, though a bishop, was an excellent poet (as were Dean Donne and Dean Swift), wrote an 'Elegy on Sir Charles Lucas and Sir George Lisle, Murdered August 28, 1649':

> We grant the war's unhappy consequence,
> With all the num'rous plagues which grow from thence,
> Murders and rapes, threats of disease and dearth,
> From you as for the proper Spring take birth:
> May bawl aloud the People's right and power
> Till by your sword you both of them devour ...
> In which, to gull the people, you pretend
> That Military Justice was your end ...
> Whence we have learned, whene'er their Saintships treat,
> The ends are mortal, and their means a cheat.

Almost every county can exhibit castles ruined in the Civil War. Not every one – in Cornwall, for instance, though Pendennis suffered a prolonged siege, it was maintained with St Mawes opposite as fortification for Falmouth harbour. The Duchy castles of Restormel and Trematon had fallen into disuse and decay; so too Launceston, though it contained the county gaol, where George Fox was imprisoned by the Commonwealth, intolerant of deviationists. Many of these castles are in romantic situations, and admired as ruins (I prefer the roof on) – even in those days a remarkable person like Aubrey, with a perceptive eye, could appreciate this. 'The castle of Montgomery was a most romancy seat', he says, with an anticipation of 18th century sensibility. Demolished, it is only a shell on its height; the church below with the mutilated effigies of the Herberts within.

In that western area Ludlow and Shrewsbury castles, also in magnificent situations above their rivers, Teme and Severn, were no longer needed after the dissolution of the Council of Wales and the Marches – they had been the residences of the Presidents with their officials. Ruined Ludlow presents a highly romantic appearance – only a few years before it had witnessed the young Milton's *Comus*, performed with Henry Lawes's music. Today, in the Feathers Inn one sees a fine panelled room, richly carved, that came out of the dismantled castle. At the mouth of the Wye ruined Chepstow presides grandly over the picturesque scene – enough of it was left to provide a home for Sir Henry Marten, the Regicide, for his last twenty years. He was lucky to escape with his life. He had been imprisoned at Windsor, but Charles II naturally couldn't bear the sight of a murderer of his father walking on the leads, so he was relegated to Chepstow. A gay spark of an openly dissolute life, he had the distinction of being disapproved of equally by Charles I and Cromwell.

In Yorkshire the ruins of Scarborough enjoy a 'romancy' situation: it was twice besieged, the choir of the neighbouring church destroyed by gunfire, St Thomas's battered down and ruined. Knaresborough and Sheffield – where the Earl of Shrewsbury had entertained Charles I's grandmother, Mary Stuart – were slighted in 1646. In the Midlands Colonel Hutchinson had held Nottingham Castle and razed St Nicholas church to make leeway for its defence, the church rebuilt in 1678. The Castle was slighted, but during 1674-9 the returned Duke of Newcastle – who suffered a great loss of pictures among his possessions, for he was a man with literary and artistic tastes – built a Restoration mansion on the site: now a museum. Neighbouring Newark, often attacked and besieged – today a mere screen of gaping windows above the Trent.

The Earl of Chesterfield's mansion at Shelford, 'a stately home' was left a blackened ruin after a siege, its defenders put to the sword: among them was the young Stanhope, mortally wounded – the Earl had three sons killed in the war.[1] William Staunton, of very ancient stock, had his home ruined. So too Colonel Hutchinson's Owthorpe; but since he was on the winning side he was able to rebuild, and furnish it with some of the King's pictures he had bought.

The demolition of Stafford Castle was ordered in 1643; then reconstructed in the 18th century, demolished again in our own ruinous time. Ashby-de-la-Zouch, of the Huntingdon family – which, in spite of their relationship to Cardinal Pole, had been Puritanical – slighted after Naseby, now rather a spectacular ruin in Leicestershire. Rockingham Castle, 'severely mutilated', but restored.

In the South the most spectacular ruin is Corfe Castle, in its dramatic situation on a steep Purbeck hill with a cleft at base. Very defensible, it was defended by a brave Lady Bankes. 'The Norman tower-keep deliberately shattered by mines and explosives after its long resistance to Parliament; down the slope to the south cascade the walls and towers of the bailey in ghastly disarray. Undermining in 1646 tipped and dislodged masonry' into the fantastic masses and shapes hundreds of tourists today come to see. How much more worth seeing if it all were complete!

'Old' Wardour Castle in Wiltshire is not open to the public – some of it blown up, masonry dangerous: it too was defended by a brave woman, Lady Arundell of Wardour. In fact it presents a rare example of a recently Jacobeanised interior, up-to-date at that time and to us original. It was wrecked by two sieges. After the first and the surrender to Parliament, the Arundell grandchildren, as Catholics, were placed under the tuition of a Puritan divine in Essex. The insolence of it, and from lower-class people! To add insult to injury the Parliamentarians carried off five wagon-loads of furniture, tapestries, and hangings to Dorchester. They burned lodges and outhouses, the palings of the deer parks, destroyed fishponds, felled timber and fruit-trees, cut up and sold lead piping that brought water from two miles away.

---

[1] A.C. Wood, *Nottinghamshire in the Civil War*, 33, 103, 112.

Then the Parliamentarians in turn were besieged, and destruction went further: gate-house blown up, a mine blew in the angle turrets. Colonel Ludlow was captured, but was subsequently exchanged – on his way to becoming a Regicide, with his belief in Millenarian nonsense, the Second Coming of Christ, etc, (disingenuously omitted from his *Memoirs* when published in the more rational atmosphere of the 18th century).

True enough, the Royalists in turn plundered their opponents when they got the chance – they did not however, wreak destruction in the churches all over the country. The house of the rich Parliamentarian lawyer, Bulstrode Whitelocke, near Henley was plundered by Sir John Byron's troops against his orders. 'They stripped the house of curtains and hangings; they broke open cupboards and chests .... They tore up such books as were left in the library and lit their pipes on precious manuscripts', etc – no surprise to see that they were smoking fools too.[1] Actually, Whitelocke was a cultivated man, like his friend Falkland on the other side. He refused to prosecute Laud, and was condemned by the strict Presbyterians as an Erastian. He was a disciple of the great scholar Selden – also a middle-of-the-road man – who had temporary charge of the Royal Library. This the Philistine Peters was in favour of selling, though himself had had a grant of £100 worth of books from Laud's library.

Ashe House near Axminster in Devon, the home of the Parliamentarian Lady Drake, was pillaged and partly burnt by the Royalists. She was the mother-in-law of the Royalist Colonel, Winston Churchill; and here in the semi-ruined house his famous children were born, John Duke of Marlborough; Arabella, mother by James II of the Duke of Berwick; Admiral George and General Charles Churchill. Today only a wing of the Elizabethan house remains. In May 1643 Prince Maurice's regiment plundered Cranborne, of the Parliamentarian Cecils, broke windows and casements, forced open chests of court-rolls, and killed 100 sheep mostly in the house, 'leaving it more nasty than any slaughter-house'.[2] Plundering was regular in 17th-

---

[1] R. Spalding, *The Improbable Puritan ... Bulstrode Whitelocke, 1605-1675*, 86-7.
[2] *Country Life*, 3 May 1973, q. p. 1221.

century warfare - and cattle were everywhere fair game for marauding armies.

At Devizes the castle was slighted; now nothing remains, except the mound where the keep was. The registers of St Mary's church note the burning of the records, and incense to cleanse the church after Cromwell's troopers. Of Chideock, slighted in 1645, nothing remains. Sherborne Castle suffered two sieges, in consequence torn apart and slighted. Much stone was used to build the New Castle and Castleton church by the gate, which remains. Dugdale tells us about the depredations at ruined Sudeley Castle: the chapel turned into a stable, the chancel a slaughter house, the communion table a chopping board. Beverstone in the Cotswolds, destroyed.

In Sussex Bramber Castle, taken by the Parliamentarians, was utterly destroyed; of the church beneath the walls, chancel and transepts were wrecked, leaving only a preaching nave and tower. The grandest loss was Arundel Castle, plundered with all its riches. At the surrender was brought out the brilliant scholar, Chillingworth, Laud's protégé, already ill; but to be teased and tormented into the grave by the odious Puritan, Francis Cheynell. Part of the fabric, notably the library, was rebuilt in Regency times; the rest of it modern on the grandest scale, by a late Victorian Duke of Norfolk, before the confiscatory taxation of modern society crippled the resources of the family.

And so the tale could be extended.

We cannot possibly enumerate the mansions of nobility and gentry ruined or so damaged as needing to be rebuilt.

In Lancashire the chief seat of the Earls of Derby - who ruled the province like princes before the war, which brought them down - was the vast mansion of Lathom House, with innumerable towers, turrets, courts. It suffered a siege, was given up to plunder, and afterwards was so completely destroyed that people have difficulty in locating its precise site and lay-out. We may imagine the spoil from so huge a place, the undisturbed accumulations of generations, as at Basing, Raglan or Arundel. Clitheroe castle was dismantled and demolished.

Bolsover in Derbyshire is one of the most romantic places in England: a half-ruined fantasy palace on the edge of a steep limestone escarpment. The Jacobean keep was built as recently as 1613–16, with its panelled and painted evocation of medieval chivalry. This was the creation of an exceptional man, Sir Charles Cavendish;

> nature having not adapted him for the Court nor camp, he betook himself to the study of the mathematics, wherein he became a great master. He had collected in Italy, France, etc, as many mathematical manuscript books as filled a hogshead, which he intended to have printed: which if he had lived to have done, the growth of mathematical learning had been 30 years or more forwarder than 'tis.[1]

To the Little Castle, with its cosy small rooms, Cavendish's brother Newcastle added the long range of the Riding School: then, along the terrace of the escarpment, a grand Gallery, with a one-storey sequence of palatial rooms. Here took place in the halcyon years of peace the magnificent entertainment of King and Queen in July 1634, the masque by Ben Jonson, 'Love's Welcome'. What one would not give to see that sleeping princess come to life again, the fairy-tale re-enacted!

Not far away, in much fought-over Nottinghamshire the losses were considerable. 'At Averham no trace remains of the Suttons' great house destroyed in the Civil War.' At Langar the mansion of the Chaworths was largely wrecked, and the family moved away to Annesley. While in Newark church an inscription tells us that 'this fonte was demolisht by ye rebels May 9th 1646. Rebuilt by the charity of Nicholas Ridley 1660'.[2] The tale of this kind of thing extends into every county of England.

In Puritan East Anglia a mob at Long Melford pillaged Lady Savage's house, for she was a Catholic, broke the glass and took her goods. Sir Francis Mannock's house was pillaged, Mr Martin's and Dr Warren's rifled. 'A great many set about the market cross, termed young minsters. This insurrection scareth all the malignant party.'[3]

[1] Aubrey, *Brief Lives*, ed. A. Clark. I. 153.
[2] Henry Thorold, *Nottinghamshire, A Shell Guide*, 36, 95, 115.
[3] *The Diary of John Rous*, ed. M.A.E. Green. Camden Soc., 121 foll.

Aubrey tells us of Bromham House in his own Wiltshire, 'Sir Edward Baynton's then a noble seat, since burnt in the civil wars.'[1] Nothing there today. At Wellington in Somerset, Popham's house, 'being a garrison was burnt'. Lord Brooke in 1642 rifled the mansion of Sir Richard Minshull, at Bourton Bucks, who had gone North to serve the King.[2] That September Essex's troops were given licence to pillage Sir William Russell's house; another Recusant's house at Birts Morton was several times thus visited. In Worcestershire Hampton Lovett of the Packingtons was burnt down; in Northamptonshire Aynhoe, of the Cartwrights, was set on fire – to be rebuilt in the reign of Queen Anne.

Apart from the destruction, either deliberate or from the chances and accidents of war, there is a whole subject in itself of the enormous losses consequent upon Royalists – 'delinquents' – having to sell their valuables, as well as lands, to pay the heavy fines to compound for their delinquency. Some Royalist families were ruined by this, others declined in wealth and went down in the world. The economics of it, and the sociological consequences, are not my subject; but it is obvious that there were enormous sales of plate and jewels, tapestries and furnishings – much of it lost to the country, as today from similar penal taxation, the constant drain of art objects that once made Britain a treasure island. From Montacute in Somerset Collinson tells us, in his history of the county, that tapestries were sold to raise money for the King; and then upon sequestration by the Commonwealth, most of the furniture in the state rooms was sold to raise fines. This must have happened fairly widely over the whole country.

What is evident is that there was a certain class element in all this, as Mrs Hutchinson noticed in regard to Nottinghamshire. The Puritan Revolution got its chance because of a division within the governing class. What Charles I's personal rule showed was that the monarchy could not rule against one half of the governing class; what the Civil War proved was that half could not permanently hold the fort against the other half. At

---

[1]Aubrey, II. 224, 160.    [2]Dugdale, *op. cit.*, 559.

the end of the Army's dictatorship, to which the Revolution had led, the two halves came together to make the Restoration.

However, we do see in the war itself that the grandest aristocrats and noblest families were, on the whole, on the side of the King. The towns, the urban middle classes, were predominantly Parliamentarian; being lower-class, they had no taste and can have cared little for the wreckage wrought, the artistic losses of all kinds. For taste is essentially aristocratic; the people have none.

# IV

# Works of Art

'And never rebel was to arts a friend.'
Dryden

In a famous passage of his Autobiography Clarendon described the blissful years of peace, the 1630s, before the unexpected storm from Scotland blew everybody off course and inaugurated revolution and civil war. 'Of all the princes of Europe the king of England alone seemed to be seated upon that pleasant promontory that might safely view the tragic sufferings of all his neighbours about him.' All Europe was involved in the seemingly endless sufferings of the Thirty Years' War – over religion, the ideology that expressed the conflict for power. England, with Charles I ruling without the distractions of Parliament, was at peace:

> His three kingdoms flourishing in entire peace and universal plenty; in danger of nothing but their own surfeits; and his dominions every day enlarged by sending out colonies upon large and fruitful plantations; his strong fleets commanding all seas; and the numerous shipping of the nation bringing the trade of the world into his ports. And all these blessings enjoyed under a Prince of the greatest clemency and justice, and of the greatest piety and devotion, and the most indulgent to his subjects, and most solicitous for their happiness and prosperity. O fortunati nimium, bona si sua norint![1]

That is the elderly Clarendon, looking back with understandable nostalgia to the happy days of his youth, when he had walked in the gardens at Great Tew, discoursing with the philosophic circle of Lord Falkland. Or again in the garden at

[1] *The Life of ... Clarendon*, (ed. 1857), I. 65-6.

Lambeth, where the young lawyer had come upon a matter of business with the Archbishop, and dared to remark on the great little man's shortness of speech. Laud took it in Christian spirit, and ever afterwards used the young man kindly, and trusted him. It is a tribute to the character of both men.

For Clarendon was not a Laudian; he was a middle-of-the-road man, consistently in favour of the King governing along with Parliament. But revolution made this impossible. The fact that it *was* revolution is witnessed by the fact that both Falkland and Clarendon (then plain Hyde) had been in agreement with Parliament against Charles I's personal rule, yet passed over to his service, on realising that the majority in the Commons under Pym's leadership were embarking on a revolutionary course.

Earlier, when writing his *History of the Rebellion*, Clarendon showed that he was capable of criticism of both Court and country. 'But all these blessings could but enable, not compel, us to be happy; we wanted that sense, acknowledgment, and value of our happiness which all but we had, and took pains to make ourselves miserable.'[1] In the first rapture of revolution, when young idealists – like Wordsworth and Coleridge later – think it bliss to be alive, they never consider what the consequences are likely to be: they learn disillusionment from misery (as in our time, in Russia). Clarendon diagnosed trouble in both Court and country. 'There was in truth a strange perverseness of understanding in most, and a strange perverseness of understanding in the rest: the Court full of excess, idleness and luxury [cf. Versailles before 1789], and the country full of pride, mutiny and discontent.'

The situation may be seen simply, without pedantic confusion: the Court was complacent, and ordinary people will never think ahead politically (cf. our own Thirties in this century, and the catastrophe that led to). This was not true of Laud, any more than of Archbishop Bancroft before him: they were both anxious, troubled men who realised what the irrepressible revolutionary spirit of the Puritans could lead to.[2]

[1] Clarendon, *History of the Rebellion*, ed. W.D. Macray, I. 96.
[2] In his will Bancroft revoked leaving his library to Canterbury: he already foresaw that the cathedrals might be despoiled; v. my *The Elizabethan Renaissance: The Cultural Achievement*, 319.

And Clarendon, though rendering Laud justice, was aware of his chief defect.

> He was a man of great parts, and of very exemplary virtues, allayed and discredited by some unpopular natural infirmities; the greatest of which was, besides a hasty, sharp way of expressing himself, that he believed innocence of heart and integrity was a guard strong enough to secure any man in his voyage through this world.[1]

In short, he was in a hurry to get his good works done, and he was naif about humans.

Charles I was essentially an aesthete, his heart in works of art, religion and his family. He was not a good politician – not to be compared as such with the experienced and crafty Pym, the turbulent genius of Cromwell, or even the good judgment of Clarendon – who said, however, that the King's own judgment was often better than the advice he took from others. He was hesitant and wanting in self-confidence – except in regard to religion and art. Moreover, he was quite un-English. Historians have not had the perception to see that on his father's side he was a Franco-Scot, on his mother's a Germano-Dane. He was not English as Elizabeth I or her father had been, with an instinctive feeling for their people.

It was said that Charles never trusted the English people after their treatment of the beloved Buckingham; it was noticed that he was apt to prefer the advice of Scots – notably from the stupid Duke of Hamilton. Thus he created mistrust about him – fatal in a sovereign: there must in authority be somewhere where the buck stops, a final court of appeal everyone can trust. In spite of all her hesitations and apparent tergiversations Elizabeth I could be trusted: Burghley always knew and relied on that.

Clarendon noticed too how much the King was under the thumb of Henrietta Maria, who had plenty of pluck and spirit, but no comprehension of, or much care for, the English people. Thus the royal couple were doubly isolated. Their outlook was not insular, patriotically *borné*, it was more cosmopolitan. This, a

[1]Clarendon, *History*, I. 120.

grave defect politically, was artistically a notable advantage. They were in touch with Europe in the arts: they were friendly with the greatest of European painters, Rubens; gave a commission to the greatest sculptor, who executed a bust of the King. As a young man in Spain, Charles had seen the treasures of Renaissance painting collected by the Spanish monarchs, and in the Escorial a model palace for a sovereign. While, in Paris, the Queen's father and brother were rebuilding the old Louvre on the grandest scale, with Perrault's classical façade. There the ministers of the monarchy, both Richelieu and Mazarin, were men of brilliant tastes, patrons of the arts and letters, collectors and builders. The first of these two was rebuilding his native town of Richelieu with classic regularity, and a splendid *château* – to be destroyed by the French Revolution.

Gothick England was backward in the visual arts, and the King undoubtedly saw a rôle for himself to bring the country abreast of Continental developments – to a discerning eye that was patriotism enough. An art-authority tells us that

> from an early age the young Prince Charles had shown marked personal tastes. During his journey to Spain with Buckingham in 1623 he bought pictures, attended auctions and sat to Velazquez. Above all he saw for the first time, in the Spanish royal collection, some of the greatest masterpieces of Renaissance painting. The experience strengthened his nascent love of the Venetian school and a personal devotion to the work of Titian: a devotion so great that Philip IV presented to the Prince Titian's *Venus of the Pardo* [now in the Louvre].[1]

All Charles's Titians are now in the Louvre, not in this country.

As with Laud's enlightened work for the Church, the experience was tragically brief, cut short by Philistine revolution. For the King's work for the arts aroused the hostility of Philistines too. 'The King's active encouragement of illustrious foreign artists, and their presence in the capital, were bitterly resented by the reactionary nationalist Company of Painter-

---

[1]M. Whinney and O. Millar, *English Art, 1625–1714* (Oxford History of English Art), 3, 6 foll.

Stainers in the City': the kind of reaction one constantly finds among the third-rate – which they were.

During the wars, and the disturbances that preceded them, the worst and most embittered prejudices found an outlet in sustained and organised iconoclasm. 'The dispersal of the Caroline collections and, above all, the King's own great collection by deliberate action on the part of the Council of State after the King's execution, involved a loss to the artistic heritage of this country which can hardly be over-estimated.' And again, in the further realm of artistic patronage, 'the Court never entirely regained the central position which it had occupied under Charles I' – not even at the Restoration, though Charles II did better in this field than he has been given credit for.

All was not lost, however. The spectacle of the King's Titians gave Van Dyke a new inspiration; while his and Rubens' landscapes led to the belated English flowering in this field, though ultimately more in that of portraiture, in which English 18th-century art became pre-eminent. Already a native genius of the first order was at work, in Inigo Jones, in various fields. The piazza he laid out in Covent Garden, with baroque church at one end (the front much altered after a fire in the 18th-century), set a model with its classic regularity, as against the higgledy-piggledy streets that were all London had to show hitherto. At the Restoration his model was followed with St James's Square, and so further forward. His fenestration of that perfect work of architecture, the Banqueting Hall in Whitehall, provided the model for that of Wren's St Paul's.

I quote from an authority. 'Inigo Jones was by far the most important English artist of the 17th century. His eminence rests not solely on his achievements as an architect. If it were so, his position might be challenged, for Wren had a far greater range.'[1] (We must not forget that Wren too was a Royalist, son of the extruded Dean of Windsor.) Inigo Jones was 'the first Englishman to have any profound knowledge of Continental art, both antique and contemporary. He was, indeed, the entirely new phenomenon in England, both as a professional architect and as a connoisseur.' Unlike an Englishman his

[1] Ibid, 15.

passion for art was philosophic and theoretical; late in life he began work on a book, with drawings, to bring together his varied interests and deeper thinking. The Civil War prevented the completion of what would have been a classic, to exert continuing inspiration. We may take his being carried out, naked in a blanket from the wreckage of Basing House, as a symbol of the age.

Inigo Jones owed his rise to the patronage of a great aristocrat, the connoisseur Earl of Arundel, who took him to Italy. There the artist imbibed the complete spirit of the Renaissance, *l'huomo universale*, and transported its expression in perfect form – hitherto rather confined to decoration and detail – to architecture in England. His grand opportunity came with the patronage of the Crown. We still have another perfect work of art of his, also of innate originality – no mere imitation, for all his knowledge of Palladio – in the Queen's House at Greenwich, completed for Henrietta Maria.

During Charles I's reign 'the most interesting and costly' of his works were for her: 'the improvements at Somerset House – the Cabinet Room, the new River Stairs, the fountains and cistern-house, the refitting of the Cross Gallery and, most important of all, the new Chapel .... For her the pergola to the Withdrawing Chamber at St James's was built; and for her, too, were the arbour and the redecorated lodging with its new balcony at Oatlands .... Works at Somerset House continued through the whole of Charles I's reign, and in 1638 there was evidently a monumental scheme for rebuilding along the Strand.'[1] There was 'an even greater palace project – that for Whitehall'. The designs for this project – of which the Banqueting Hall was to constitute a small section, the whole palace to run the length of Whitehall today – still exist. The far smaller resources of the English Crown, compared with France or Spain, prevented this from ever being built – or we might have had something to compare with Escorial or Louvre – or even the Tuileries (burnt down by the vandals of the Commune in 1871).

Nevertheless we can see something of the continuing influence

---

[1] J. Summerson, *Inigo Jones*, 11 foll.

of this man of genius among his fellow artists and persons of discernment. The angle-towers at Holkham derive from Jones's work at Wilton, as again at Rokeby, as well as in the decorative ceilings in the latter, or that of the great hall at Wentworth Woodhouse, inspired by the Queen's House at Greenwich. A ceiling at Nuneham Courtenay was derived from the Banqueting Hall, while at Trafalgar House in Wiltshire we see a tribute to the master in the bust looking down upon us in the entrance hall.[1]

Hardly anything of all the work accomplished exists now – except for drawings, like those for the masques which were such a feature of Charles I's Court and in their splendour rivalled those of Italy. For they united the arts, poetry, music, architectural scene, stage machinery; the antique and the contemporary, the classic and the romantic. We know what Puritan Philistines thought about it all – 'braveries and vanities, old rotten pictures and broken-nosed marbles'. They themselves cared only for play-acting in the pulpit, not in its proper place – on the stage.

All of that vanished like a dream – and indeed there is a dream-like quality about Caroline art, part of its charm for the elect – not only in the ethereal masques but in the music and poetry, not least in the wonderful dream-world Van Dyke created in his portraits of King and Queen and the figures of their Court, in which we see them still as in a mirage.

We probably owe Van Dyke to the propulsion of Rubens, who much appreciated his visit in the summer of 1629: 'the beauty of the countryside, the charm of the people, the magnificence and splendour of their exterior culture – extreme, as of a nation rich and enjoying profound peace; but also on account of the incredible wealth of excellent pictures, sculptures and antique inscriptions to be seen in this Court.' He praised Arundel's collection of marbles, never having seen anything more rare than the statues from Smyrna and Magnesia. He regretted that Selden, 'to whom we owe the publication of these texts and a

[1]Christopher Hussey, *English Country Houses: Early Georgian*, 134, 140, 154; *Mid Georgian*, 116.

[93]

commentary', was now involving himself in politics and incurring the King's displeasure. 'I wish he would devote himself entirely to the well-defined life of contemplation.'

Rubens reported that the inventor Drebbel was living outside London and had produced a microscope, which magnified things enormously – though his machines had not functioned on the fireships recently at La Rochelle. Sir Dudley Carleton, the diplomat, was a patron of the arts, and a collector of antiquities: Rubens offered him some of his pictures in exchange for a number of those.[1]

In England in the 1630s Van Dyke evolved a new style different from his earlier Flemish and Italian phases, one 'particularly suited to the ephemeral civilisation of the English Court'. It may have been 'ephemeral', but its influence lasted. 'Van Dyke's portraits are, with their withdrawn grandeur, frigid magnificence, [is that the right word? I should say 'elect' – nothing frigid about Henrietta Maria] and brittle elegance [why should elegance be 'brittle'?] a penetrating commentary on the Caroline court.'[2]

'Van Dyke's English period is the most important single factor in the development of portrait-painting in this country'; and again 'the most dramatic in the history of English painting'.[3] After a first visit Van Dyke remained in touch with English travellers and collectors. He painted Nicholas Lanier abroad, a figure of significance in Caroline art, a close adviser of the King, who entrusted him with missions collecting works of art abroad. Lanier eventually brought off the grand *coup* of purchasing the whole Gonzaga collection from Mantua, when others were after it, and transporting it to England. Lanier was both composer and painter in his own right: we have an excellent self-portrait in the Music School at Oxford, and his music should be collected and published. He was a cousin of the royal musician, Alphonso Lanier, husband of Shakespeare's Dark Lady and old friend of the musical Archbishop Bancroft.[4]

A Van Dyke *Madonna and Child* was given to the King by his

---

[1] *Letters of the Great Artists*, ed. R. Friedenthal, 1. 150, 155.
[2] M. Whinney and O. Millar, *op. cit.*, 60.
[3] O. Millar, *Van Dyck in England*, 9.
[4] cf. my edition of *The Poems of Shakespeare's Dark Lady*.

Lord Treasurer Portland, another connoisseur, who had a magnificent classical tomb in Winchester cathedral. Before returning to England on the King's invitation Van Dyke painted for him 'the sumptuous *Rinaldo and Armida,* which is now in Baltimore'.[1] Neither the 'tender and very personal charm' of his religious pieces, nor the romantic *brio* of the mythological, would appeal to the uncultivated. But the melancholy detectable underneath the surface brilliance, perhaps the nostalgia for a never-never world of perfection, had an echo in the King's own heart. (Also King and painter were small men, with beautiful manners – unlike the potent, blustering Cromwell.)

When Van Dyke came to England 'he saw one of the finest collection of Titians that has ever been made, he was in the service of one of Titian's most passionate admirers', and the effect may be seen in his subsesquent work. The connoisseur monarch was equally *au fait* with Titian and Van Dyke: when one of the set of Titian's Emperors was irreparably damaged he ordered Van Dyke to fill the gap. Titian's grand portrait of the *Emperor Charles V with a Dog* the King had brought back from Spain.

Our authority says well of Van Dyke's famous equestrian portrait of the King with M. St Antoine, 'its effect at the end of the Gallery at St James's must have been most spectacular, as if Charles were riding out through the arch to join the Roman Emperors of Titian and Julio Romano'.

So too with the characteristic figures of the Court: the double portrait of the brothers Lord Bernard and Lord John Stuart in all the pride and flourish of their youth, the former to be struck down at Chester, to the grief of the King, who had by then so much to mourn. Or the monumental portrait of Southampton's friend, when they were young, Henry Danvers, Earl of Danby (now in Leningrad). He it was who gave the Botanical Garden to Oxford, first such in England, with its grandiose gateway by Nicholas Stone. Many of these portraits used to remain in the houses of their descendants – today being dispersed in the social revolution of our time, like Van Dyke's 'nostalgic, Arcadian' *Lord Wharton,* now in Washington.

[1]M. Whinney and O. Millar, *op. cit.,* 68, 69, 72.

Even more pertinent to our theme is the fate of the religious pictures which Van Dyke painted: 'a *Crucifixion*, a *Deposition* [from the Cross], *St John the Baptist in the Desert*, *The Magdalen listening to a Harmony of Angels*, and *Judith and Holofernes*, all for Sir Kenelm Digby; a *Crucifixion* for the Earl of Northumberland, and for the Queen *The Rest on the Flight*' (into Egypt). All these pictures have disappeared. 'So have the mythologies which were painted for the King: a *Dance of the Muses on Parnassus*, *Apollo and Marsyas*, some *Bacchanals* and a *Venus and Adonis*.'[1]

This underlines our theme and brings home to us the ideological element in the Puritan Revolution; for it was the religious pictures that were destroyed, like the grand Rubens altar piece. Even when they were sent abroad the fanatics laid down that 'no superstitious images should cross the seas' – for fear of encouraging Continental souls in their errors. Nor were pagan mythological subjects well seen. The victors in the Revolution were not all of them uncivilised, some of them, apart from their Puritanism, were cultivated men. Even the Regicide Colonel Hutchinson, otherwise a gentleman, bought a number of the King's pictures after his execution. But such people preferred sedate portraits, and far more of these were allowed to remain in the country 'widowed of the arts and muses'.

Not all Van Dyke's sitters were friendly to Charles and Henrietta Maria, but they were all aristocrats, or had aristocratic tastes, like the musicians and poets. This was what the eminent painter's own nature was attuned to and perfectly equipped to portray. Our authority speaks of 'the supreme distinction, reticence, and refinement which made him so aristocratic an artist'.[2] No other was so celebrated by the poets – Waller, Cowley, Herrick. They responded no less visually to the cultured world conjured up by King and Queen. Here is Thomas Randolph, on a Maid-of-honour walking in the gardens of Somerset House, 'where glittering courtiers in their tissues stalked' –

> away she slipped,
> And in a fount her whitest hand she dipped.

[1] Ibid, 73-4.    [2] O. Millar, *Van Dyck in England*, 20, 24, 26, 36.

The splendour that surrounded the monarchy was 'displayed with an imaginative power and a technical brilliance which had never been seen before in this country'. The irony of it! – for it was a civilisation brutally challenged, and on the point of collapse before *bourgeois* revolutionary force.

In addition to the dispersal of art objects – paintings, sculptures, medals, coins, tapestries, books and manuscripts – a further effect was the dispersal of the artists. 'The Civil War shattered the civilisation which Van Dyke recorded and affected the careers of many painters in England. It was the cause of Johnson's [Cornelius Janssen] return to Holland', as probably of younger native painters, like Michael Wright and William Sheppard, hiving off to Italy.[1] We have seen that Hollar and Faithorne went abroad. At Oxford John de Critz the younger, who was to have succeeded his father as Serjeant-Painter, was killed; while the Royal capital during the war witnessed the brief, meteoric career of Dobson, 'the most accomplished native portrait painter before the advent of Hogarth'. There he painted in all the *fougue* of war – storm clouds, guns, armour, military accoutrements – the Royalist warriors, peers and commanders. Upon the surrender of Oxford in 1646 he went to London, and shortly died in want, not yet thirty-six.

This underlines for us that Caroline culture – painters and poets alike – had portrayed England at peace, an atmosphere 'under whose benign and fruitful influence the arts could flourish'.[2] In vain.

We cannot go in detail into the extensive subject of the dispersal of the King's collections, we can only summarise and choose representatively. Other great collections were dispersed too: second in size and importance was the Duke of Buckingham's, third was the Earl of Arundel's, who had been first in the field as a connoisseur. We are told by an authority that probably no collection escaped unscathed, except possibly the Earl of Northumberland's. I doubt that statement, for the Earl of Pembroke's also would have come through undamaged, since both those peers were on the safe side, as were the Cecils at

[1]Ibid. 84.　　[2]O. Millar, *Van Dyck in England*, 9.

Hatfield. The subject is indeed full of pitfalls – first the problem of attributions, difficult to make out from the rough-and-ready descriptions of the inaesthetic commissioners to whom were entrusted the sales; and this apart from the numerous changes of attribution, and disputes concerning them since. A plain historian, however much a lover of the arts, cannot hope to solve the problems of the art-experts.

Charles I, greatest collector of the age, had keen rivals in the European capitals; notably Philip IV of Spain, who continued the aesthetic tradition of his house, patron of Velazquez; and in France, Richelieu and Mazarin. On Charles's execution the Spanish and French ambassadors moved quickly in, and some of his grandest pictures are to be seen today in the Louvre or in the Prado.

As one walks round the Prado today, one notes the pictures that were once Charles I's. Raphael's 'Holy Family', for example, known as 'La Perla', for on acquiring it Philip IV exclaimed, 'He acqi la perla de mis cuadros.'[1] Among the Titians, and copies of Titian, we find the splendid portrait of the Emperor Charles V with his dog, which Charles had brought to England when prince; another is that of the 'Marquis del Vasto with his Soldiers'. There are two Veroneses, 'The Wedding Feast at Cana', and 'Jesus with the Centurion'; Mantegna's 'Assumption of the Virgin', Tintoretto's 'Christ Washing the Feet of the Apostles', and Dürer's splendid Self-Portrait, which had been given by the City Council of Nuremberg to Arundel, thence to the King. I noted too Correggio's 'Noli me tangere', all delicate greens and blues, with his exquisite soft colouring. Philip IV had given Charles I Titian's 'Diana and Actaeon', and 'Diana and Calisto', retaining only copies. It is interesting that for centuries, right into the 19th, collectors were so interested in *subjects* of pictures that they often had copies made – heresy today.

Charles I's collection contained a number of copies; alas, all the Titians in the Louvre that came from him were originals. The splendid *Venus of the Pardo* was sold in the year of the King's execution to Colonel Hutchinson the Regicide, for the then very large sum of £600, the biggest for a picture in the sales. I do not

[1] *Museo del Prado: Catalogo de los Cuadros*, 490.

know when it left this reprobate's possession: he must have sold it to France at a profit, or it would have been taken back from him at the Restoration – when, like Milton (who was not a Regicide, but had defended it), he was lucky to escape with his neck.

The King had collected hundreds of pictures, besides those that had come down to him from his predecessors; Raphael's famous panel of St George, for example, which Baldassare Castiglione (of the *Book of the Courtier*) had brought as a present to Henry VII from Florence. This made the fair sum of £150: I do not know how it got to Washington. Among the painters represented, and paintings sold, besides those already mentioned, we find Bellini, Paris Bordone, Bronzino, the Breughels, Caravaggio, Annibale Carracci, Clouet, Cranach, Dossi, Giorgione, Julio Romano, Guercino, Holbein, Honthorst, Lucas van Leyden, Palma Vecchio, Parmigianino, Perugino, Pordenone, Guido Reni, Schiavone; besides many lesser mortals, and those to whom the King gave his patronage, like Artemisia and Orazio Gentileschi.

When the sales came along it is noticeable how many of the lesser pictures were bought in by former officials of the Royal Household, by painters of the royal entourage, by Nicholas Lanier, and two of his cousins, by Emmanuel de Critz, even the young beginner Peter Lely makes an appearance.[1] Such people could not compete with the grandees abroad: they could not reach the heights, but they did their best – not only out of love of the arts, but partly no doubt out of devotion to the King who had been their best friend. Emmanuel de Critz, whose brother had been killed, was said to have three rooms full of the King's pictures in his house in Austin Friars, and this is corroborated by the number of his purchases recorded. Thus it came about that a large number of lesser pictures remained in England, for at the Restoration there was a concerted drive to bring back what had been lost during the pinchbeck Revolution. The Cromwellian Lord Lisle, for example, returned at the Restoration the King's pictures which he had acquired; and from Charles II acquired a pardon.

---

[1] cf. *The Inventories and Valuations of the King's Goods, 1649–51*. ed. O. Millar. *Walpole Soc.*, vol 43.

In addition a certain amount of the King's possessions was reserved to furnish the offices of the Commonwealth Council of State - £10,000 worth for Whitehall; and when Cromwell became Lord Protector, to the scandal of Mrs Hutchinson, more was 'reserved for his Highness'. (He became a more absolute, and more capable, monarch than ever Charles I had been.) Hence Hampton Court was saved, and with it the historic Mantegna Cartoons and much else that remains there today.[1]

Let us look, for a specimen, at the purchases of the Laniers. Nicholas's most expensive purchase was the Giorgione 'Picture of Music' for £100 - probably the marvellous *Concert Champêtre* now in the Louvre - naturally that would appeal to him most, composer as well as painter. His next dearest purchases were two pictures, for £55 each, of Julio Romano - the Mannerist painter celebrated by Shakespeare. He bought two paintings, one a Flemish landscape, by Bartholomew Breenbergh, a Caracci, and a portrait Van Dyke had done of him 'to the knees'. Lanier's own painting of 'Mary, Christ and Joseph' - nothing of Virgin or Saint - was bought by the lawyer Jackson, a keen purchaser. Also Nicholas made a large buy of arras hangings, portraying 'Triumphs', 48 ells, and a wood carving of a man.

Alphonso Lanier had two brothers, Jerome and Clement who emigrated to America to become the founder of the numerous clan of Laniers there; they include the poet and musician Sidney Lanier, and Thomas Lanier ('Tennessee') Williams. Clement Lanier's chief purchase was a Polidoro 'Gods in the Clouds' for £40; he also bought a limning, i.e. a miniature of 'Diana in a Golden Shower' for £20, and an inexpensive 'Queen Anna in a blue mantle'. Jerome Lanier bought much more: the most expensive being two of the favourite Julio Romanos and the Correggio 'John Baptist' - that expressively handsome body! - from Somerset House. He paid rather more for a Polidoro in fresco, then £20 for a Tintoretto 'Susanna'. He bought too a Flemish landscape, by Nieuwlandt, that had come up from Oatlands, a Laocoon statue from Somerset House, a 'naked body without a head' from Whitehall, and a more expensive tapestry of St George. It appears that the Laniers had

---

[1]cf. C.H. Collins Baker, *Catalogue of the Pictures at Hampton Court.*

some difficulty in getting all their purchases delivered by the Council of State.

John Evelyn knew the Laniers, being a connoisseur himself. '1 August 1652: came old Jerome Lanier, a man greatly skilled in painting and music .... 2 August. I went to see Jerome Lanier's rare collection of pictures, especially those of Julio Romano, which surely had been the King's and an Egyptian figure, etc. There were also excellent things of Polidoro, Guido [Reni]. Raphael, Tintoretto, etc'.[1] Evelyn and the Commonwealth Sales Accounts corroborate each other. In the New Year, '14 January 1653: I went to Greenwich to see again Mr Lanier's Collection, who showed me Queen Elizabeth's head, an intaglio in a rare sardonyx, cut by a famous Italian. Mr Lanier, who had been a domestic servant of that Queen, assured me it was exceedingly like her.' In his *Sculptura* Evelyn adds, 'I think it is now in his Majesty's cabinet.'

Among the Titians was the 'Mary, Christ and Joseph' – ultimately bought by Mellon for his National Gallery in Washington, where it now reposes.[2] So too Veronese's resplendent 'Finding of Moses', which the young Lely had the taste to buy for £55. He also bought a Tintoretto 'Susanna', but gave more for a 'landshape with Rewins' by Breenbergh. A painter who made more than a score of purchases was Remigius Van Leemput, whom the King had employed as a copyist, to copy Holbein and Van Dyke, whom Remy (as he was known) chiefly admired. He bought a Van Dyke of the King on horseback, perhaps that now at Windsor. His collection was sold on his death in 1677 – buried in Inigo Jones's church in Covent Garden.

Richard Symonds at the time noted the number of pictures bought by artists – they knew their value. Shortly after the King's execution sales of his goods raised some £30,000 for the new Republic's fleet. Commissioners for the sales included the graceless poet Wither, one expert Jan van Belcamp, and Anthony Mildmay, a former gentleman of the Privy Chamber whom Charles disliked – it fell to him to convey the King's body

---

[1] *The Diary of John Evelyn*, ed. E.S. de Beer, III, 74-5, 79-80.
[2] *Paintings and Sculpture from the Mellon Collection*. (National Gallery of Art, Washington, D. C.)

to Windsor. Sales continued through 1650 and 1651; in 1653 the Council of State permitted the Spanish ambassador to export without licence twenty-four chests of pictures, tapestries and household goods. Think, if only all these things had remained in England, it would have made a treasure-house comparable only to Italy – as Charles I intended.

The King's passion for painting, particularly for Titian, and his superb taste may be gathered from a peep into the first room only of his suite at Whitehall, the Privy Lodgings – and also what we lost from the dispersal. There hung six or seven Titians alone: *The Pope presenting Jacopo Pesaro to St Peter*, now in Antwerp; *St Margaret* and *The Allocution of the Marquis del Vasto*, now in the Prado; the *Entombment*, the *D'Avalos Allegory* and *The Supper at Emmaus*, now in the Louvre; *The Woman in a Fur Cloak*, now in Vienna.[1]

The incomparably handsome Buckingham – of whom Clarendon said that his manners were of 'an elaborate and overflowing courtesy' – had been assassinated in 1629, but his collection was kept together for a time at York House. (We still have Nicholas Stone's monumental gateway to it on the Thames Embankment.) Buckingham was the only man the reserved Charles ever loved, apart from his clever father, James I: they made an inseparable trio. The trip to Spain has always been regarded as foolish, as it was politically fruitless: we have seen that, from the artistic point of view, it could not have been more fruitful. Its influence upon Buckingham was hardly less marked than upon the Prince; and the Duke gathered further impressions from his missions abroad. It was he who persuaded Rubens to come to England, and also to sell him, for £10,000, the great painter's personal collection, containing works by Titian, Tintoretto, Veronese, Raphael, Leonardo; along with statues, busts, reliefs, gems. The Ashmolean at Oxford has an exquisite ivory statuette of Venus and Cupid – contemporary German workmanship, which was in Rubens' personal collection, bought by Buckingham. It is a small, but precious, example of the numerous things lost to this country by the Civil War.

This was a *coup* almost as remarkable as his friend, the King's

[1] M. Whinney and O. Millar, *op. cit.*, 5.

purchase of the entire Gonzaga collection. At one stroke England acquired another astonishing addition to its art treasures, and Buckingham went on collecting with such rapidity, as if he had not many years before him – nor had he. He had an agent in Balthasar Gerbier, another foreigner in that aesthetic entourage: again a Renaissance all-round man, amateur architect, painter, diplomatist – as was Rubens himself. Parliament regarded Gerbier as a spy, of course, and threw out a bill for his naturalisation; the King knighted him. Another in this intensely cultivated circle was Endymion Porter, who acquired pictures for both King and Duke, friend of the poets, who addressed verses to him as he to them. He knew Spain well and conducted the Duke's correspondence thither. Philistines in Parliament, the pure-minded Republicans, so much hated all this circle, that Endymion Porter was one of the few exempted from pardon after the war; and the memory of Buckingham was so detested that, years after his death, his splendid tomb in Westminster Abbey, bronzes by Le Sueur, was damaged.

Gerbier was able to compliment Buckingham on the speed with which he had built up his huge collection: 'out of all the amateurs, and princes and kings, there is not one who has collected in forty years as many pictures as your Excellency has collected in five'.[1] This was no mere flattery, he fully appreciated their value; he had been made Keeper of York House. 'Our pictures, if they were to be sold a century after our death, would sell for good cash, and for three times more than they have cost. I wish I could only live a century, in order to laugh at these facetious folk who say, "It's only money cast away for baubles and shadows." '[2] In the event these works of art, cast upon the market in a hurry, were sold much below their value – which today would be astronomical. Gerbier himself bought several pictures at the sales.

'In 1621 Gerbier sent over to Buckingham from Venice a consignment which included Titian's great *Ecce Homo* – now in Vienna.'[3] In Spain two years later the King gave Prince Charles

[1] O. Millar, *The Age of Charles I. Painting in England, 1620–49*, 5.
[2] W. Gaunt, *Court Painting in England*, 72.    [3] O. Millar, *op cit.*, 17–18.

Giovanni da Bologna's sculpted *Samson and the Philistine*; on their return the Prince gave it to Buckingham: it was placed in the garden of York House. The Duke's taste was infallible (where, in politics, his touch was very fallible). Of all contemporary painters he admired Rubens most, and commissioned him to paint the splendid equestrian portrait of himself that hung in the Great Chamber at York House. This grandest of baroque portraits in the country survived, to be bought by the rich banker Child – and be destroyed in our own destructive age, by fire, shortly after the second German war.

Rubens appreciated the peace of those halcyon years in England, as against the horrors of the Thirty Years' War on the Continent. He paid tribute to it in his allegory of *Peace and War*, and to 'the charms of the English scene in that magical idyll, the *Landscape with St George*'.[1] He was greatly impressed by the concentration of treasures in London: 'when it comes to fine pictures by the hands of first-class masters, I have never seen such a large number in one place as in the royal palace and in the gallery of the late Duke of Buckingham'.

His taste was comprehensive (unlike Philip II's, who could not take El Greco): Buckingham appreciated Flemish painting as well as Italian. Earlier, his own beauty had been rendered by painters as varied as Larkin, Janssen, Mytens and Miereveld – thence his taste was to take flight, with the King's, to higher spheres. Honthorst painted an Allegory of the Duke as Mercury, presenting the Liberal Arts to the King and Queen as Apollo and Diana. It is comparable to the scenes of the Court Masques – we can imagine how grievous to Puritans on all grounds.

As a patron Buckingham lured Gentileschi from the French Court in 1625, to come and paint in England, where he painted the ceiling of the saloon at York House with the Nine Muses. When Inigo Jones saw Titian's 'Portrait of a Secretary' there, he practically threw himself on his knees before it. Nor did Buckingham confine himself to the arts: he was the patron of the remarkable gardener, John Tradescant, who collected rare plants for the Duke's country houses at New Hall and Burley-on-the-Hill.[2] For Cambridge, of which he was Chancellor, he

[1] M. Whinney and O. Millar, *op. cit.*, 5.
[2] R. Lockyer, *Buckingham*, 214, 239, 409, 411.

purchased a whole collection of Arabic manuscripts, for his projected university library to parallel the Bodleian.

Altogether he had a collection of at least a couple of hundred pictures, besides other art objects. Since it was private property, the Commonwealth seems not to have laid its dead hand upon much of it, but to have allowed the impoverished family to sell pictures and treasures to live on abroad in exile. However, in 1645 Parliament did order the religious pictures at York House, those representing the Trinity, the Virgin Mary, etc to be burnt – in accordance with their idiotic ideological views. And Buckingham's son, in exile, in 1648 sold at Antwerp a large number of pictures, many of the finest thus passing into European collections. The lovely Rubens sketches for the Whitehall ceiling are in private hands, some abroad; his splendid portrait of the King's eminent doctor, Sir Theodore Mayerne, is now in North Carolina; his chalk-drawing of Buckingham's head, in Vienna. Not long before his death, Envy had figured in pursuit of him, in a masque presented to King and Queen at York House; his widow, much in love with him, described him in his epitaph as the 'spotless Sacrifice to ravenous Envy'.

Envy, as I have said, is a strongly operative motive in all the revolutions of our day. It is odd that historians should not give it its due – Clarendon did – familiar enough in the academic ambience.

The third great collection in London at the time was the Earl of Arundel's, the noble aristocrat, between whom and the new Duke no love was lost: Buckingham set out to rival the older man of the spreading Howard upas-tree. We have a portrait of the connoisseur Earl in his gallery at Arundel House, with long wand pointing to the serried rank of antique busts arrayed along it. His large collection had a very different character from that of the younger, more fashionable men, though he too commissioned portraits of himself from Rubens. His special interests were ancient sculpture and gems, and German painters, especially Holbein and Dürer. He had an agent, at Rome too, to whom he wrote in 1636:

I wish you saw the picture of a Madonna [of Dürer], which the bishop of Würzburg gave me as I passed by that way; and though it were painted at first upon an uneven board and is varnished, yet it is more worth than all the toys I have gotten in Germany. For such I esteem it, having ever carried it in my own coach since I had it. And how then do you think I should value things of Leonardo, Raphael, Correggio, and such like?[1]

We can see in this the intimate feeling for pictures this reserved aristocrat had.

At Nuremberg he bought the whole Pirkheimer library, which, through Evelyn's efforts, came to the Royal Society after the Restoration. From Daniel Rice he acquired his collection of medals and intaglios. In Brussels he patronised the painter Vanderborcht, and employed his son to collect for him. He is said ultimately to have owned some 37 statues, 128 busts, 250 inscribed marbles, besides sarcophagi, Roman altars, pictures and gems. He died at the end of the first phase of the Civil War, in 1646. Much of his statuary, the famous and much-studied 'Arundel Marbles', were given to Oxford university after the Restoration: a safer repository, when all is said – as Laud found for his gifts of precious manuscripts. Sales by the family from his immense collections went on for the best part of a century; it was due to his discernment that the Leonardo drawings at Windsor and the famous bust of Homer in the British Museum came to this country. But what a place Charles I's London was, with three such treasure-houses!

In miniatures – the art of 'limning' as it was called – Elizabethan painting reached its highest quality in little.[2] This standard was maintained well into the 17th century.

> The surpassing excellence of miniature painting in England in the lifetime of Charles I is owing partly to the delight which patrons and connoisseurs took in the ingenious and the 'curious' – in fine workmanship on an intricate scale – and partly to the nature of the miniature itself as a form of portraiture. It was at once more precious and more portable than a portrait in 'large'.

[1] *Dict. Nat. Biog.*, sub Thomas Howard.
[2] cf. Sir Roy Strong, *The Elizabethan Miniature*.

Actually, Charles I was probably the first collector to form, in the modern sense, a collection of miniatures. In his 'new erected' Cabinet Room at Whitehall, in which he had put together his smallest, highly prized and most exotic possessions, were cupboards in which were laid out nearly 80 limned pieces: set in simple turned 'boxes' of ivory, amber, ebony, jet and boxwood; in 'a round golden blue-and-white enamelled ring', or 'a golden square enamelled wrought case', specially made to hold a miniature of the Queen.[1]

Not all of these appear in the sales, though when they do they fetch good prices: eight miniatures of James I's family sold for £100, and eight of Tudor monarchs for another £100. A miniature of a dish of fruit was bought by Colonel Hutchinson for £25; the 'Burying of Christ done in limning by ould olyiver' i.e. Isaac Oliver, made as much as £100; whereas 'A naked Venus asleep and a satyr by her', by the same artist, not a miniature, went for £6.

We need not depreciate Caroline sculpture for not reaching the heights of its painting and architecture – having no Inigo Jones or Van Dyke. Here also the Reformation had done irreparable damage, not only destructively but positively. The Reformation killed medieval English sculpture, which could show such masterpieces as the headless woman's figure in Winchester cathedral, or the beautiful headless figure of the Church in the Judgment porch at Lincoln,[2] which can compare with the best at Chartres. Everywhere are the reredoses and niches emptied of their proper statues; gone are all the alabaster reliefs which were a pride of the country, when England could export works of art to Europe. The masons' yards by the cathedrals were all closed down. Maniac Puritans wanted to 'complete' the Reformation, i.e. complete the destruction.

The damage was positive too. For Protestantism forbade religious painting and images in the churches. Thus, with men's instinct to create –

---

[1] O. Millar, *The Age of Charles I*, 110.
[2] v. L. Stone, *Sculpture in Britain: The Middle Ages*, plates 86 and 99.

> I too will something make
> And joy in the making –

and with the increasingly secular inflexion of the Tudor age
sculpture took the form of monuments, tombs, effigies: where
had been altars and shrines, in place of the Saints we have
everywhere memorials of the gentry, who profited so largely
from the Reformation – hundreds of them.

Here also Charles I was engaged in a conscious work of
reparation – no less than his Archbishop was in the Church.
After all, the Reformation had done more than enough damage,
as visitors to England noticed, seeing the ruins of abbeys and
churches all over the country, even in London still. The King,
however, was going further to bring England in touch with
Continental developments in this field too. The leading native
sculptor, Nicholas Stone, was aware of them, himself moving
out of traditional Gothic into classical forms, and well capable of
expressing emotion in marble. His beautiful figures of Lady
Carey at Stowe-Nine-Churches[1]and of Sir William Curle at
Hatfield lie there on their graves in relaxed free-flowing lines as
if they had just fallen asleep. His exquisite monument in
Magdalen College chapel at Oxford, to the two young Lyttelton
brothers drowned in the Isis, have a moving lifelikeness, a
modernity which might be of the 18th century. Naturally,
Philistines care for none of these things; and, when low-grade
humans show themselves to be fools, it is the duty of the historian
to describe them as such.

Charles I could not get the greatest sculptor of the age,
Bernini, to come to England, though he invited him; so he did
his best with what he could get. Bernini was asked to execute a
portrait bust of the King, and for the purpose Van Dyke made a
triple sketch of his features, two in profile. When Bernini saw it,
he said it was the most tragic countenance he had ever seen.

[1]When I went to see this work of art, shortly after the war, an American soldier
had been discovered in the church, with a crowbar ready to 'lift' the figure. In the
despicable demotic society of today churches have to be kept closed on account of
the depredations of vandals. And this apart from deliberate destruction – for
example, in Cornwall alone, the burning down of St Dennis church and of the
fine painted reredos of St Mary's, Penzance.

Artists are those who have real perception – not ordinary humans – but Bernini cannot have intuited the last tragic scene, the King stepping out from his own palace at Whitehall to the scaffold.

Three foreign sculptors of distinction were recruited by the Court, of whom the best known is Le Sueur. One does not need to criticise Le Sueur for the impassivity of his bronze portrait busts of the King: he was rendering majesty. In actuality, there was an impassivity in his character and conduct: when the news of the beloved Buckingham's murder was brought to the King in chapel, he expressed no emotion but fell forward on his knees in prayer. (On the human plane, the Duke's children were brought up much with Charles's own.) In fact, there is no impassivity in Le Sueur's figure of Pembroke in the Bodleian quadrangle at Oxford: he looks positively brisk. Le Sueur did enable us to recall these men as they were in life. As often as I pass within the gates into Duke Humphrey's Library, by the bust of the King which Laud presented, they come back to mind. Or again, in the exquisite quadrangle which the Archbishop gave to his old college of St John's, there are the properly hierarchical figures of King and Queen architecturally posed.

The King collected hundreds of pieces to enliven his palaces and courts, and to decorate his gardens. When it came to disperse them, they made fair prices, statues on average more than pictures; so that whatever Philistines might say about the King's old 'broken-nosed' antiques, there were connoisseurs about who knew better. By far the highest price was paid, by an artist of discernment, de Critz, for the Bernini bust: £800, an enormous sum then. The work came back to the Crown after the happy Restoration – to be destroyed, along with much else, in the fire that consumed Whitehall Palace in 1698. This bust had been at Greenwich, from which came 36 statues, making higher average prices; though a modern Lucretia fetched only £30.[1]

From St James's, palace and gardens, came no less than 256 pieces. The life-size figures fetched high prices: Selina, 'bigger than the life', and a Sabine in flight, 'so big as life', £600 each; Tiberius, 'bigger than the life', £500; Seneca, 'so big as the life,

[1] O. Millar, *Inventories, loc. cit.*, *passim*.

[109]

sitting and pedestal', 'Pompey, at length, sitting and the pedestal', £250 each. One sees the classical influence at every point.

From Somerset House came altogether 120 pieces, making an average price of some £50, the top price being for a Commodus at £150. The statues from the gardens and terraces there made more: an Augustus, more than life-size, £200; while the fountains, with 4 sea monsters, 4 sea shells, '4 boys with dolphins', 3 turtles and the great statue, together with the bronze Mercury from the upper terrace, made £500. Reserved were '8 scrolls weighing about 8000lb weight, and all which did belong to the two fountains in the Garden' – I suppose a use could be found for them, by utilitarian souls.

Charles I was not merely a mass-collector, like a William Randolph Hearst, but a discerning patron. He was not taken in: in many cases he reduced the prices asked, and occasionally would annotate, 'This I will not have.' So the country would have had immeasurably good value for its money. Upon the outbreak of the Civil War Le Sueur left the silly country, as so many of the intelligent did – including the greatest intellect of them all, the philosopher Hobbes (as I would have done: there is a limit to what one can put up with from ordinary humans).

Two other foreign sculptors of some eminence left too. The discriminating Arundel ordained that his tomb be made by Fanelli, 'the figure of white marble or brass sitting and looking upwards'.[1] Owing to circumstances it was never executed: 'so English sculptors were deprived of the example of a seated figure, as in life, designed by an Italian'. However, the Italian executed the pretty bust of the young Prince Charles aged ten – approved by the expert Miss Whinney, and the big Diana fountain, originally at Hampton Court, 'all that now remains of the wealth of garden sculpture made for Charles I'.

The Flemish Dieussart executed busts of the King, and of his nephew, the Elector Palatine: whom some Parliamentarians fancied for Charles I's throne. In the end his descendants came to it, for the present royal house are descended from him. Dieussart's major work was a grand monstrance for the Queen's chapel at

[1] M. Whinney, *Sculpture in Britain, 1530–1830*, 37–9.

Somerset House, which 'combined a full Baroque panoply of architecture, sculpture, and painting. Its existence was, however, short for it was destroyed during the Commonwealth.'
To sum up, in expert words:

> During the period between the outbreak of the Civil War and the Restoration no marked developments occur in English sculpture. This is not surprising, for Court patronage was at a standstill, and though many tombs were made, these were for the most part for middle-class patrons, and therefore conservative in character. Aristocratic tombs are relatively rare, and it is not unusual to find that a member of a great family had no memorial erected to him for many years.

In short, there *was* a class element in the Revolution – as people saw at the time, and as only the imperceptive fail to see today. And in the arts, there was a hiatus.

A Renaissance connoisseur collected also medals, reliefs, casts, drawings, tapestries, carvings, coins, ivories, amber, gems, jewels – one cannot cover, let alone itemise, all the King's possessions. There were drawers full of antique and Renaissance medals; boxes of coins; silver plates in relief. Of these there were half-a-dozen of James I, useful for family presents, and one of Charles's gallant sister, Elizabeth, the Elector's wife, mother of Prince Rupert and Prince Maurice, also of clever Sophia, through whom the Hanoverian line descends.

Nor can we cover regalia, the Crown Jewels, and plate – though these contained some works of fine art and craftsmanship. Sir John Eliot, who was possessed of a venomous hatred of Buckingham, whom he had formerly served, burst out in one of his flights of rhetoric against the King in the Commons, urging a commission to search for Elizabeth I's jewels: 'O those jewels! the pride and glory of this kingdom! which have made it so far shining beyond others! [We observe the Puritan chauvinism.] Would they were here, within the compass of these walls, to be viewed and seen by us, to be examined in this place! Their very name and memory have transported me.'[1]

---

[1] q. *Jewels and Plate of Queen Elizabeth I.* Ed. A.J. Collins, 3.

Charles I had had to sell or pawn some of these jewels, to pay for the wars against France and Spain which the Commons urged upon him and then would not pay for. (Those were the fatal mistakes the young and inexperienced Charles and Buckingham made, hoping in vain for popularity.) Also we must bear in mind the marked change of taste. Charles sold the resplendent chain of rubies we see on Henry VIII's portraits – with his refined taste Charles would have thought it rather barbarous.

As early as 1644 the Commons passed an ordinance to melt down all the gold and silver plate in the Tower, to raise money for their war. The few Lords who remained at Westminster demurred: 'For that the Plate is ancient Plate, the fashion of it and the badges upon it more worth than the Plate itself. Also the Parliament hath expressed affection to the King, and to take care of his Children. And that this Act would be somewhat incongruous, now to sell his Plate, which that Ordinance requires.'[1] This exposes the humbug of the Commons' claim – past-masters of propaganda as they were – that they were fighting *for* the King, as well as his Parliament, against his evil advisers.

With the success of the Revolution, the King's execution and the inauguration of a republic, the regalia was broken up and dispersed, hitherto kept in Westminster Abbey. The Imperial Crown raised £1110; the solid gold melted down, the pearls and sapphires sold. The Queen's Crown made £338, 'King Alfred's' with a network of gold wire, apparently an earlier work, £248. There went too the ancient chalice of St Edward, for £110.15, the Queen's ivory sceptre, the ampulla with the dove, which contained the oil for the anointing, with all the Coronation vestments. When Charles II came back to his own, all the regalia had to be made anew: nothing remains from the medieval kings.

Similarly at Windsor. Charles I had furnished St George's Chapel with a splendid set of gold plate, made by the leading designer in that kind, Vianen. All melted down: at the Restoration the Chapel was re-equipped, with plate naturally less good. We have details of the breaking up of Henry VII's

[1] q. Ibid, 188.

great image of St George there: 'Item, part of a George head,
which came from the College of Windsor, being the remain
upon the defacing of the same; viz. in coarse gold 5¼ oz, in collets
of gold set with coarse stones and in coarse gold, part in
crampions of gold, 7¼ oz, and in broken silver 1½ oz. In all 14
oz.'[1] We learn that, altogether from Royal sources, some 13,000
oz. of plate, gold and silver, were melted down – for the idiotic,
but very human, purposes of war.

Many pieces of plate had historic associations. The big
'Morion', for example, which Henry VII took over from
Richard III: 'one salt of gold with a cover borne up with a
Morion [helmet], having about the neck 5 coarse rubies and
garnishing pearls, about the foot 12 coarse rubies and 11 coarse
garnishing pearls [they must have been set alternately]. The
cover having 19 coarse rubies, 12 coarse garnishing pearls, and
about the border 6 coarse diamonds, 6 coarse rubies and 11
coarse garnishing pearls. 46½ oz.'[2] On returning from his
Voyage round the World, Sir Francis Drake had presented a
splendid salt to Queen Elizabeth: 'one salt of gold like a glove,
standing upon two naked men, being the history of Jupiter and
Pallas, with a woman in the top thereof having a trumpet in her
hand, the foot enamelled with divers flowers.' What a piece!
Converted into coin.

A considerable amount of plate and jewels had been extracted
by King and Queen to finance their cause. Henrietta Maria
took a number of Crown jewels abroad, to sell or pawn for
munitions of war. One touching item was the handsome set of
buttons of pearl the King had worn: 'I gave them up with no
small regret' she wrote; along with such items as his ruby collar,
pledged in Antwerp, and his largest collar of gold, in Denmark.[3]
I have myself seen the fine silver box, in the form of a large shell,
which the Goldsmiths' Company presented to Elizabeth I on the
defeat of the Armada – in the possession of the Buccleuchs; and
held in my hand the George, which Charles I wore upon the
scaffold – come down to the Duke of Wellington.

[1]Ibid, 273.    [2]Ibid, 290, 192.
[3]Ibid, 181-2.

And so we might go through all Charles I's possessions entered for sale and dispersal: the cups of gold – like that which Harington saw Elizabeth I drinking out of in her very last days – of silver, crystal and agate; the gold candlesticks; the flagons and spice-plates, like those decorative platters upon which sweet-meats were handed round at the Elizabethan Court (the Pierpont Morgan Library has such a set, in New York); the bowls and basins, ewers and salts, the table furniture – need one mention spoons? (but think of the value of Apostle spoons today!); the tapestries, arras hangings and carpets; the embroidered book-covers with gold and silver thread; the 17 volumes with the illuminated coats-of-arms of the Order of the Garter; down to 'one feather bed and bolster of CP', which commanded its price.

To anyone who cares for the arts, or of any sensibility, it is a desolating picture.

# V

# Music and Theatre

The Puritan Revolution and its consequences are no less evident in the realms of music and drama, perhaps even more so; for it closed down the Court and the cathedrals, those nurseries of music, as well as the theatres. The consequences were catastrophic at the time; but, because the revolution failed, as the love of music never did, the traditions reasserted themselves when these nurseries of the arts were restored, but naturally in changed forms, and with notable losses. The death of the most brilliant of Caroline composers, William Lawes at only forty-two, was taken as a symbolic event by his fellows: it was signalised by an unexampled outpouring of elegies and tributes to his genius. The fact that he was hailed as the 'Father of music' – as Byrd had always been – means that they looked upon him as a leader. There is no knowing what he would have accomplished if he had lived to eighty, as Byrd did. But William Lawes was already prodigiously prolific. Revolution and civil war broke the chain of continuity; with the Restoration came a change of taste, and earlier Caroline music to some extent went out of fashion. However, Lawes was not only a precursor of Purcell: he *was* a Purcell in himself, borne down by the deluge.

The question is sometimes put – Did the Puritans kill music in England?

Put in that simple form, the question is silly, for of course they did not – nothing could. The question is more complex, and the answer far more interesting. We have to be more discriminating, and investigate just what they did do. It is not enough to think to answer the question by pointing out that there were Puritans who liked music – that Oliver Cromwell did, for example. When the organ at Magdalen College, Oxford, was dismantled Cromwell had it brought to Hampton Court, where 'his Highness' the Protector lived in some state. An aristocrat himself, he appreciated the polyphonic motets of Richard Dering, the Catholic organist of Henrietta Maria's Chapel. We all know how devoted Milton was to music. Though a middle-class man, as an artist his tastes were aristocratic; Republican as he was, with more than Republican pride, no one had more contempt for the people or the average man (which he was far from being). The Parliamentarian Whitelocke, a cultivated man, was a connoisseur of music, and on a mission to Sweden pleased the Court there with the performance of English music. John Browne, a clerk to Parliament, was a devoted copyist, who preserved in manuscript much music which might otherwise have been lost – there was a great scattering.

None of this affects the main conclusion, which is indisputable: the Puritans shut down the music of the Court, the Church, and the Theatre.

When we go further into the matter we shall see that there was a class element in all this too. 'When the last remnants of Court and High Church [theatre also] were suppressed, only the simplified art of middle classes was left. A fresh impetus that might have brought new life by developing the vital productive powers of the people themselves disappeared among the social changes that took place.'[1] These, never wholly quenched, were to surface again, but with a change. Folk-song and folk-melody, which had been a source of inspiration to Elizabethan composers, ceased to inspire on a higher level.

Meanwhile, the consequences were shocking. 'Composers, organists, and singers were turned adrift and had to seek precarious livelihoods by teaching, or else escape starvation by adopting some occupation other than that for which they were fitted by talent or education. Others had to emigrate to other countries or to retire to the countryside. William Child devoted his time and talent more to farming. Thomas Tomkins retired to the country; John Jenkins, Henry Lawes, Charles Coleman, Christopher Gibbons, Simon Ives, all former members of the Chapel Royal, became private teachers.' Four of these were distinguished composers, three of them of the first rank of talent,

---

[1] E.H. Meyer, *English Chamber Music*, 198-200.

if not men of genius like William Lawes. The establishment of the King's Music, the Court instrumentalists, contained some fifty musicians – all turned adrift. A few emigrated, like the artists we have named; 'Benjamin Rogers spent much of his time abroad, as did also William Young', who entered the service of the Archduke Ferdinand. The Queen had an English musician as her organist in exile. 'Many composers were lost sight of completely.' A few of them collaborated with the new régime – three of them important musicians, John Wilson, John Hingston, Davis Mell. That happens in all revolutions.

We have a touching reminder of the straits to which players and musicians were reduced, in 'The Actors' Remonstrance for the silencing of their Profession', 1643:

> Our music that was to delectable and precious that they scorned to come to a tavern under 20 shillings' salary for two hours now wander, with their instruments under their cloaks – I mean such as have any – into all houses of good fellowship, saluting every room where there is company with 'Will you have any music, gentlemen?'

What would have happened to William Lawes, if he had not been killed? With his strongly defined personality, his originality, and his aggressive Royalism (for which he sacrificed his life), he could never have become a collaborator – any more than Shostakovich could.

The sophisticated music of Court, Church and Theatre was in marked contrast with that of people and Puritans, and increasingly in conflict – to the loss of both. The greatness of Elizabethan music and drama, the 'Golden Age', lay partly in the fact that it was an expression of an integrated society – integrated in the national struggle against Spain. With the long peace, things fell apart and the split in society became evident: the later drama no longer had the integrated wholeness of Shakespeare. Sophisticated Blackfriars for the upper classes, the Globe rather more for the people: not so good – and for music similarly. We might call the age of Charles I a 'Silver Age'.

Change comes about naturally in the arts, in accordance with their own internal developments, but also in response to the changes in the society of which they are an expression. Curiously enough, the accession of young Charles I to the throne coincided with the removal from the scene of those most distinguished composers who carried on the Elizabethan tradition to new flowering. Orlando Gibbons was a genius, not inferior to Byrd in the quality of his work; he created a specifically Anglican character in his church music, which is alive today. He accompanied Charles I to Canterbury for the reception of his young French bride in 1625; there Gibbons died suddenly on Whit Sunday, only forty-one. Next year a fine bust, by Nicholas Stone, was erected in the cathedral – the nose broken off subsequently, and characteristically.[1]

The no less original Thomas Weelkes, of the splendid, complex madrigals and anthems – still alive today – organist at Chichester and also at the Chapel Royal, had died 'untimely' in his forties in 1623.[2] These eminent musicians often combined their post in a cathedral with attendance for special occasions at the Chapel Royal, a signal honour. Alfonso Ferrabosco II spent all his life in England, the character of his music English; he was a close friend of Ben Jonson, and wrote the music for several of his masques, for which Inigo Jones devised the spectacle. Honoured as 'composer of music to the King' in 1626, Ferrabosco died in 1628.

Ferrabosco succeeded Coperario, whose real name was John Cooper, who died in 1626. Cooper was so addicted to Italian music that he chose to be called Coperario, by which name he is generally known, so I suppose we must conform. He was a brilliant composer of fantasies – not at all irregular in form, but pointing towards the subsequent development of sonata form. 'The importance of Coperario and Ferrabosco in the development of early English baroque instrumental style is paramount. They may be said to have taken the first significant steps in transforming the older "motet style for instruments" into characteristically instrumental writing.'[3] Earlier instrumental

[1] cf. E. H. Fellowes, *Orlando Gibbons*; P. Vining, 'Orlando Gibbons: the Portraits', *Music and Letters*, Oct. 1977, 415 foll.
[2] cf. D. Brown, *Thomas Weelkes*.
[3] M. Lefkowitz, *William Lawes*, 9-10.

'consort' music. i.e. for several instruments, had meant a transcription from the vocal, motets or madrigals. Now instruments, chiefly viols of different pitch, were to be written for for themselves, developing their own musical idiom.

In short, the 'New Music' as it is called; or the transition from High Renaissance to Baroque. These terms are never defined, and indeed it is difficult to do so - one can never express the experience of music satisfactorily in words. But we can *see* the transition to baroque in architecture or sculpture, in the work of the greatest baroque artist, Bernini. To put it simply, it shows a transition from regular, controlled expression to more irregular, free-flowing expression - we might usefully call it Expressionism.

Thus there was a new impulse in music, in which Charles I participated. Coperario had been his teacher, and there survives an early composition of the King's, 'Mark how the blushful morn' - one notes his characteristic delicacy of sentiment. He was fond too of taking part in 'consort' playing, especially 'those incomparable Phantasies [regular fantasies, not just 'fancies'] of Mr Coperario to the organ', i.e. the organ accompanying the strings.

We should remember here that the earlier organ had a sweet diapason tone, not the reedy brilliance of modern organs. And also cultivated people preferred the quieter music of the whole family of viols to the more shrill tone of the violin: they considered the violin lower-class, as indeed the fiddle was popular and fiddlers often vagrants. The adoption and promotion of the violin is a later 17th-century development.

One figure of prime importance survived from the Elizabethan age into this new world, and to write its epitaph. This was the long-lived Thomas Tomkins (1572-1656), pupil of Byrd and continuator of the polyphonic tradition in his prolific work, in almost every field.[1] He was organist of Worcester cathedral, and the bulk of his work is church music, motets, anthems, services; he also wrote fine keyboard music, for he was a foremost executant on the organ. He belonged to the most numerous family of musicians in the history of English music, all of them

[1]cf. D. Stevens, *Thomas Tomkins, 1572-1656*.

connected with the Church and Court. It originated in Cornwall – the Cornish form of the name is Tonkin – whence the father moved to become a vicar choral at St David's. A fossil of the connexion remains in the son's 'Toy – made at Poole Court', then the home of the Trelawnys near Menheniot. An elder brother was killed with Sir Richard Grenville on board the *Revenge*. Another brother, John, friend of the poet Phineas Fletcher, was organist of St Paul's and of the Chapel Royal; while Giles was organist of Salisbury cathedral, which reared a number of eminent musicians, composers as well as performers. Giles was much favoured by Charles I for his skill on the virginals; and both he and John accompanied the King, with the Chapel Royal, to Scotland for his coronation there – which Archbishop Laud performed regularly in a cope, to the scandal of the Elect.

Robert Tomkins was a viol player in the King's Consort (i.e. orchestra). Brother Nathaniel was a canon of Worcester, in sympathy with Laud's mission for order and decent ritual, when some of the citizens objected to choral services and preferred preaching. The dispute came up, as everything did, to the worried archbishop; Bishop Thornborough, a left-over from the Elizabethan age, advised him to let the 'fools' have their way – and Laud, who was not unreasonable, complied.

Thomas Tomkins was the last of the great Elizabethan madrigalists, but he was capable of moving with the times and wrote a number of fantasies, consort music for viols in the new fashion. But much more organ music, where he was pre-eminent; among this one notes a voluntary for the consecration of the chapel at Auckland Castle on St Peter's day, 1635. (The Laudians were restoring the rite of consecration for churches – the Church *was* becoming more Catholic once more.) Next year was a Plague year, which Tomkins commemorated with a tremendous Offertory, for keyboard.

At Worcester he had an exceptionally fine organ, towards which over a hundred people had subscribed. Tomkins was in the habit of composing special works for the greater feast-days of the Church – soon to be suppressed. In 1643, his house was wrecked by a cannon shot, 'when Waller attempted the taking of the city', and on Essex's incursion into it the organ was

damaged. On Parliament's victory in 1646, the diarist
Townshend tells us,

> July 20: the organs were this day taken down out of the cathedral
> church. Some Parliamenters, hearing the music of the church at
> service, walking in the aisle, fell a-skipping about and dancing as
> it were in derision. Others, seeing the workmen taking them
> down, said 'You might have spared that labour: we would have
> done it for you.' 'No', said a merry lad, 'for when the Earl of
> Essex was here, the first man of yours that plucked down and
> spoiled the organs broke his neck here.'[1]

Three days later the services were suppressed; there is a
touching note of the last to be held. 'July 23: this day at 6 of the
clock prayers, many gentlemen went to take their last farewell
and meeting at the college, at the Common Prayers of the
Church, and to receive the Bishop's blessing.' This was Bishop
Prideaux, who died practically penniless, a year after Charles I's
martyrdom.

Tomkins did indeed retire to the country and, without organ
or choir, gave himself up to composing for keyboard. Most of
these manuscripts disappeared, only one in eight have survived;
one of them his 'Sad Pavan for these distracted times', a fine
work still performed and admired today. Tomkins composed it
within a matter of days from the last terrible scene outside the
Banqueting House in Whitehall. Tomkins' loyalism is expressed
also in those few pieces he named, the pavans in memory of
Strafford and Laud, two other martyrs to the Revolution - both
of them condemned by Act of attainder, since no evidence
forthcoming was sufficient to impeach them. The King always
regarded his consent to Strafford's execution - wrung from him
by mob-pressure - as a sin; it was worse - a profound political
mistake.

Nathaniel Tomkins, as a canon, was sequestrated, turned
out: as a 'delinquent', i.e. loyal to the King, he underwent a
heavy fine. For these people music was dumb during the bad
times:

[1]Ibid, 58-9.

> Although the cannon and the churlish drum
> Have struck the choir mute and the organs dumb,
> Yet music's art, with air and string and voice,
> Makes glad the sad, and sorrow to rejoice.

As Feltham said well (and William Shakespeare before him): 'I think he hath not a mind well-tempered, whose zeal is not inflamed with a heavenly anthem.' One cannot think that the minds of Puritans in general were 'well-tempered'. When the good times came back, all was to do again: organs restored, considerable payments for song-books, i.e. anthems, and service books for the choir. It was not until the Restoration that a large collection of Tomkins' church music, the *Musica Deo Sacra*, was published in 1668.

We have an authoritative estimate of Tomkins from our own day.

> Wherein lies the greatness of Thomas Tomkins' art? To some extent it resides in the shape and beauty of his melodic lines, and in his contrapuntal ingenuity. But more especially his genius is to be found in the unusually bold and rich harmonic progressions, achieved by free use of passing and anticipatory notes, chromatic intervals, and frequent false relations. Such works as 'A Sad Pavan: for these distracted times' and 'When David heard that Absalom was slain' are unsurpassed for poignancy of musical expression.[1]

In short, Tomkins was essentially a polyphonic composer.

We do not have to disparage Puritan music: civilised persons can include both. We still appreciate the grave simplicity of hymns like the Old Hundredth, with which Cromwell's Ironsides marched in unison to victory at Naseby:

> All people that on earth do dwell,
>     Sing to the Lord with cheerful voice;
> Him serve with fear, his praise forth tell,
>     Come ye before him, and rejoice.

[1] Ibid, 94.

[122]

> The Lord, ye know, is God indeed,
> Without our aid he did us make;
> *We are His folk*, he doth us feed,
> And for his sheep he doth us take.

This expressed their spirit: *they* were his folk.

Persons of taste liked neither the spirit, nor the rough and rude verse of Old Sternhold and Hopkins in which it was expressed.[1] Charles I, for one, did not. He much preferred the translation of the Psalms by George Sandys, an experienced and practising poet, to which he gave his patronage.[2] Sandys' *Paraphrase* was published in 1636, with dedicatory poems to King, Queen, the unfortunate but courageous Elizabeth, the 'Winter Queen' of Bohemia, as well as to the Archbishop. Sandys spoke of the encouragement he had received of the King, and prophetically, referring to the Winter Queen's troubles:

> Crowns are the sport of fortune.

Two years later the book was given a further resonance, being 'Set to new tunes for private devotion; and a thorough bass for voice or instrument, by Henry Lawes, Gentleman of his Majesty's Chapel Royal.' It was sped on its way by tributes from the poets, Bishop Henry King, Sidney Godolphin, Thomas Carew, Waller, as well as by Dudley Digges and Sir Henry Rainsford (of associations with Shakespeare and Drayton).

The book never took on, for all its superiority to the uncouth metrics of Sternhold and Hopkins, or of Francis Rouse. It was not to be expected that the people at large would give up what they had been used to – what was in any case more suited to their uncouth taste. Sandys' version of the Psalms was a product of the Court – anathema to Puritans; it retained its favour with the King, who consoled himself with it during his imprisonment in the Isle of Wight – as he entertained himself reading Shakespeare, in the recent Second Folio, during his confinement at Hampton Court.

---

[1] This is the meaning of the word 'Old' attached to these tunes; they had appeared in the original publication of Sternhold and Hopkins at the Reformation.
[2] R.B. Davis, *George Sandys, Poet-Adventurer*, 236 foll.

One sees the conflict of taste no less with regard to music itself. Hitherto music in cathedral, church or chapel, was sung from 'prick-song', i.e. manuscript pricked for notation. This entailed a great deal of work and expense – it also, by the way, is the reason why so much earlier church music disappeared, with the dispersal of the choirs and their manuscripts. Puritan singing was simple and congregational; the elaborate music of the Church, on a much higher plane artistically, was for the elect and there was a 'scarcity of auditors that understood it'.

In 1641 a musical canon of St Paul's, John Barnard, did his best to help here with a comprehensive collection of church music from the greatest Elizabethan composers, *The First Book of Selected Church Music.* He expressed the purpose of the publication: 'Whereby such books as were heretofore, with much difficulty and charges, transcribed for the use of the Choir are now to the saving of much labour and expence published for the general good of all such as shall desire them, either for public or private exercise.'[1] He evidently intended to follow up with a second volume, a further selection coming up to contemporary composers, from Tomkins onwards.

All to no avail. It was already too late; that glorious tradition of music went underground during the Revolution – to emerge with the Restoration of the Church. Witness of its undying vitality is the fact that it is the staple of cathedral music today, and not only in England but in the Episcopal Church in the United States in 'such places where they sing'. The Presbyterian Kirk sticks to its ancient doggerel; the Anglican Church, in its comprehensiveness, includes these tunes – not only the Old Hundredth but the Old 120th, 124th, 137th etc – along with the even more moving plainsong of the Catholic Church through all the ages.

Conflict is to be seen in regard to secular music no less. The trade union of musicians in London, the City Gild of Musicians, was jealous of the favoured circle of musicians at Court in Westminster, and which followed the Court wherever it was. At any rate they should not play in the City. (How sickeningly one recognises the spirit from the amenities of contemporary

---

[1]J. Pulver, *A Biographical Dictionary of Old English Music*, 39.

trade-union society!) Roger North, in his account of the music of the time, makes the point that only the music of the Court could compare with that of Italy. For a century past the Court had employed a large number of foreign musicians, whole families of them like the Bassanos, Lupos, Ferraboscos, mainly Italians, though the numerous Laniers were French by origin. These 'Gentlemen of the Chapel Royal' wrote themselves, and were recognised, as gentlemen; they were noticeably uppish, and the records of the Elizabethan age show them not infrequently scuffling with native citizens in the streets of London. Something may be imputed to their Italian temperament (Emilia Bassano, Alphonso Lanier's wife and Shakespeare's young mistress, exhibited plenty of it); but the English of those days were just as quick on the draw.

One such scuffle on Cornhill in February 1629 involved no less a person than Nicholas Lanier.[1] We have seen how close he was to Charles I as art-adviser, his agent in procuring the Gonzaga collection from Mantua. Lanier was primarily a musician though also a good amateur painter, thus indispensable in the production of the Court masques, for which much of his music was written. Quarrelling with a citizen in the street, Lanier and his fellows drew their swords – characteristically; the gathering crowd, no less characteristically, resorted to sticks and stones and overbore Lanier's little group.

More important than the fracas in itself, the City Gild, trade-unionwise, responded by insisting on the Court musicians submitting themselves to the Gild and its regulations, or otherwise be debarred from teaching or practising in the City. This was highly inconvenient, for there were occasions when the Court musicians would be needed and called upon, Inns of Court masques, Blackfriars plays – very much a Court venue. The Crown responded by annulling the patent the Gild had received from James I, and incorporating the Court musicians as 'Marshal, Wardens and Commonalty of the art and science of music in Westminster, with authority in the country, no one to practice the profession without licence'. Nicholas Lanier,

---

[1] cf. G.A. Phillips, 'Crown Musical Patronage from Elizabeth I to Charles I', *Music and Letters*, Jan. 1977, 38.

Master of the King's Music, was announced as Marshal of the Incorporation.

One sees yet again the King's desire to impose order and control, in this sphere too; but the edict was unenforceable – just as the Archbishop, for all his ceaseless care and worry, could not enforce order on the Puritans, either in Church or in the press. There was a mutinous spirit abroad, as Clarendon said, in every sphere; and direct confrontation was increasing, always the prelude to revolution.

Puritan feeling had been expressing itself about music also for the past three generations. There was the nasty-spirited Stubbes, in his *Anatomy of Abuses* (1583):

> Every town, city and country [i.e. county] is full of these minstrels to pipe up a dance to the Devil; but of divines, so few there be as they may hardly be seen. May you, as rogues extravagants and stragglers from the heavenly country, be arrested of the High Justice of Peace, Christ Jesus, and be punished with eternal death, notwithstanding your pretensed licences of earthly men.

One recognises the language. Elizabeth I had known how to deal with a Stubbes, when he interfered in her affairs. With regard to preaching, she knew that there were only 500 clergy in the whole country capable of preaching, out of some 9000 parishes. With the marked increase of university education for the clergy, many more had become preachers – let alone the large addition the Commonwealth was to make from the ranks of cobblers and such. Stubbes was one of those who could not keep his mouth shut: there is a direct line of continuity between such as he and Prynne, a similarly sour, embittered Philistine.

The attack on the cathedrals was equally an attack on their music. A number of the most eminent organists doubled with the honour of their appointment to the Chapel Royal. We may look at Salisbury to see what creative schools of music the cathedrals were, producing composers as well as executants. Family tradition and succession were important, naturally from the point of view of training. Salisbury had had a line of distinguished organists in the Farrants, and now came a fine flowering with Henry and William Lawes, composers of prime importance, their brother John a 'singing-man' at Westminster Abbey. Edward Lowe became organist at Christ Church, Oxford, and kept the torch flickering during dreary Commonwealth days with private concerts, until with the Restoration he was promoted to the Chapel Royal in the old manner. Nearby at Wilton House the Earl of Pembroke, and not far afield the Earl of Hertford, were notable patrons, particularly of Ferrabosco and Coperario. It all constituted a musical culture, of which George Herbert was the poet, the Lawes brothers prime figures in the music of the age.

They were devoted to each other, Henry six years older than William, born in 1602: sons of a lay vicar, and trained in the cathedral. Because Henry Lawes was associated with Milton and wrote the music for *Comus*, he was for long thought the more important of the two. Now that it is recognised that William Lawes was the original genius, people are apt to under-rate Henry, who certainly had first-rate talent. William was the most important dramatic composer before Purcell; but since he wrote so much for the stage, with the suppression of the theatre most of that music was buried - and, in the conditions of the time, much else too.

He was prodigiously prolific, pouring his genius into almost every form. Characteristic of it was his romantic *fougue*, a restless passionateness, turbulence of spirit underlined by melancholy: a combination to appeal to the Caroline Court, the romantic melancholy particularly to the King. The range itself bespoke greatness: music for sixteen stage plays, three Court masques, one Royal entertainment: altogether 136 vocal works; 41 fantasias for viols in five and six parts.[1] He wrote much dance music for the Court, some 66 pieces; his is the earliest music written for the harp; he even wrote a little for the violin, only then moving up in the social scale. In church music he favoured the 'Lamentations of Jeremiah' (as Tallis had done), which gave opening to his inner emotions. When he set the Psalms, he used the Prayer Book words of the Church, not the Authorised

[1] M. Lefkowitz, *William Lawes, passim.*

Version. A favourite key with him was C minor (as it was with me in early musical days).

William Lawes's fate was in keeping with his spirit. Fuller describes it:

> In these distracted times his loyalty engaged him in the war for his Lord and Master; and though he was made a Commissary on design to secure him – such officers being commonly shot-free by their place, as not exposed to danger[1] – yet, such the activity of his spirit he disclaimed the covert of his office. And betrayed thereunto by his own adventurousness was casually shot at the siege of Chester, the same time when the Lord Bernard Stuart lost his life. Nor was the King's soul so engrossed with grief for the death of so near a kinsman but that, hearing of the death of his dear servant William Lawes, he had a particular mourning for him when dead, whom he loved when living and commonly called the 'Father of Music'.

Several of the Royal musicians enlisted on the King's side: Orlando Gibbons' son Christopher and Henry Cooke; Christopher Simpson, an able composer and exceptionally a violinist, joined up under the Earl of Newcastle.[2] It was natural enough that the Royalist cause should be theirs by conviction, but it is evident that they had a personal devotion to the King whose soul was in the arts, not politics, where he was no match for Pym or Cromwell – for what that was worth *sub specie aeternitatis*.

That their leader should have fallen in the field of battle was taken as a symbol, for never was there a greater outpouring of tributes, from musicians and poets alike. One has the strong sense of a confraternity – Lawes himself had written a beautiful elegy for John Tomkins. Now all the leading musicians paid tribute to their fellow. John Jenkins was hardly less distinguished than Lawes, and almost as prolific. We may regard him as second to the master, and quote his elegy as an example of the dialogue which was a new feature in Caroline music:

[1] cf. the action of the civilised Russian Court under Nicholas I to keep the young Tolstoy out of the first line in the Caucasus.
[2] P.M. Young, *A History of British Music*, 222.

| | |
|---|---|
| Treble: | What caused his fate? |
| Bass: | A fatal breath of honour |
| | Challenged death with death. |
| Treble: | What tempted? |
| Bass: | Virtue. |
| Treble: | Why? |
| Bass: | To have a loyal fame, |
| | A royal grave. |

Jenkins generously hailed his junior as 'the soul of mine and all our harmony'. Elegies were contributed by, among others, five distinguished composers: William's brother Henry, John Wilson, Simon Ives, John Hilton, and Jenkins who was William's senior by ten years yet a close friend. Their music might be said to be complementary: where Jenkins had almost as wide a range, he had a quieter spirit – one might compare him with George Herbert, Lawes with Donne. Jenkins had an 'infinite flowing vein', where Lawes was more rugged and daring, often improvisatory, though elaborated in texture and harmony.

John Hilton set a long piece beginning,

> Bound by the near conjunction of our souls . . .

The poets were not far behind, with Herrick and Aurelian Townsend, who had collaborated with Lawes in creating Court masques. He paid tribute to the brothers' settings of the Psalms:

> Brothers in blood, in science and affection,
> Beloved by those that envy their renown.
> In a false time true servants of the crown:
> Laws of themselves, needing no direction.

Since none of his brother's music had been printed, Henry Lawes chose to commemorate him by publishing their *Choice Psalms* in 1648, which 'I have been much importuned to send to the press, and should not easily have been persuaded to do it now, especially in these dissonant times, but to do a right, or at least to show my love, to the memory of my Brother, unfortunately lost in these unnatural wars – yet lies in the bed of honour, and expired in the service and defence of the King his Master.' To him the work was dedicated: 'I could not answer mine own conscience, most gracious Sovereign, should I dedicate these compositions to any but your Majesty. They were born and nourished in your Majesty's service. Many of them were composed by my brother, whose life and endeavours were devoted to your service: whereof I, who knew his heart, am a surviving witness, and therein he persisted until that last minute when he fell a willing sacrifice for your Majesty ... from whose Royal bounty both of us received all we enjoyed.'

The brothers' Psalms were set to Sandys' verses, which the King preferred. The surviving brother daily prayed that 'the King of Heaven and Earth restore your Majesty according to your own righteous heart'. By this time this was what the country wished. The King was still alive, held in captivity at Carisbrooke; but it was not to be: shortly the Army struck.

A new development was the declamatory solo-song, probably in response to the lead given from Italy. This also reflected the extremely close association between the musicians and the poets. Elizabethan song-writers were nothing like so choosy about words: words took second place – hence the inferior quality of much madrigal verse. This was not good enough for Caroline poets, not only more sophisticated but aiming at conciseness and metrical perfection. There was both loss and gain: against Elizabethan simplicity, freshness and innocence we have more subtlety and precision. With the new form of the musical dialogue we have argument, and that set the composer more of a problem.

It is on account of this, not seeing the music in its proper perspective, that critics, with 19th-century prejudices – and unconscious that their own views are time-conditioned – depreciate Caroline music, especially the declamatory of which Henry Lawes was the chief exponent and practitioner.[1] He left a vast body of work, one recently discovered manuscript containing no less than 300 songs. And he was greatly esteemed

[1]E.F. Hart, 'Introduction to Henry Lawes', *Music and Letters*, 1951, 217.

in his own day, by poets and musicians and the general public. A recent writer, rendering him justice, asks pertinently 'who is in a better position to judge a musician's declamation than his contemporaries, especially the poets whose verses he sets?'[1] It all goes to show how important a sense of historical perspective is to the understanding of historic arts.

Hence we may see that Milton's too-famous tribute to Henry Lawes has been doubtfully understood:

Harry, whose tuneful and well-measured Song
First taught our English music how to scan
Words with just note and accent . . .

It is really a tribute to Lawes's art of declamatory song, in which the music is made to follow the words justly. At this time, too, bar-accent was coming in to regularise the measure; Henry Lawes was an innovator in this field too.

Lawes's popularity is attested to by the number of his published works. While public performance was suppressed, the native love of music was unquenched and partly met by private gatherings, out of which grew the first public concerts; still more by publications, for which there was a marked demand - and John Playford cashed in on it. Three books of Henry Lawes's Airs and Dialogues were published during the Commonwealth; nicer still to think that he survived to write the Coronation anthem, 'Zadok the Priest', for Charles II.

The prolific John Jenkins was also lucky enough to survive. He was an easy-going personality, 'neither conceited nor morose but very much a gentleman', i.e. of Court breeding; highly intelligent and witty, so that 'in most of his friends' houses

---

[1]Critics! cf. a composer of genius today on the subject. Michael Tippett: 'Music should speak to us as far as possible immediately, directly, and without analysis.' Or the earlier 'often highly resisting criticisms of Britten's music that seem to have soured the composer's attitude to musicology for life in a way'. They were genuinely 'attempting to put their finger on aspects of Britten's technique that caused then unease, trying to pin down something that was not quite right about the way he composed music'! As if they could! I recall a detailed analysis of Britten's music by an academic, in the *Cambridge Review*, reducing it to nullity. Or cf. the incomprehension with which Elgar was treated by the academic, which so much embittered him.

there was a chamber called by his name, and he was always courted to stay'. Thus Roger North, who was taught by him at Kirtling. Earlier he had been given refuge by the L'Estranges in Norfolk, and taught the famous Tory pamphleteer, Roger L'Estrange. Long-lived, at the Restoration Jenkins was reinstated in the Royal Music.

Others who were not so prominent were less lucky. Some maintained themselves by private teaching, as many of the dispossessed clergy did, or by practising medicine. Benjamin Cosyn, a graceful composer for the virginals, was organist at Charterhouse until 1643; thrown out, he was left destitute, until the school awarded him a tiny pension.[1] The organist and the master of the choristers at Westminster Abbey were both thrown out. And so it went. John Hilton, a distinguished composer, had been organist at St Margaret's, Westminster; at his funeral in 1657, his fellows – since singing at burials was silenced as Popish – 'sang the anthem in the house over the corpse before it went to church, and kept time on his coffin'.[2]

Some sense of the devastation in English music came to the surface with a public petition, under the Protectorate, for a state academy to come to the rescue. Nothing came of it; but rescue was on the way with the Restoration.

Justice cannot be done to the Caroline masques on purely literary grounds, for in them the spectacle came first, the words were secondary, supplying simply a scenario for the stage effects and the music. It was precisely over this that Ben Jonson quarrelled with Inigo Jones: Ben was not the man to take second place to anybody. In the event he was forced to: others could supply words for a masque, but no one could compete with Inigo in stage-craft, the designing of scenery, costumes, etc. The masque presented a fusion of all three arts, the music hardly less than the spectacle. In this the composer could collaborate. For Shirley's *Triumph of Peace* in 1634 Henry Lawes wrote most of the music, seconded by Simon Ives and others. Thomas Carew wrote the words for *Coelum Britannicum* in the same year, Henry

[1]M.H. Glyn, *Elizabethan Virginal Music*, 118–19.
[2]P.M. Young, *op. cit.*, 222.

Lawes again writing the music, as he did shortly after for Milton's *Comus*. Meanwhile William Lawes wrote the music for Davenant's stage play, *Love and Honour*, for the King's Men at Blackfriars, which had become more and more closely associated with the Court.

A strong element of propaganda pervaded the masques presented for Charles I. The *Triumph of Peace* put the case for those peaceful years enjoyed by England while the Thiry Years' War still raged on the Continent. Aggressive Protestantism wanted to push England into the conflict, and – when they were young and foolish – Charles and Buckingham, for the sake of popularity, had involved themselves in conflict with Catholic France and Spain, been left in the lurch by Parliament and come out ingloriously – that overmighty subject, the Duke, a victim. After that, the King's motto appears to have been 'Never Again' – neither war nor Parliament. But there were people about spoiling for both. One must reflect that, after the long Jacobean peace, plenty of aggressive masculine types were spoiling for action; and that it has always been a point of policy with governments to deflect popular discontent at home into campaigns abroad. One sees this displayed, too, in the enthusiasm with which the brilliant (and foolish) young courtiers flocked to the Borders in 1639 – to receive their come-uppance from the embattled Scots.

Undoubtedly Charles I and his father were men of peace – James I passionately so (a clever, timorous homosexual), whose great ambition was to leave a name in history as *Rex Pacificus*. He deeply wanted to bring about peace in Europe, but this was beyond him; his son gave up the attempt, content to maintain peace at home. This was the theme of the masque, the *Triumph of Peace*, which was also intended as a demonstration of the loyalty of the Inns of Court, after one of their members, the odious Prynne, had attacked stage, Court and Church, and libelled the Queen, in his *Histriomastix*.

This masque was the most elaborate and extravagant of all those produced, but paid for by the wealthy Inns of Court. It employed no less than forty lutes, along with the (unpopular, of course) French musicians of the Queen's Chapel. It was preceded by a procession of some hundreds in fur and feather, silver and gold trimmings, which marched from Chancery Lane to Whitehall, where King and Queen were so courteous as to ask that 'the whole show might fetch a turn about the Tilt-yard, that their Majesties might have a double view of them ... In the meantime the Banqueting-house was so crowded with fair ladies, glittering with their rich clothes and richer jewels, and with lords and gentlemen of great quality, that there was scarce room for the King and Queen to come in.'[1] (What memories the King would have on the fatal day, fifteen years ahead, when he would step out of a window there to his execution!) Then the masque proceeded, 'dancing, speeches, music, and scenes ... all of them exact, none failed in their parts, and the scenes were most curious [i.e. ingenious] and costly'.

In some of these spectacles at Court King and Queen danced – almost a ritual act. Henrietta Maria herself adored dancing, music and plays; in one or two of the masques she and her ladies acted, and on four occasions she attended performances at Blackfriars. It is true that these were private performances – all the same, attending a theatre would have been unthinkable for Elizabeth I. All this scandalised the Puritans. We must in justice allow that they had a point – the sheer extravagance of spending so much on anything so impermanent, so ephemeral, as a masque. The Court, however, was keeping up – as in the other arts – with the European culture of the Courts abroad. 'Here one clearly sees the influence of Renaissance festivals and carnivals, especially the masquerade and the Florentine *trionfo* which was so popular with Lorenzo dei Medici.'[2] Perhaps it was all rather un-English.

For whom was the propaganda intended? It was only preaching to the converted, and for the rest of no effect, or, rather, counter-productive. It is sad to have to confess that the horrid Prynne was more English, in tune with popular feeling, at any rate Puritan feeling. He had for years been trying to get his book against the stage, plays, actors, masques, strollers, the whole theatrical profession, into print and could not get it licensed. An Oxford man, alas, a barrister of Lincoln's Inn, a

[1] q. from Whitelocke, in Lefkowitz, *op. cit.*, 212-13.
[2] Ibid, 206.

learned man widely read in theology and Church history, he had for some years been attacking the Church. He was both vehement and determined, and at last got his book into print.

Laud, as archbishop, was officially concerned with censorship of the press – part of his burdensome duties. In this field the Church had had, on the whole, a markedly tolerant record. It was said that the King and Queen would have overlooked the libels and aspersions in the book, but Laud was not the man to neglect any part of his duty. He brought the matter to the attention of the Privy Council.

> Mr Prynne hath been a malignant man to the state and government of the realm, a mover of the people to discontent and sedition; and to put this his resolution into practice he hath compiled a book called *Histrio Mastix*, and therein he hath presumed to cast aspersion upon the King, the Queen, and the Commonwealth, to infuse an opinion into the people that it is lawful to lay violent hands upon Princes that are either actors, favourers or spectators of stage plays.[1]

Prynne had cited such cases as Nero, Caligula, Commodus, Heliogabulus, and others to that effect.

The Privy Council did not concern themselves with his remarks on Bishops as 'Devils masks' and that Christ was a Puritan etc, as more properly belonging to the Church, i.e. the Court of High Commission. They confined themselves to the secular: his charge against the 'French women, or monsters rather', who dared to act a French play at Blackfriars, 'an impudent, shameful, graceless, if not more than whorish attempt ... Dare then any Christian woman be so whorishly impudent as to act or speak publicly on a stage, perhaps without hair [cf. St Paul on that subject], and in man's apparel, in the presence of sundry men and women. Dancing, even in queens themselves and in the very greatest persons, who are commonly the most devoted to it, have been all ways scandalous and of ill report among the Saints of God', i.e. Prynne and his like. In his Index Prynne had listed 'delight and skill in dancing: a badge of lewd, lascivious women and strumpets'.

[1] *Documents relating to ... William Prynne*, ed. S.R. Gardiner. Camden Soc., 1, 10 foll.

Prynne cited the condemnation of dancing by those European Puritans, the Waldenses (whom Milton was to salute, 'Avenge, O Lord, thy slaughtered Saints'): 'the dancing wantons – that I say not whorish-Herodiases, the effeminate cinquapace – coranto-frisking gallants of our age; together with our rustic hobbling satyrs, nymphs, and dancing fairies, who spend their strength, their time, especially the Easter, Whitsuntide etc in lewd, lascivious dancings.' This condemnation of poor rustics would lead, when Prynne and his like got their way, to the suppression of maypoles, Whitsun and hock-tide celebrations, church-ales, keeping Christmas, etc, in every parish in England, so far as they could.

'By Herodias, whom he meant, his malice may easily discover him' – he meant the Queen, as everybody knew. The Privy Council imposed upon him a severe sentence: life imprisonment, £5000 fine, his ears to be clipped, a custom of the time. The sentence was unanimous, except for the Archbishop who dissented from the clipping of the ears – I suspect on anthropological, rather than humanitarian, grounds. Today we should think the sentence barbarous, and Prynne a case for psychiatry rather than the pillory; Soviet Russia would give him prolonged treatment in one of their asylums for dissidents.

After the *Triumph of Peace* the Queen danced in the revels 'until it was almost morning', and was so pleased with its success that a repeat performance was arranged for the City, at Merchant Taylors' Hall. The aesthete in the King, anxious lest the smoke of so many torches and candles should damage the paintings in the Banqueting Hall, ordered a new temporary hall of timber from Inigo Jones for subsequent masques. William Lawes wrote the music for Davenant's *Triumphs of the Prince d'Amour*, which was put on for the visit of the King's nephew, the Elector Charles Louis, brother of Prince Rupert. The more important *Britannia Triumphans* of 1638 – Davenant, Jones, William Lawes working together – also had a propaganda point, relating to the immense outcry raised over Ship Money.

After the long peace the fleet was in disrepair and needed replacements, while the King wished not only to clear the Channel of Algerine pirates but to assert sovereignty over it. Ship money had been customarily levied on coastal counties;

why should it not be extended to inland counties, which profited also from the protection of the fleet? Significantly enough – though it has not been noticed – this bright idea occurred to a Cornishman, William Noy, the Attorney General. Resistance to it was led by a rich Buckinghamshire squire, John Hampden, one of the numerous cousins of Oliver Cromwell, and Hampden gained a national reputation by fighting Ship Money through the courts. To my mind the most pointed word was said about it by Thomas Hobbes: worth £500 a year, and to boggle at 10 or 12 shillings!

John Hampden succeeded in raising hell, and becoming a popular hero, for the country was more and more mutinous. However, money was raised and the fleet renewed – to go over to Parliament when revolution raised its standard. Really, Charles I had no luck – and for success in politics one needs luck most of all.

The masque sought to vindicate the King's policy, his renewal of the fleet and assertion of sovereignty over the seas – the theme should have been as popular as it was patriotic. Charles himself appeared as 'Britanocles, who hath by his wisdom, valour and piety, not only vindicated his own but far distant seas, infested with pirates; and reduced the land, by his example, to a real knowledge of all good arts and sciences'. All to no avail. The work was performed on the Sunday after Twelfth Night, and this too gave offence: it came up against the crazy sabbatarianism of the Puritans, which was against any jollity on Sundays. All round the country Puritan preachers had inveighed against the royal Book of Sports giving leave to honest entertainment on that one day out of the week's work.

The masque touched on the conflict, for it began with an argument between Action – what the King was trying to do – and Imposture, a character which Puritans in power were going to fulfil in overflowing measure. Leaders of rebellion were ominously recalled from the past, Jack Cade, Kett of the Norfolk Rising of 1549, Jack Straw. The ancient magician Merlin was called up to raise the standards of 'the mean and low', the multitude who care neither for learning nor the arts and sciences. All this was true enough – and rather too near the bone.

Most of the music written by William Lawes has managed

to survive – unlike the Puritans: symphonies, declamatory songs, ballads, choruses and Valediction. It is pleasant to record that it was revived for performance in the Coronation year of Elizabeth II, 1953.

The public theatre continued to be dominated by the King's Men, Shakespeare's old company – formerly the Lord Chamberlain's – but even more than before. It had been the favourite company playing at Court in his time, but in the new conditions of Charles's Court the association became very close. For one thing the private theatre at Blackfriars had become far more important to the Company: it dominated its interests, financially and socially; and in many respects, in regard to the plays performed, their authors and performances, Blackfriars twinned with the Court. The Globe continued during the summer months for the general public; Blackfriars for the rest of the year, an enclosed theatre in which music was an important feature. More expensive, its clientèle was aristocratic and markedly Courtly: there were 'the silks and plush and all the wits', the precinct blocked with their coaches.

There remained a good deal of continuity from Shakespeare's later days. His fellow, John Heming, was still business manager; John Lowin, a big fellow who could play Henry VIII, was the leading actor; Christopher Beeston carried on for years – to whom we owe the information that Shakespeare had briefly been an usher in a school in the country. A new age brought a new atmosphere, a change of taste. Charles I's Court was immeasurably more refined and delicate than his undignified father's, more elegant as well as sophisticated. Even Lucy Hutchinson allowed that it was chaste. All the talk was of love, as usual in Courts, but it was a cult of platonic love; and the favourite plays at Blackfriars now were not Shakespeare's, but Beaumont and Fletcher's.

One remarkable survivor from Elizabethan days was old Thomas Heywood, who took – as Ben Jonson did – to writing masques. He had much success with his masque, *Love's Mistress*, which the Queen laid on to entertain the King on his birthday, 19 November 1634. Heywood himself was delighted by the splendid sets Inigo Jones devised for it. The old man had this gratifying success just after young William Davenant's play, *The Just Italian,* had been a failure. Like others, Davenant turned his pen to masques as well as to stage plays. He wrote the words – we might almost call it the libretto – for the last masque to be presented at Court, *Salmacida Spolia* in 1640, when the spirit of rebellion was abroad and Court masques no longer feasible.

James Shirley and Richard Brome are the leading professional Caroline dramatists; i.e. they made their living by writing for the theatre,[1] each of them contracted to write two plays a year: Shirley at first for the Cockpit in Drury Lane; Brome for the Queen's Men, Henrietta Maria's Company. Shirley spent some years in Ireland under Strafford, where he gave the first important impulse to the Dublin theatre. A Catholic convert, Shirley was a favoured valet of the Queen, for whose Company he wrote a few realistic plays of London life, *Hyde Park* and *The Lady of Pleasure,* the latter his finest comic work. He dedicated *The Bird in a Cage* ironically to Prynne: 'The fame of your candour and your innocent love to learning, especially to that musical part of humane knowledge – poetry; and in particular to that which concerns the stage and scene – yourself, as I hear, having lately written a tragedy. . . .'[2] And so on: things were coming to open confrontation.

Shirley himself wrote tragedies, notably *The Traitor* and *The Cardinal,* but more comedies, like the very successful *The Gamester.* It was said of this that the King suggested the plot. We know that Shirley could be a fine poet, from his moving dirge, 'The glories of our death and state', written about the time of the death of Cromwell. A prolific and successful writer – no less than sixteen of his plays were published in London – he was promoted to succeed Massinger as dramatist for the King's Men in 1640. Like other artists he felt the difficulties under which they worked:

> We have named our play
> *The Example* – and for aught we know, it may

[1] v. the important distinction made by G.E. Bentley, *The Profession of Dramatist in Shakespeare's Time,* ch. 1.
[2] q. G.E. Bentley, *The Jacobean and Caroline Stage,* III.

> Be made one; for at no time did the laws,
> However understood, more fright the cause
> Of unbefriended poesy.[1]

On the outbreak of war he raised a troop for the King and joined the Earl of Newcastle, serving him on campaign from 1642 to 1644. That rich Cavendish potentate – Bess of Hardwick had made the fortunes for all of them[2] – was an unsuccessful commander in the field; and no more with his pen – Shirley helped him with his plays. After the war Shirley taught school in Whitefriars – he was a university man – and published school books to live, his poems for consolation. At the Restoration and the revival of the theatre his plays were for a time the favourites. Good as his best work is, it would be interesting to have a few of his plays revived for us today.[3]

Davenant would have regarded himself, as Ben Jonson had done, as primarily a poet rather than a professional playwright, though ultimately no one played a more important part in the transition, through the bleak Commonwealth days, from the Caroline to the Restoration stage. He began his career writing masques for the Court, then turned to plays for the King's Men, in closest association with courtiers, Endymion Porter and Harry Jermyn, close friends with Suckling and Carew, chaffing each other – very un-Puritan-wise – on being clapped. Davenant wrote a play called *The Platonic Lovers*, which, however much in keeping with Court taste, was very far from his own practice (he lost his nose to syphilis, caught in France).

Dashing and intrepid, Davenant had a tempestuous career. Recovering from his illness – and the mercury treatment it involved – he fatally stabbed an ostler, and fled abroad to Holland. After publishing *Madagascar*, a volume of poems, with tributes from his poetic friends, he was pardoned and made poet laureate with a pension. His most sparkling comedy, *The Wits*, was corrected by the King himself at Newmarket, who struck

---

[1]q. *James Shirley*, (The Best Plays of the Old Dramatists. Mermaid Series), ed. Edmund Gosse, xxii.
[2]v. 'Bess of Hardwick', in my *Eminent Elizabethans*.
[3]Theatre producers, in want of something original, please note!

out some passages, 'This is too insolent, and to be changed.'[1] Nothing daunted, Davenant has brazen references to the treatment for pox, losing one's nose, etc – enough to make the Puritans right. But we are reminded that Shakespeare always referred to the pox, 'French crowns' etc as good for a laugh, and that Davenant in his cups liked to give out that he was William's by-blow from passing through Oxford. (It was not impossible: Shakespeare was on friendly terms with the Davenants; William, born 3 March 1606, would have been conceived in the high summer of 1605. Shakespeare went back to the country once a year in summer, according to Aubrey.)

'The King's men were at the beck-and-call of the Sovereign for performances at Court', as well as at Blackfriars, and the Court musicians supplied music for the plays, notably William Lawes, but occasionally too Nicholas Lanier and the excellent song-writer, Robert Johnson. When the Scots initiated war with the solemn League and Covenant – against bishops and a sensibly revised Prayer Book, an improved version of the Anglican, designed to bring both communions ecumenically together – Davenant joined up with his friends, who all thought that going to the Borders they were out for a joy-ride. They were 'the Wits'. After the surprise they got, the crumbling of the Royal cause confronted by the embattled Long Parliament and the imprisonment of the King's chief minister, Strafford, in the Tower, Davenant entered, with his friends Jermyn and Suckling, into the Army Plot to liberate Strafford. That too failed – through the Queen's friend, the beautiful bitch Lady Carlisle, Pym learned every move of the Court beforehand.

Davenant was bailed, next year was in Holland with the Queen, who was raising munitions for war, and Davenant came back to serve in the army; knighted at the siege of Gloucester in 1643. Setting out as Royal Governor of Maryland, he was captured in the Channel and had the narrowest escape from execution as a proclaimed traitor – to Parliament a dangerous 'malignant'. In prison he began his long heroic poem *Gondibert*, the finest in that *genre* before Dryden: for which Thomas

---

[1] Bentley, *op. cit.*, I. 61.

Hobbes, of all people – the least poetic of men – wrote a long reasoned argument in approbation.

Davenant made two marriages, one to the widow of the Queen's Catholic physician, who died shortly after, and in France he married a French aristocratic lady. (He must have been irresistible, or how could they have taken the risk?) Back in England he at once took up his artistic schemes with his usual enterprise. Since drama and public performances of music were prohibited, private 'entertainments' took place in grandees' houses, like Rutland House or Holland House in Kensington (which survived to our own time, to be destroyed by the barbarians in the Second German War). Sometimes poor players were smuggled in.

Davenant thought up something more ambitious, which he advertised as a 'First Day's Entertainment', a sedate sequence of speeches and dialogues, with songs and instrumental pieces by the unemployed musicians, Henry Lawes among them. Having got away with that, Davenant went on to something bigger, *The Siege of Rhodes* in 1656: something between a masque and an opera – always considered a forerunner of the latter; music by the previous composers, plus young Matthew Locke, himself an important link musically between the Carolines and Purcell. The scenery was designed by Inigo Jones's pupil, John Webb. Things were on their way back.

The authorities were alerted, and a committee of the Council was appointed 'to consider by what authority the opera in Drury Lane is shown, in imitation of a play; and what the nature of it is'.[1] Davenant was forced to draw in his horns, and next resorted to tableau representation without action, but with music, probably by Locke. He adroitly chose subjects to appeal to the authorities, for Cromwell was now engaged in his imperialist war with Spain, hoping to conquer the West Indies. So Davenant, with pardonable effrontery, presented scenes of 'The Cruelty of the Spaniards in Peru', and 'The History of Sir Francis Drake'. We must remember that the Puritans were the leaders in colonial enterprise; Pym, Lord Saye and Sele, Lord Brooke, John White of Dorchester all were active members of

[1] P.M. Young, *A History of British Music*, 235-6.

the companies pushing colonisation, Pym's step-father, Sir Anthony Rouse, a friend of Drake's. The humbugs were the imperialists.[1]

Davenant got away with it, and at the Restoration was in clover once more. Two new companies were established by Royal order to take the place of the old ones. In place of the King's Men Tom Killigrew – of that ardent Royalist family, and a crony of Charles II – had the Theatre Royal in Drury Lane; Davenant's, the Duke's Company, had the Queen's Men's Salisbury Court. Davenant's was the better managed and more successful; notable too for its series of Shakespeare adaptations – *Hamlet*, *Macbeth*, *The Tempest*, etc – which Will Davenant made a special feature.

Another of these gentleman amateurs who made good poets was Sir John Denham, of whom Aubrey gives us a charming biography, for he knew him well. They were both Trinity men at Oxford, where Denham's tutor said that 'he was the dreamingest young fellow: he never expected such things from him as he has left the world'. In 1640 he wrote a play for Blackfriars, *The Sophy*, which 'did take extremely'. Mr Edmund Waller said then of him that 'he broke out like the Irish Rebellion, three-score thousand strong, before anybody was aware'.[2]

Denham's poem 'Cooper's Hill' had lasting importance, for its description of landscape looked forward to the later eighteenth century and Wordsworth. Aubrey thought it 'incomparably well described by that sweet swan', printed at Oxford shortly after Edgehill, 'in a sort of brown paper, for then they could get no better'. The King much enjoyed his company 'for his ingenuity'. When the Parliamentarian poet, Wither, turned up a prisoner there, Denham begged the King to pardon him, for while Wither lived, he (Denham) 'should not be the worst poet in England'.

Denham, like the most cultivated gentlemen of the time, had a good knowledge of architecture, and at the Restoration was made Surveyor-General of Works, to which office Charles I had

[1] cf. A.P. Newton, *The Colonising Activities of the English Puritans*.
[2] Aubrey, *Brief Lives*, ed. cit. I. 216 foll.

promised him the reversion. In 'Cooper's Hill' Denham had paid tribute to the King's generosity in paying for Inigo Jones's magnificent portico at St Paul's. In 1660 John Webb, as a professional architect, protested that 'though Denham may have, as most gentry, some knowledge of the theory of architecture, he can have none of the practice'. However, Denham took his duties seriously and supervised new brick buildings in Scotland Yard – by which he recouped himself financially from his losses by gambling and the war – and latterly had the sense to take on Wren as his deputy.

Altogether he had a fascinating and *mouvementé* life, as a confidential agent of both Charles and Henrietta Maria, entrusted with their correspondence at home and abroad.[1] Aubrey – as usual, and as so few do – tells us what he looked like: 'he was of the tallest, but a little incurvetting at the shoulders ... his gait was slow and was rather a stalking (he had long legs). His eye was a kind of light goose-grey; not big, but it had a strange piercingness ... when he conversed with you, he looked into your very thoughts.' Evidently the light of intelligence shone there. He too took to satirical squibs against the Presbyterian humbugs, to amuse the Royalists at Oxford; I am sorry not to have read the 'indecent doggerel poem' he wrote about a Colchester Quaker on the eve of the Restoration.

The Queen's Men were second of the Companies in importance, with a good writer, Richard Brome, as their regular dramatist. He had been a servant of Ben Jonson, and learned from him; like him, he wrote realistic comedy as well as romantic. Brome had good success with his *Lovesick Maid*, just after Jonson's failure with *The New Inn* at Blackfriars: thought to be one of Brome's best, it was a casualty of the times, now lost. His *Northern Lass* was very popular too, as also *The Sparagus Garden*, spectacularly so, a comedy of intrigue spiced with farcical satire.

The Queen's Men played at the Phoenix until the prolonged plague of 1636-7 closed down the theatres, and after that came a reorganisation. They came to Salisbury Court, and the

---

[1]Another good subject for a biography wanted, as against nonsense about Ranters, Diggers etc.

experienced Beeston formed a new Company, Beeston's Boys. After the break came *The Antipodes*, which Bentley describes as one of Brome's cleverest and most entertaining comedies. One would like the chance of seeing some of them. He did not live to see the Restoration: older than Shirley and Davenant he died about 1652/3.

Courtiers themselves took a hand in the sport of writing plays: all three Killigrews, for example, though their plays belong to the period of exile and the Restoration. Thomas Carew, a better poet, wrote a play that is lost, and his friend Suckling's tragedy, *The Sad One*, remained unfinished. Three plays of his were performed at Blackfriars: *Aglaura*, tricked out with extravagant splendour, especially in costumes, which cost a fortune in themselves, music by Henry Lawes. The spectacular extravagance – for Suckling was rich – was much commented upon, with some envy; inevitably it was performed again at Court. Brome, the professional, reflected upon the amateur Suckling:

> Opinion, which our Author cannot court –
>> For the dear daintiness of it – has of late
> From the old ways of plays possessed a Sort
>> Only to run to those that carry state
> In Scene magnificent and language high –
>> And Clothes worth all the rest, except the Action:
> And such are only good those Leaders cry,
>> And into that belief draw on a Faction
>> That must despise all sportive, merry wit,
>> Because some such great Play had none in it.[1]

The Faction would be Suckling's grand friends who boosted his work. He was not in the least out-faced; his next play, a comedy, *The Goblins*, in the Prologue lets us know precisely what the Caroline writers thought was new about their work in a more sophisticated age:

> Wit in a prologue poets justly may
> Style a new imposition on a play.

[1] q. G.E. Bentley, *op. cit.*, I. 59.

When Shakespeare, Beaumont, Fletcher ruled the stage,
There scarce were ten good palates in the age;
More curious cooks than guests; for men would eat
Most heartily of any kind of meat.[1]

Caroline audiences wouldn't. Significantly enough, both Suckling and Brome, otherwise differing – Brome of the older generation, Suckling of the younger – both admired Shakespeare, were indebted to his work and made use of it in their own.

Suckling's last completed work was a tragedy, *Brennoralt,* or *The Discontented Colonel.* Suckling served in the King's army on the Scottish Borders in 1639, and the play reflects the Rebellion of the Scots, under the guise of Lithuanians, against their King:

The Lithuanians, sir,
Are of the wilder sort of creatures, must
Be rid with cavilous and harsh curbs ...
    Religion
And liberty – most specious name – they urge,
Which, like the bills of subtle mountebanks,
Filled with great promises of curing all –
Though by the wise passed by as common cosenage,
Yet by the knowing multitude they're still
Admired and flocked unto.
*King:*      Is there no way
To disabuse them?
*Melidor*:    All is now too late;
The vulgar in religion are like
Unknown lands: those that first possess them have them.
When things are risen to the point they are,
'Tis either not examined or believed
Among the warlike.[2]

This then was how the Court viewed the mutinous spirit abroad, the mutterings preliminary to revolution:

---

[1] *The Works of Sir John Suckling*, ed. A. Hamilton Thompson, 163.
[2] Ibid, 241-2. The word cavilous is misprinted 'cavilons'.

This late commotion in your kingdom, sir,
Is like a growing wen upon the face,
Which as we cannot look on but with trouble,
So take't away we cannot but with danger.

After the failure of the Army Plot, charged with treason by
Parliament, Suckling escaped abroad, where, penniless and
without hope, he took poison and died. He was about
thirty-two; so, with his brilliant gifts, he accomplished all that
he did in his twenties.

For the past century the universities had been an important, if
secondary, scene of stage plays and dramatic efforts, though the
plays were naturally academic and the actors amateurs. With
Laud as Chancellor and the university devotedly loyal, Oxford
was to the fore, particularly Christ Church with its great hall
much used for such productions. Here the leading figure was
young William Cartwright, a Westminster Student of the
House,[1] much admired as preacher and poet. He was a good
Laudian, who hated Puritans. In the high summer of 1636 Laud
laid on a grand entertainment of the King and Queen for the
opening of his Canterbury quadrangle at St John's (to which
Charles had contributed timber from the Royal forests –
another bone of contention). Plays always formed a regular
feature of Royal visits and Cartwright was called upon to
provide one. (This too was made a charge against Laud, by
Prynne, later – the Archbishop too civilised a man to have any
objection to plays as such).

Cartwright answered the call with *The Royal Slave*, the songs
set by Henry Lawes, splendidly mounted and costumed by Inigo
Jones: 'very well penned and acted, and the strangeness of the
Persian habits gave great content'.[2] 'All things went happy',
recorded the anxious Chancellor, who worried over everything.
In fact the play pleased the Queen so much that she asked Laud
if the Persian costumes might be lent to her own Queen's Men

---

[1]Christ Church, *Aedes Christi*, is referred to by Oxford men as the House;
Westminster School has always enjoyed closed scholarships there, and at Trinity,
Cambridge.
[2]*The Life and Poems of William Cartwright*, ed. R.C. Goffin, xxi.

for a performance by them at Hampton Court. The Chancellor agreed, provided that the play, exotic clothes and stage effects were for private performance there only. Apparently it was considered that the Oxford production was the better one. Cartwright wrote three more plays, *The Lady Errant*, based on an idea from Fletcher's *The Sea Voyage*, thought to be the best. Then he died, quite young, of a fever contracted in crowded war-time Oxford in 1643. He was thirty-two. In the glad days of 1636 another play had been presented to the King and Queen, *The Floating Island* by William Strode, another Westminster scholar at Christ Church and canon of the cathedral, where he was 'a most florid preacher'.[1] As an undergraduate he had played a female part in Burton's *Philosophaster*, and this kind of ambivalence had long given offence to Puritans and provided them with ammunition. (What *did* it lead to? Christopher Marlowe had been such a bad example.) As Public Orator Strode had received the King and his consort with an oration at Christ Church gate – after the happy Restoration, to be finished with Wren's Tom Tower. As for Strode's play, Lord Caernarvon said that it was fitter for scholars than a Court, 'the worst that ever he saw but one that he saw at Cambridge'.

Meanwhile the too successful King's Men at Blackfriars were winning unpopularity from the citizenry. The coaches of the aristocracy crowding to it blocked the precinct and the street leading to it. In 1619 the City Council had gone beyond themselves and ordered the King's Men to cease to play.[2] King James had replied shortly with a new licence to his 'well-beloved servants'. In 1633 complaints came up again from the inhabitants of Blackfriars: there was a genuine and increasing parking problem. The Court responded sensibly by forbidding parking in the precinct of Blackfriars, and ordering that coaches should be parked in St Paul's churchyard, Fleet Street and neighbouring lanes.

In 1641 the agitation reached Parliament, and this was

---

[1] cf. *The Poetical Works of William Strode, 1600-1645*, ed. by Bertram Dobell. He is not to be confused with William Strode, M.P., a leading Parliamentary opponent of the King, though both Strodes came from the Devonshire stock, were about the same age and died the same year.

[2] G.E. Bentley, *op. cit.*, 4-5, 31-2, 64 foll.

serious. A city alderman preferred a petition from the inhabitants not only of Blackfriars but of the parishes of St Martin's, Ludgate and St Bride's. Moreover, he and others spoke up to the sympathetic assembly extending the attack to playhouses in general: they were a hindrance to trade. From Sir Simonds D'Ewes' laconic notes one can gather only the drift of the discussion, with its Puritan overtones: 'God's house not so near Devil's: this is particular grievance, and the other a general .... Others spake against this playhouse and others.'

The players knew what to expect from a Parliament dominated by Pym, who had already disposed of the King's chief minister, with the grim words: 'Stone-dead hath no fellow.' The stage players' Complaint assured themselves that ' 'tis to be feared, for monopolies are down, projectors are down, the High Commission Court is down, the Star Chamber is down and some think Bishops will down – and why should we then, that are far inferior to any of those, not justly fear lest we should be down too?'

As revolutionary feeling grew with the concessions forced from the King, the appetite for more growing all the time – a characteristic of revolution, every concession taken advantage of to press for more – in Parliament in February 1642 'there was a great complaint made against the Playhouses, and a motion made for the suppressing of them'. In September that year they were suppressed, in the humbugging language employed by such people for such purposes.

Whereas the distressed state of Ireland, steeped in her own blood, and the distracted estate of England, threatened with a Cloud of Blood, a Civil War, call for all possible means to appease and avert the Wrath of God appearing in these Judgments – amongst which Fasting and Prayer have been often tried to be very effectual [!] and whereas public Sports do not well agree with public calamities, nor public Stage-Plays with the Seasons of Humiliation, this being an Exercise of sad and pious solemnity, and the other being Spectacles of pleasure, too commonly expressing lascivious Mirth and Levity: It is therefore thought fit and ordained by the Lords [a small minority of them] and Commons [a small majority] in this Parliament assembled that, while these sad Causes and set times of Humiliation do continue, public Stage-Plays shall cease and be forborne.

There is the delightful Puritan spirit in the full bloom of its purity. And to add insult to injury, 'all the apparel, hangings, books and other goods seized were sold and converted', by those who seized them, 'to their own uses'.

# VI

# Poets and Persons

The Caroline age was, like the Elizabethan, an age of music and poetry; but, we have seen, with a difference in the artistic achievement in all the arts. Having looked at the work, we should look a little into the men who accomplished it. What were they really like? What their fates?

Today, the present generation, for reasons more sociological than intellectual, is fixed on expounding for us the 'thought' of the Puritan Revolution. We have scores of books and articles on the fantasies of Ranters, Fifth Monarchy men, Millenarians, Seekers, Quakers, Anabaptists, Levellers, Diggers, Muggle-tonians – all the scum thrown up by revolution. For of what value is the 'thought' of people who can hardly think? – as most people cannot, in the precise meaning of the word. Far more valuable, in their realm, are the works of men's hands and, in the intellectual field, the thought of distinguished minds.

Then, too, in endlessly chewing the chaff of those people's nonsense, they fail to tell us what these and those were really like. It is people who are real, not the nonsense they think: people are the real, tangible facts of history, of flesh and blood, and understanding them goes a long way to understanding their work. The work of artists, whether poets or dramatists, painters or architects, is not 'a ballet of bloodless categories' (the contrasting personalities of Inigo Jones and Wren are *visible* in their work, to persons of perception). We should not waste time on the propositions of nonsense, which has the characteristics of being both interminable and self-proliferating. Poetry is a different matter. In the confusion and impermanences of time, only art lasts.

The Caroline generation was, unlike the Elizabethan, an unfortunate one. They were mostly young, and many of them died young, even apart from those who died in the wars, killed in the field or on the scaffold. Charles I, born with the century, was in his twenties and thirties in the years we have been portraying, from his accession in 1625 to the outbreak of the Revolution. Henrietta Maria, born in 1609, was a girl of fifteen when she came to England to become Queen. The Parliamentary leader, 'King Pym', was an experienced man of an older generation: born in 1584, he was more of an Elizabethan.

It is not always possible to give the precise ages of those who were lost, and here we have not to do with politicians. Moreover, those who fought on the King's side were more often persons of quality, their lives – if they were men of genius – more valuable. Others recur, and are forgotten. Lord Falkland was not really a politician; he accepted the King's call to become his Secretary of State with the greatest reluctance, out of a sense of duty. He hated the war, and – despairing of peace – deliberately threw his life away at the battle of Newbury, 'ingeminating "Peace! Peace!" ' He was thirty-three. He was of a philosophic turn of mind, already writing prose and verse, and a generous encourager of other men's work. No knowing what he might have accomplished, if he had lived. Of others who walked and talked in his gardens at Great Tew, gallant little Sidney Godolphin, admirable poet and man, whom all reverenced for his character, was thirty-two when he was killed at Chagford in 1643. William Chillingworth was Laud's godson and one of those whom the Archbishop brought back from Rome – to write his classic *The Religion of Protestants a safe Way of Salvation.* Captured at Arundel Castle, ill from the siege and harassed by the fanatic Cheynell, he died shortly after at forty-one or two.

Brought out fatally wounded from the appalling wreckage of Basing House was young Thomas Johnson, the brilliant botanist, who had greatly enlarged and corrected Gerard's famous *Herbal* and published the first local catalogue of plants issued in England, besides other works. An Oxford man and Royalist, the genus *Johnsonia* was named in his memory. He would have made a prominent figure in the Royal Society at the Restoration. Nor was he the only loss to science. William Gascoigne was the inventor of the micrometer: killed at Marston Moor, on the Royalist side, aged thirty-two. The astronomer Flamsteed's brother told Aubrey that Gascoigne 'found out the way of improving telescopes before Descartes'.[1] What more might have been expected of him!

Nor were such remarkable men the only loss. The greatest of English physiologists, Sir William Harvey, suffered an irreparable loss 'when his lodgings were plundered in the time of the rebellion'.[2] For many years he had been making researches in anatomical observations on insects, and had written his book, *De insectis*. 'He had made dissections of frogs, toads, and a number of other animals: which papers together with his goods were plundered, he being for the King and with him at Oxon. He could never for love nor money retrieve them or hear what became of them.' He told Aubrey ''twas the greatest crucifying to him that ever he had in all his life'. While at Oxford the King had the good taste to make the great scientist Warden of Merton – though this did not last long. Harvey had already had the experience of having his discovery of the circulation of the blood rejected by inferior minds. He told Aubrey that after his book came out 'he fell mightily in his practise ... all the physicians were against his opinion, and envied him. With much ado at last, in about 20 or thirty years time, it was received in all the universities in the world.' (As, in time, the commonsense solution to the 'problems' of Shakespeare's biography will come to be.)

We are concerned here with the artists, and have seen that the chief composer of the time was about thirty-two when he was killed, his friend Suckling was the same age when he took his own life in exile. Cartwright was thirty-two; the poet Thomas Randolph, a Westminster and Trinity man, only twenty-nine or thirty. Thomas Carew, John Cleveland and Strode were in their early forties; so too Aurelian Townsend, a favourite writer of masques. The poet Francis Quarles was not much over fifty; like Harvey, he had had his manuscripts destroyed by Parliamentary soldiers. His son was banished for life for fighting for the King.

We see that it was a youthful world upon which the shadows fell, and that most of those artists whose lives were darkened or extinguished were Royalists.

---

[1]Aubrey, *op. cit.*, I. 261.    [2]Ibid, I. 297, 303.

Sir John Suckling has always been taken as a characteristic Cavalier, carefree, light-hearted and light-headed, rather a scapegrace. In some respects, not all, the stereotype fits. His father was a Secretary of State, his mother a sister of the enormously rich Lionel Cranfield;[1] his dull parent made a fortune, the brilliant son wasted it. Aubrey learned from Davenant that Suckling was 'the greatest gallant of his time and the greatest gamester, both at bowling and cards'.[2] He played for high stakes and was no less extravagant. For the Scottish expedition he raised at his own expense 'a troop of 100 very handsome young proper [i.e. tall] men, whom he clad in white doublets and scarlet breeches, and scarlet coats, hats and feathers, well horsed and armed'. One way and another he ruined himself: it is difficult to understand how anyone so intelligent could be so foolish.

His loyalty appears in a New Year's salute to the King in 1640 after the fiasco on the Borders:

> May no ill vapour cloud the sky,
> Bold storms invade the sovereignty . . .
> May all the discords in your state –
> Like those in music we create –
> Be governed at so wise a rate
> That what would of itself sound harsh, or fright,
> May be so tempered that it may delight.

Suckling's celebrated *Session of the Poets*, much imitated by others, called them all around him. They mostly called themselves the 'sons of Ben' (Jonson), to whom many tributes were written: Suckling is witty about Ben's high opinion of himself:

---

[1]For him v. R.H. Tawney, *Business and Politics under James I*. Tawney, with his Leftist bias, embarked on this study with the aim of exposing Cranfield as Lord Treasurer, and catching him out, but had the honesty to admit that he was mistaken and Cranfield a better man and minister of the Crown than he had expected.

[2]Aubrey, II. 240 foll.

Prepared before with canary wine,
He told them plainly he deserved the bays,
For his were called *Works*, where others were but plays;

Bid them remember how he had purged the stage
Of errors that had lasted many an age,
And he hoped they did not think *The Silent Woman*,
*The Fox*, and *The Alchemist* outdone by no man.

Tom Carew[1] was next, but he had a fault
That would not well stand with a laureat:
His muse was hide-bound, and th'issue of's brain
Was seldom brought forth but with trouble and pain.

Will Davenant, ashamed of a foolish mischance
That he had got lately travelling in France
Modestly hoped the handsomeness of's muse
Might any deformity about him excuse.

Suckling wrote a similarly graceless poem 'Upon T.C. having the Pox':

Truth, Tom, I must confess I much admire
Thy water should find passage through the fire ...
Sure then his way he forces, for all know
The French ne'er grants a passage to his foe. etc.

We have a fashionable dialogue poem between these two wits, 'Upon my Lady Carlisle's Walking in Hampton Court Garden', when after some high-flown lines about the flowers, the beauty of the scene, and of the lady, Suckling gets down to it:

Alas! Tom, I am flesh and blood,
And was consulting how I could
In spite of masks and hoods descry
The parts denied unto the eye:
I was undoing all she wore –

[1]The correct pronunciation is Cary.

And, had she walked but one turn more,
Eve in her first state had not been
More naked, or more plainly seen.

This is in some contrast with Milton's description of that apparition.

Suckling is best recognised today for such a poem as

Out upon it! I have loved
  Three whole days together,
And am like to love three more,
  If it prove fair weather.

Time shall moult away his wings
  Ere he shall discover
In the whole wide world again
  Such a constant lover.

It is fairly clear from his poems that Suckling had no intention of being roped and tied in matrimony. Lord Broghill can hardly have been complimented by the poem on his wedding:

Broghill, our gallant friend,
  Is gone to church as martyrs to the fire:
Who marry different but i' th'end,
  Since both do take
The hardest way to what they most desire.

We have heard more than enough of the Cavalier poets as poets of love, and indeed we have more than enough of their poetry on that subject, whether platonic and ideal, passionate and consummatory, witty and erotic, or simply pornographic – and very un-Puritan. It is true that there was a cult of women among the Cavaliers, whether placed on a pedestal or lower down. And this was very different from the Puritan attitude, which placed women far below the angels the Cavaliers made them into. In fact the Puritans approximated to the old German ideal of the province of women being *die Kinder, die Küche, und die*

*Kirche.* Milton was hardly exceptional in holding to the inferiority of women:[1]

> Whence true authority to men: though both
> Not equal, as their sex not equal seemed ...
> He for God only, she for God in him.

At least the Cavaliers did not think that – too civilised.

The serious side to their poetry has been overlooked, though not in such wholly religious poets as George Herbert or Richard Crashaw. There is a serious side to Suckling even when he is joking:

> Hales, set by himself, most gravely did smile
> To see them about nothing keep such a coil;
> Apollo had spied him, but knowing his mind
> Passed by, and called Falkland that sat just behind.
>
> He was of late so gone with divinity
> That he had almost forgot his poetry;
> Though to say the truth – and Apollo did know it –
> He might have been both his priest and his poet.

Surprisingly, Suckling himself wrote a *Discourse on Religion*, and a most powerfully argued tract it is, showing both intellectual power of a high order and a rational approach to the subject, even anthropological in a way.[2] He begins with the position: 'That there is then a God will not be so much the dispute as what this God is, or how to be worshipped is that which hath troubled poor mortals from the first; nor are they yet in quiet. So great has been the diversity.' He discusses earlier, ancient religions, and then, 'Let us inquire whether those things they have in common with us we have not in a more excellent manner; and whether the rest, in which we differ from all the world, we take not up with reason.'

'That we have the same virtues with them is very true; but

---

[1] cf. my *Milton the Puritan: Portrait of a Mind*, 230 foll.
[2] *Works, ed. cit.*, 343 foll.

who can deny that those virtues have received additions from Christianity, conducting to men's better living together.' For example, 'we extol patient bearing of injuries', and he gives other instances of the superiority of Christian ethics. He has no difficulty in pointing to the barbarous savagery of the Old Testament, though he is too polite to say so; he merely says, 'Revenge of injuries Moses both took himself and allowed by the law to others.' He could have said that the Old Testament Jehovah enjoined upon the Jews, several times over, the extermination of their enemies, and awarded them punishment for neglecting their duty to do so. We must remember how the Puritans inspired themselves with their mania for the Old Testament; again Suckling does not say so, he says nothing against them.

However, he makes a relevant point most strongly when he says, 'the strangest, though most epidemical, disease of all religions has been an imagination men have had that the imposing painful and difficult things upon themselves was the best way to appease the Deity, grossly thinking the chief service and delight of the Creator to consist in the tortures and sufferings of the creature'. This knocks the ground away from the Puritan position, with its constant Fastings and Humiliations, such tortures as the ghastly Cheynell inflicted upon the dying Chillingworth (who appears in Suckling's poem). A coarser spirit than Suckling's, when all is said, Samuel Butler tilted against those

> That with more care keep Holy-day
> The wrong, than others the right, way:
> Compound for Sins they are inclined to
> By damning those they have no mind to;
> Still so perverse and opposite
> As if they worshipped God for spite.

Lastly, Suckling goes on to the position, 'That God has lived with men has been the general fancy of all nations, every particular having this tradition that the Deity at some time or other conversed amongst men. Nor is it contrary to reason to believe Him residing in glory above, and yet incarnate here.'

[158]

Thence Suckling accepts the Christian position: Incarnation, Resurrection, the Trinity (which Newton did not), and an altogether more kindly Anglican doctrine of rewards and punishments. This rational account of religion was condemned as Socinianism; ignorant and ill-educated Puritans called it atheism. Actually, it was the intellectual position, undogmatic and rational, of the cultivated Falkland circle.

It is a succinct and concise statement of Suckling's belief, written in prose of fine economy and elegance – Aubrey tells us where. Suckling, Davenant and another went on a jaunt to Bath. 'Sir John came like a young prince for all manner of equipage and convenience, and Sir W. Davenant told me that he had a cart-load of books carried down, and 'twas there at Bath that he writ the little tract in his book about Socinianism.' On the way they were well entertained for several days at Sir Edward Baynton's, Bromham House, 'then a noble seat, since burnt in the Civil Wars'.

A more touching statement of Christian belief in one of the Falkland circle appears in several of Sidney Godolphin's poems:

> Wise men in tracing nature's laws
> Ascend unto the highest cause:
> Shepherds with humble fearfulness
> Walk safely though their light be less:
> Though wise men better know the way,
> It seems no honest heart can stray.
>
> There is no merit in the wise
> But love – the shepherd's sacrifice.
> Wise men, all ways of knowledge past,
> To the shepherd's wonder come at last;
> To know can only wonder breed,
> And not to know is wonder's seed.

We glimpse in this something of the philosophical interests of that circle.

Something of their practice is to be seen in good John Hales of Eton, a man whom everybody loved. He was 'the common godfather there, and 'twas pretty to see, as he walked to Windsor, how his godchildren asked his blessing. When he was bursar he still [ever] gave away all his groats for the acquittances to his godchildren, and by the time he came to Windsor bridge he would never have a groat left.'[1] Hales was of a philosophic cast of mind too; he had been with Hall at the Synod of Dort and shocked by the venom of the Calvinists. Hales's Broad-Churchmanship did not commend itself to the more orthodox Laud, who once called him to account. Hales gave such a good account of himself that the Archbishop ceased to question him – Laud being more broad-minded than he has been given credit for. Hales would not publish, but after the Restoration the *Golden Remains of the ever-memorable Mr John Hales* were put together and became something of a best-seller.[2]

His pride was in his noble library, which, after his ejection from his Fellowship, he was forced to sell – for some £700, when it had cost him not less than £2500. A widow woman, whom Hales had helped bountifully in the good days, told Aubrey that 'she was much against the sale of 'em because she knew it was his life and joy. He might have been restored to his Fellowship again, but he would not accept the offer.' Like Bishop Wren, good Anglicans would not accept the conditions of either Commonwealth or Protectorate, either the Presbyterian Covenant or the Engagement. They waited for the country to return to its senses – as Clarendon had the admirable confidence that it would. Hales did not live to see it.

A far greater influence, a writer with a touch of genius, was Jeremy Taylor, a Cambridge man whom Laud, as Visitor, imposed upon an unwilling All Souls. (Who was right about that?) Like Laud himself, Taylor was a lower-class man, and none the worse for it. It used to amuse the King to see the grandees of the Privy Council take a superior line about the Archbishop's ungracious manner; however, he had precedence before them, and the envy of aristocrats was one of the motives for dislike of him. Another was the fact that he had the King's

[1]Aubrey, *op. cit.* I. 278 foll.
[2]A second impression, of 1673, gives Hales's letters from the nasty Synod, with his statement of the Anglican position regarding Grace for poor sinners extending beyond the Predestined Elect, i.e. the Calvinists themselves.

complete confidence; they were at one with regard to policy, and towards the end Laud was operating as a virtual prime minister. Especially after he got another ecclesiastic made Lord Treasurer, Bishop Juxon, unself-seeking, absolutely upright and incorruptible. Those who wanted the job were of course furious – like Lord Saye and Sele, who – on becoming commissioner of the treasury, in the first moves towards revolution – got an enormous hand-out. With his financial interest in New England he proposed the establishment of an hereditary aristocracy there – turned down by Massachusetts; Lord Saye and Sele thereupon relinquished his intention of settling there. As Clarendon said of Cromwell's similar intention of going to America if the Grand Remonstrance had not been passed – 'so near was this poor country to its deliverance'.

Jeremy Taylor was made chaplain to Laud and to Charles I, and was of course thrown out of his Fellowship, along with most of the Fellows of Oxford and Cambridge colleges during the Interregnum. Taken prisoner at the capture of Cardigan Castle, he was allowed to retreat to Golden Grove, where he wrote his most famous books, *The Liberty of Prophesying, Holy Living* and *Holy Dying*. Charles I, shortly before his execution, sent him his watch and some trinkets for keepsakes. Taylor was imprisoned once again, before the Restoration, where he dedicated his *Doctor Dubitantium* to Charles II – it did not resolve *his* doubts: he had had enough of people's certainties about religion. Taylor was made bishop of Dromore in Ireland, where he built the Protestant cathedral.

Clarendon himself adhered to the tolerant Broad-church-manship of the Falkland circle; at the Restoration he was in favour of an accommodation with the stiff-necked Presbyterians (as was the sceptical Charles II, who thought what fools people were to fight over religion). Clarendon was not himself responsible for the repressive 'Clarendon Code', which bore hardly on the Dissenters: this was imposed upon him by the Cavalier Parliament, in its reaction against the rule of the Saints – very understandable after all they had had to put up with.

One can read the Anglican position, as one can virtually write the history of the time, in its poetry. Even the merry-hearted Herrick had his serious side: read 'His Litany, to the Holy Spirit':

In the hour of my distress,
When temptations me oppress,
And when I my sins confess,
      Sweet Spirit comfort me!

When I lie within my bed,
Sick in heart, and sick in head,
And with doubts discomforted,
      Sweet Spirit comfort me!

I do not think that the Puritans thought of the operations of the Holy Spirit as a 'sweet' comforter, and it would have been better for everybody, themselves included, if they had been discomforted by some doubts.

However, we really turn to Herrick for his advice 'To live merrily, and to trust to Good Verses'; for his celebration of the charming side of Caroline country life:

There's not a budding boy or girl this day
But is got up and gone to bring in May.
      A deal of Youth ere this is come
      Back, and with white-thorn laden home.
      Some have dispatched their cakes and cream
      Before that we have left to dream;
And some have wept and wooed, and plighted troth,
And chose their Priest ere we can cast off sloth.

May-day celebrations and maypoles, Saints' days and Feasts, were suppressed by the Saints of God – all to come back at the Restoration, as was Herrick. Ejected by Parliament from his living at Dean Prior, he was restored to it, to end his days there. I always think of him as I pass his little church by the roadside, and sometimes call in to remember him there at his memorial by the altar he served.

And why should he not believe in the fairies? –

If ye will with Mab find grace,
Set each platter in his place:
Rake the fire up, and get

> Water in, ere sun be set.
> Wash your pails, and cleanse your dairies –
> Sluts are loathsome to the Fairies:
> Sweep your house – Who doth not so,
> Mab will pinch her by the toe.

In that simple invocation, or imprecation, there is a good deal of Shakespeare: not only the Mab of *Romeo and Juliet* but the fairies of *The Merry Wives of Windsor*.

Surely belief in the fairies was better, and less harmful than, belief in witches – to which Puritans were addicted. Under their rule the persecution of witches proliferated all over the country, though at its worst in Puritan Essex. Some two hundred poor old beldames were strung up. There was little persecution of witches under the civilised rule of Charles I and Laud.

All the Carolines were devotees of Shakespeare, even Milton, who stands at the utterly opposite pole to him in outlook. Milton, the idealogue *par excellence*, thought a great deal of pure nonsense; one of the extraordinary things about William Shakespeare is that he seems to have thought no nonsense of any kind whatever.[1] However, the Carolines preferred Ben Jonson, whom they knew, and Beaumont and Fletcher. Here is Cartwright on the last:

> Shakespeare to thee was dull, whose best jest lies
> I' th' ladies' questions and the Fool's replies –
> Old-fashioned wit, which walked from town to town
> In turned hose, which our fathers called the Clown:
> Whose wit our nice times would obsceneness call,
> And which made bawdry pass for comical.
> Nature was all his art, *thy* vein was free
> As his, but without his scurrility.

Here was Caroline taste, and something of the difference between Elizabethan and Caroline.

Many of Francis Quarles's famous *Emblems* were inspired

---

[1] cf. my *Shakespeare's Globe: his Moral and Intellectual Outlook* (US title, *What Shakespeare Read and Thought*).

from the Bible, especially those parts favoured in Anglican worship, the Psalms and Canticles. One sees the High Anglican inflexion in such verses as –

> He is my Altar; I, his Holy Place;
> I am his guest, and he my living food;
> I'm his by penitence, he mine by grace;
> I'm his by purchase, he is mine by blood;
> He's my supporting elm, and I his vine:
> Thus I my best-beloved's am, thus he is mine.

Quarles had been a servant of the Royal family, cup-bearer to the Princess Elizabeth, whom he accompanied to Germany after her marriage to the Elector Palatine. When Quarles later wrote in defence of the King, his manuscripts were destroyed by Parliamentary soldiers.

Even Davenant was orthodox enough in religion, as in 'The Christian's Reply to the Philosopher':

> Frail Life! in which through mists of human breath
> We grope for truth, and make our progress slow,
> Because by passion blinded; till by death
> Our passions ending, we begin to know ...
>
> O harmless Death! whom still the valiant brave,
> The wise expect, the sorrowful invite,
> And all the good embrace, we know the grave
> A short dark passage to eternal light.

Davenant's gay friend, Tom Carew, recognising himself as a sinner, at least had Anglican humility:

> I press not to the choir, nor dare I greet
> The holy place with my unhallowed feet:
> My unwashed muse pollutes not things divine,
> Nor mingles her profaner notes with thine –

He was paying respect to Sandys' *Paraphrase of the Psalms* –

[164]

Here, humbly at the porch, she listening stays
And with glad ears sucks in thy sacred lays.

Along with Ben Jonson, Donne stood at the head of those the
Carolines admired; and Carew wrote an Elegy on him which is
also a penetrating example of good criticism, though the
religious aspect is naturally to the fore:

But the flame
Of thy brave soul, that shot such heat and light
As burnt our earth and made our darkness bright,
Committed holy rapes upon our will,
Did through the eye the melting heart distil;
And the deep knowledge of dark truths so teach
As sense might judge what fancy could not reach,
Must be desired for ever.

Many of these poets had tasted of the Royal bounty, some of
them supported by it. With his care for all the arts Charles I
raised the fee of the Poet Laureate from 100 marks to £100 a
year, with a tierce of wine: 'a revenue in those days', says Dr
Johnson, 'not inadequate to the convenience of life.' Inevitably
there are poetic addresses to the King, or to the Queen, like
Davenant's 'To the Queen, entertained at night by the Countess
of Anglesey':

Fair as unshaded light; or as the day
In its first birth, when all the year was May, etc.

Several of his poems are addressed to his patron, the courtier
Endymion Porter, who was favoured for his culture and taste by
the King. Porter was much in love with his wife, the lady Olivia;
Davenant celebrated this in one of the fashionable Dialogue-
songs:

From this vexed world when we shall both retire,
Where all are Lovers, and where all rejoice,
I need not seek thee in the heavenly choir,
For I shall know Olivia by her voice.

Charles I's execution naturally called forth verse, like Henry King's long Elegy 'upon the most Incomparable', though rather less than one might expect, people were so stunned by it. Sir Richard Fanshawe had been an emissary for him to Spain, and later was taken prisoner at the battle of Worcester, where he fought for Charles II. In 1649 he wrote:

> The bloody trunk of him who did possess
> Above the rest a hapless happy state,
> *This little stone* doth seal, but not depress,
> And scarce can stop the rolling of his fate ...
>
> Ten years upon him falsely smiled,
> Sheathing in fawning looks the deadly Knife
> Long aimèd at his head – that so beguiled
> It more securely might bereave his life:
>
> Then threw him to a Scaffold from a Throne –
> *Much Doctrine lies under this little Stone.*

The finest lines of all were written by one who was no servant of the Stuarts but became one of Cromwell's: Andrew Marvell. Ironically they occur in a poem in praise of the victorious General; his victim

> But with his keener eye
> The Axe's edge did try;
> Nor called the gods with vulgar spite
> To vindicate his helpless Right,
> But bowed his comely head
> Down as upon a bed.

Charles I's surpassing dignity through all his trials, especially the majesty of his behaviour in that last public scene, were worth a victory in the field and contributed largely to the restoration of the monarchy. After that crime, his blood ran for ever between the revolutionaries and the English people.

Meanwhile we can read the history of the time in the poets:

Though for a time we see Whitehall
With cobwebs hanging on the wall,
Instead of silk and silver brave,
Which formerly it used to have,
   With rich perfume in every room
     Delightful to that Princely train:
   Which again you shall see, when the time it shall be,
    *That the King enjoys his own again.*

This poem became enormously popular, with its repeated
refrain sung all over the country, in the streets, in inns and
taverns, in country manors where healths were drunk to the
King overseas – it too was worth a victory in the field. As the
perceptive Selden remarked, 'more solid things do not show the
complexion of the times so well as ballads and libels'. We shall
come to those.

The dramatist Shirley, done out of his living, took to writing,
and publishing, poems:

Victorious men of earth, no more
   Proclaim how wide your Empires are . . .
Devouring Famine, Plague, and War,
   Each able to undo mankind,
Death's servile Emissaries are . . .

At last, before Cromwell's death, Shirley came up with his
superb valediction to it all: 'The glories of our blood and state,
Are shadows, not substantial things' –

Some men with swords may reap the field,
   And plant fresh laurels where they kill,
But their strong nerves at last must yield,
   They tame but one another still . . .

The Garlands wither on your brow,
   Then boast no more your mighty deeds,
Upon Death's purple altar now
   See where the Victor-victim bleeds,
    Your heads must come

> To the cold tomb:
> Only the actions of the Just
> Smell sweet, and blossom in their dust.

The poet obviously had Cromwell in mind – so much so that people said that the great man trembled at hearing it. I do not believe this, though significant as folklore; true it is that Cromwell was in a doubtful state of mind on *his* death-bed: he was fearful about whether he was still in a state of grace.

One is reminded of Cleveland's superb Epitaph on Strafford:

> Here lies wise and valiant dust
> Huddled up 'twixt fit and just:
> Strafford, who was hurried hence
> 'Twixt treason and convenience ...
> The Prince's nearest joy and grief,
> He had, yet wanted, all relief:
> The prop and ruin of the state,
> The People's violent love and hate:
> One in extremes loved and abhorred,
> Riddles lie here, or in a word,
> Here lies blood; and let it lie
> Speechless still and never cry.

This was accompanied by 'Pym's Anarchy', which he let loose and then controlled, probably by Thomas Jordan, a former actor:

> Ask me no more why th'Gaol confines
> Our Hierarchy of best divines –
> Since some in Parliament agree
> 'Tis for the Subjects' Liberty.
>
> Ask me no more why from Blackwall
> Great tumults come into Whitehall –
> Since it's allowed by free consent
> The Privilege of Parliament.
>
> Ask me not why to London comes
> So many muskets, pikes and drums,

> Although you fear they'll never cease –
> 'Tis to protect the kingdom's peace.

The poets perceived, and underlined, the humbug of Parliament which held to the slogan that they were fighting *for* the King, against his ill advisers.

The war itself brought forth not much in the way of verse: perhaps Cartwright's best poem on 'The Death of Sir Bevil Grenville', killed at Lansdown: a noble character, and nobly described by Clarendon.

> Whence in a just esteem to Church and Crown
> He offered all, and nothing thought his own.
> This thrust him into action whole and free,
> Knowing no interests but loyalty:
> Not loving arms as arms, or strife for strife,
> Not wasteful, nor yet sparing, of his life;
> A great exactor of himself, and then
> By fair commands no less of other men.

Today we remember the war more from a few lines of Lovelace: on 'Going to the Wars',

> Tell me not, sweet, I am unkind,
>     That from the nunnery
> Of thy chaste breast and quiet mind
>     To war and arms I fly.
>
> True: a new mistress now I chase,
>     The first foe in the field,
> And with a stronger faith embrace
>     A sword, a horse, a shield . . .
>
> I could not love thee, dear, so much,
>     Loved I not honour more.

Those lines have entered into the nation's tradition and inspired many going to fight for it, as the following have consoled others in trouble:

> Stone walls do not a prison make
> Nor iron bars a cage ...

Lovelace was younger than most of those we have cited, but was twice imprisoned. At Oxford he was 'accounted the most amiable and beautiful person that ever eye beheld',[1] and was only twenty when he served, like so many of the Wits, on the Scottish Borders in 1638 and was again in the second expedition in 1639. While there he wrote a tragedy, *The Soldier*, which was lost in the confusion of the times. We learn his interest in the stage from his address 'To Fletcher, Revived', and he befriended the dramatist Henry Glapthorne – out of work and down on his luck. Glapthorne responded by dedicating his poem, 'Whitehall', to him.

Born of good Kentish family to a considerable estate, Lovelace was a patron of the arts, a friend to the young Lely. We have a poem on the portrait the painter did of the King with his son, the Duke of York, while confined at Hampton Court:

> See, what a clouded Majesty! and eyes
> Whose glory through their mist doth brighter rise!
> See, what an humble bravery doth shine,
> And grief triumphant breaking through each line.

A long 'panegyric to the best picture of Friendship, Mr Pet. Lely' tells us something of what the English poets thought of the sister art, 'Peinture':

> Where then when all the world pays its respect
> Lies our Transalpine barbarous neglect?
> When the chaste hands of pow'rful Titiàn
> Had drawn the scourges of our God and Man ...
> But Holbein's noble and prodigious worth
> Only the pangs of an whole Age brings forth ...
> O sacred *Peinture*! that dost fairly draw
> What but in mists deep inward *Poets* saw.

---

[1] q. *The Poems of Richard Lovelace*, ed. C.H. Wilkinson, xix.

When Edward Phillips, Milton's far from Puritan nephew, commented on Lovelace's poetry, he put his finger on what was true of many of the Cavaliers: they were amateurs, in the best sense of the word, not dedicated professionals like his severe uncle.

Lovelace was first imprisoned for the part he played in presenting the notorious Kentish Petition, which so enraged Parliament in 1642. The county had presented a protest against Parliament assuming command of the local militias in every county: a revolutionary measure, for command of the militia was by law the Crown's prerogative. Further, the county asked 'that the Book of Common Prayer established by law might be observed'. But revolution was well on the way: the Puritans had no intention of abiding by the law, they intended to lay down the law, and did – until the revolution broke down of its own dissensions. Only its Army could hold the country down. On the threshold of revolution Parliament itself had used the tactic of petitioning for propaganda purpose, and it was well known that their agents, popular preachers like Marshall and Burgess, boosted the numbers of the petitioners.

Lovelace lost at least one brother in the war: 'To his dear Brother Colonel F.L. immoderately mourning my Brother's untimely Death at Carmarthen' – apparently the younger William had been serving under Colonel Francis, himself a versifier and artist, capable of executing the portrait for Lovelace's posthumous poems:

> If tears could wash the Ill away
> A pearl for each wet bead I'd pay;
> But as dewed corn the fuller grows,
> So watered eyes but swell our woes.

A fatality indeed fell upon that generation. Lovelace himself had to sell the family estate and ended his days in penury, after a second imprisonment:

> What fate was mine when in mine obscure cave –
> Shut up almost close prisoner in a grave –
> Your beams could reach me through this vault of night,
> And canton the dark dungeòn with light!

This was written to Charles Cotton, a younger man who was able to help Lovelace in his last days of indigence: he was not forty when he died.

Lovelace bore an unblemished character, no scandal ever attached to his name, for all his parts. Cotton paid tribute to this in a poem to his memory:

> Such was thy composition, such thy mind
> Improved to virtue, and from vice refined:
> Thy youth an abstract of the world's best parts
> Inured to arms, and exercised in arts ...
>
> In fortune humble, constant in mischance,
> Expert of both, and both served to advance
> Thy name, by various trials of thy spirit,
> And give the testimony of thy merit.
>
> Valiant to envy of the bravest men,
> And learnèd to an undisputed pen,
> Good as the best in both, and great; but yet
> No dangerous courage, nor offensive wit.

As a young man Cotton can comment on later events during the Interregnum. We have a poem commemorating the Earl of Derby, who had survived the civil war. Virtually a prince in Lancashire and Cheshire – he held the title of King of the Isle of Man – he had raised hundreds of troops from his tenantry for Charles I, like those comparable potentates, the Earls of Worcester and of Newcastle. We have seen that his historic house, Lathom, was razed after siege; Derby held out for some years in the Isle of Man, until Charles II invaded from Scotland, to be defeated at Worcester. Derby had been captured, and was executed in 1651:

> To what a formidable greatness grown
> Is this prodigious beast Rebellìòn?
> When sovereignty and its so sacred law
> Thus lies subjected to his tyrant awe ...
> In this great ruin, Derby, lay thy fate –

Derby unfortunately fortunate –
Unhappy thus to fall a sacrifice
To such an irreligious power as this.
And blest as 'twas thy nobler sense to die
A constant lover of thy loyalty . . .

And first, the justest and the best of kings,
Robed in the glory of his sufferings,
By his too violent fate informed us all
What tragic ends attended his great fall.
Since when his subjects, some by chance of war,
Some by perverted justice at the bar
Have perished: thus what th'other leaves, this takes,
And whoso scapes the Sword falls by the Axe . . .

The poet thus describes the rule of the Saints:

In this false Age, where such as do amiss
Control the honest sort, and make a prey
Of all that are not villainous as they . . .
Blood-thirsty tyrants of usurpèd state!
In facts of death prompt and insatiate . . .

We observe in the poetry of the age, as in its history, the
transition from romance and comedy to tragic passion, and
eventually satire. Cotton wrote a vitriolic poem upon Waller's
'Panegyric' to Cromwell on becoming Lord Protector. Waller
had had a very narrow escape through involving himself in
politics. A rich man, owner of Beaconsfield and married to an
heiress, he was a cousin of John Hampden and Cromwell, and
therefore a Parliament man. He was really a middle-of-the-road
figure, opposed to war and Parliament's raising of troops against
the King – one cannot but sympathise with him. Appointed
commissioner by Parliament to treat with Charles at Oxford in
1643, Waller came to sympathise with him and entered into
some plot to bring the war to an end. No one seems to know the
ins-and-outs of it, except that Waller was forced to reveal the
names of his fellow plotters and pay an enormous fine to save his
life from a charge of treason (to Parliament). Imprisoned for a

time in the Tower, he was then banished and lived for some years in exile. There he was free to publish his Poems (1645).

These celebrated the former glad days and read ironically now: 'To the Queen, occasioned by her Majesty's picture':

> Well fare the hand! which to our humble sight
> Presents that beauty which the dazzling light
> Of royal splendour hides from weaker eyes,
> And all access, save by this art, denies.

Waller was a man of taste, delighting alike in music and painting. 'To Van Dyke':

> Rare Artisan, whose pencil moves
> Not our delights alone, but loves!
> From thy shop of beauty we
> Slaves return, that entered free ...
> Strange that thy hand should not inspire
> The beauty only, but the fire;
> Not the form alone, and grace,
> But act and powèr of a face.

And equally 'To Mr Henry Lawes, who had then newly set a song of mine in the year 1635':

> Verse makes heroic virtue live,
> But you can life to verses give ...
> You by the help of tune and time
> Can make that song that was but rhyme.
> Noy[1] pleading, no man doubts the cause.
> Or questions verses set by Lawes.
>
> As a church window, thick with paint,
> Lets in a light but dim and faint,
> So others, with division,[2] hide
> The light of sense, the poet's pride.

---

[1] Attorney-General Noy, of Ship Money fame, had been a brilliant lawyer.
[2] i.e. variation.

[174]

> But you alone may boast
> That not a syllable is lost:
> The writer's, and the setter's, skill
> At once the ravished ears do fill.

More ironically still reads, 'Upon his Majesty's Repairing of Paul's' – we recall that the King had given the monumental portico:

> That shipwrecked vessel which the Apostle bore,
> Scarce suffered more upon Melita's shore
> Than did his temple in the sea of time,
> Our nation's glory, and our nation's crime.

Or again that 'To the King, on his Navy':

> Where'er thy Navy spreads her canvas wings,
> Homage to thee, and peace to all she brings;
> The French and Spaniard, when thy flags appear,
> Forget their hatred, and consent to fear.

Alas, the Navy, for which the King had incurred so much unpopularity by raising Ship Money to build it – fomented by Waller's cousin, John Hampden – was by now, 1645, a weapon under Parliament's control against him. After a number of years in exile Waller was at length pardoned by cousin Cromwell's influence. So it was natural enough that the returned exile should greet the newly made Lord Protector with a panegyric. It turned out to be one of the most remarkable poems of the Interregnum: again naturally enough, for the astonishing career of the man was enough to inspire heroic verse. There was something indubitably heroic about Oliver Cromwell, even his opponent Clarendon paid tribute to his greatness. From a simple country gentleman he had now risen to a far more absolute monarchy than ever Charles I enjoyed, and showed to Europe and the world how capable he was of exercising it.

> While with a strong, and yet a gentle, hand
> You bridle faction and our hearts command,

> Protect us from ourselves and from the foe,
> Make us unite, and make us conquer too ...

The country could, and did, certainly conquer under the dictator, but he could never unite the country, or get it to accept his rule, which depended simply on force, the Army.

> Your drooping country torn with civil hate,
> Restored by you, is made a glorious state:

That at any rate was true.

> The seat of Empire, where the Irish come,
> And the unwilling Scotch to fetch their doom.

The Irish have never forgotten or forgiven him to this day – any more than those devoted to the King he had had put to death. His subjugation of the Scotch, however, was popular in England, for they had started it all, were the trouble-makers. On setting out to conquer Scotland Cromwell was cheered by the populace. He turned to his companion (I think, Lambert) and said that those would cheer as heartily if these were setting out for the gallows. He had no more illusions about the people than Charles I had (or for that matter Milton, or Shakespeare, a kindlier spirit, either).

> The Sea's our own, and now all nations greet
> With bending sails each vessel of our fleet:
> Your power extends as far as winds can blow,
> Or swelling sails upon the globe may go.
> – Heaven, that has placed this Island to give law,
> To balance Europe and her states to awe,
> In this conjunction does on Britain smile,
> The greatest Leader, and the greatest Isle.

The complacency of it! Here is the true Puritan spirit – they were the imperialists. The religious Milton, who served the dictator though a Republican, held the same intolerable view –

'God, that revealed Himself first to his Englishmen'! The cosmopolitan Charles I never thought that.

> Whether this portion of the world were rent
> By the rude ocean from the Continent,
> Or thus Created, it was sure designed
> To be the Sacred Refuge of Mankind.
> Hither th'oppressed shall henceforth resort,
> Justice to crave, and succour at your Court.

Something in that. From the time of Elizabeth I – whom the Protector admired and regarded himself as *her* successor – England had been the refuge of persecuted Protestants from abroad; and now Cromwell allowed back the Jews – if for financial reasons, appropriately enough for devotees of the Old Testament.

England's age-long insular security (alas, no more) is thus expressed:

> Angels and we have this Prerogative
> That none can at our happy Seat arrive,
> While we descend at pleasure to invade
> The Bad with vengeance, or the Good to aid.

We may adduce here Milton's similar complacency: 'Let not England forget her precedence of teaching nations how to live'! (Today that precedence has passed to the United States.)

> To dig for wealth we weary not our limbs,
> Gold, though the heavy'st metal, hither swims:

(Alas, no longer.)

> Ours is the harvest where the Indians mow,
> We plough the Deep, and reap what others Sow.

Here we have the theory of economic imperialism summed up in a couplet – Lenin should have known it.

Scotland, 'from all ages kept for you to tame', was really held down by the Army – in spite of their common Puritanism, and Cromwell speaking their own Biblical jargon in sermons to the Scots.

> They, that henceforth must be content to know
> No warmer region than their hills of snow –

Cromwell had certainly stopped their invasions of England to interfere in English affairs –

> May blame the sun, but must extol your Grace,
> Which in our Senate has allowed them place;
> Preferred by Conquest, happily o'erthrown,
> Falling they rise, to be with us made one –
> So kind Dictators made, when they came home,
> Their vanquished foes free citizens of Rome.

True enough: briefly, under the Protectorate, the two countries were united, and Scotland allotted seats in Cromwellian 'Parliaments'. But the dictator could no more agree with his 'Parliaments', though selected and chosen by him, than Charles I could, with his more representative assemblies.

> Lifting up all that prostrate lie, you grieve
> You cannot make the dead again to live –

Did the great man never have remorse for what he had done? He did recognise that it could never be forgiven by 'the young Man' – his term for the dead King's son; to himself he must have had some afterthoughts about the King's difficulties with Parliaments, when he found it impossible to deal with those even of his own choosing.

Cromwell's well-publicised virtues as a family man are duly celebrated, in Biblical terms:

> Your private life did a just pattern give
> How Fathers, Husbands, pious Sons should live,
> Born to command, your Princely virtues slept
> Like humble David's, while the Flock he kept.

But now –

> But there, my Lord, we'll bays and olive bring
> To Crown your Head, while you in triumph ride
> O'er vanquished nations, and the sea beside;
> While all your Neighbour Princes unto you
> Like Joseph's Sheaves pay reverence and bow.

This was true too: it was noted at the time how European monarchs, who privately hated his guts, sued to him. In history power talks.

And what did the vanquished Royalists think of this remarkable effort? Here is young Cotton:

> From whence, vile Poet, didst thou glean the wit
> And words for such a vicious Poem fit?
> Where couldst thou paper find was not too white,
> Or ink that could be black enough to write?
> What servile Devil tempted thee to be
> A flatterer of thine own Slavery.
> To kiss thy Bondage, and extol the deed
> At once that made thy Prince and Country bleed?
> I wonder much thy false heart did not dread
> And shame to write what all men blush to read;
> Thus with a base ingratitude to rear
> Trophies unto thy Master's Murderer?

There could be no reconciliation so long as Cromwell lived and the Regicides ruled. When the inevitable Restoration came about, it was from agreement between the Royalists and the (comparatively) respectable Parliamentarians who had opposed the King's execution – as even Cromwell's superior, the Lord General Fairfax, had done.

The defeated side in revolution finds expression in satire – as we note with Soviet Russia today, the only outlet being verses like those which Mandelstam wrote and circulated about the Man with bicycle-handlebar moustaches, murderer of a million

peasants.[1] During the Interregnum the Royalists were entertained by Cleveland's poems, which were very popular; and
after the Restoration by Samuel Butler's *Hudibras*, which has
won a permanent place in literature, as well as other brilliant
pieces of his in both prose and verse. Those two give us the
'complexion of the times' very well: the failure of the Puritan
experiment, the revelation of its hypocrisy and self-seeking
(Milton, one of its most committed supporters, agreed about
that), disillusionment all round, especially with the pretences of
religion, the fixation on nonsense and disputes about nonsense
propositions, a *désabusé* cynicism about men and public affairs.

Cleveland and Butler were cronies, according to Aubrey, and
'had a club every night'. They were exactly of an age, from the
same part of the country – Cleveland from Warwickshire, Butler
from Worcester. Cleveland was a Cambridge man who, turned
out of his fellowship at St John's (over 200 Fellows were ejected
from Cambridge colleges, and over 300 from Oxford), made for
Oxford during the Royalist occupation where he was much
'caressed'. He made them laugh amid their misfortunes, and
there was plenty to laugh at.

There was the attack on the bishops by those eminent divines
whose initials formed the monstrous word of their publication,
*Smectymnuus,* who wanted their jobs. These were Stephen
Marshall, who had 'grown very rich' with preferments, like his
large salary of £300 a year as preacher at St Margaret's,
Westminster. Edmund Calamy had refused to read 'that wicked
Book of Sports'; he suffered from giddiness so that he could not
preach from a high pulpit, but from the desk below. He was
against the divine right of bishops, but asserted the divine right
of ministers of the gospel, since he was one. Thomas Young had
the rich living of Stowmarket at £300 a year, and was intruded
into the place of the Master of Jesus at Cambridge. (They had all
made a point of attacking pluralism.) They were all Cambridge
Puritans. Matthew Newcomen was 'sanctified by divine grace',
according to his brother-in-law, Calamy. William Spurstow was

---

[1]cf. Mrs Mandelstam's Memoirs. It is noteworthy that when Stalin learned that
Mandelstam was regarded as a genius, he minuted, 'Isolate, but preserve.' It
reveals his scale of values, since he had no compunction in annihilating millions
of ordinary people.

intruded as Master of St Catharine's, instead of its properly elected occupant.

Cleveland went for this set of humbugs in his poem 'Smectymnuus, or the Club-Divines':

> Smectymnuus! The goblin makes me start.
> I'th' name of Rabbi Abraham, what art?
> Syriac? or Arabic? or Welsh? what skill't?
> Ap all the bricklayers that Babel built,
> Some conjurer translate and let me know it:
> Till then 'tis fit for a West Saxon poet.

Then there was the blessed Westminster Assembly of Divines which had been called by Parliament, as part of its bargain with the Scots, and to provide a directory of public worship in place of the despised Book of Common Prayer – which nevertheless was the law of the land, and was ultimately proved to have its consensus with it. We have already observed the orgies of preaching and extempore prayer these divines indulged themselves in, in the dismantled and disgraced Abbey. Now they made themselves comfortable in Jerusalem Chamber with big fires and tapestries to keep out draughts (from outside), while they disputed interminably their Predestination nonsense, who had Divine Grace and who had not – they had no doubt that they were the Elect.

As a Parliamentarian Selden had been appointed a member. As the most learned scholar in England he gave them trouble, querying the meanings of words, for he knew far more Greek and Hebrew than they did. It must have contributed something to his disillusionment. In the end the Elect Parliament, now down to a mere Rump of its members, got sick of the Assembly, which kept pressing for the full Presbyterian discipline over the laity. Parliament was too sunk in English Erastianism – Selden was a complete Erastian – to stand for that. The Scotch dominie, Baillie, who kept a diary of the proceedings, went home fed up with the carnal English. Presbyterianism never had a chance of becoming the religion of the English people; and now the victorious Puritans were splitting in two, between Presbyterians and Independents (of whom the Lord Protector was one) and

quarrelling like mad among themselves.[1]
Cleveland on 'The Mixed Assembly':

> Flea-bitten[2] synod, an assembly brewed
> Of clerks and elders *ana*, like the rude
> Chaos of Presbyt'ry, where laymen guide
> With the tame woolpack clergy by their side:
> Who asked the banns between these discoloured mates? ...
>
> A jig! a jig! and in this antic dance
> Fielding and Doxie Marshall first advance.
> Twisse blows the Scotch-pipes, and the loving brace
> Puts on the traces and treads the cinque-a-pace.
> Then Saye and Sele must his old hamstrings supple,
> And he and rumpled Palmer make a couple.
> Kimbolton, that rebellious Boanerges,
> Must be content to saddle Dr Burgess.[3]
> If Burgess get a clap, 'tis ne'er the worse,
> But the fifth time of his compurgators ...
>
> Pym and the members must their giblets levy
> To encounter Madam Smec, that single bevy.
> Thus every Ghibelline has got his Guelph
> But Selden – he's a galliard by himself –
> And well may be: there's more divines in him
> Than in all this, their Jewish Sanhedrim.

There they are, and more too: flies stuck in the amber of
Cleveland's verse.
Marshall appears again in a poem, 'The Rebel Scot':

> Or roar like Marshall, that Geneva bull,
> Hell and Damnation a pulpit-full.

[1]Thomas Edwards, whom Laud had tried to silence, attacked as an orthodox
Presbyterian the sins of his brethren, who were Independents, in his well-named
*Gangraena ... or a Discovery of many Errors, Heresies, Blasphemies, and pernicious
Practices* (1646) in other sects than his own.
[2]I suspect that this was literally exact.
[3]Cornelius Burgess, among other jobs, was Vice-President of this delightful
assembly.

Anti-Scotch feeling was increasing mightily in England, since it was too obvious that they had been bought by Parliament to overwhelm the King. The cunning Pym, a pastmaster at political intrigue, had kept the Scots' army in being in the North to exert pressure on Charles. Since the King's cause proved stronger in the field than Parliament, with all its resources, ever expected, Pym bought the intervention of the Scots for £300,000, and the imposition of their Solemn League and Covenant in England. That turned the scales at Marston Moor. Later, the Scots sold their King – who foolishly entrusted himself in their hands – to Parliament for another £200,000. The Scots were a poor people, and they were hungry.

> No, the Scots-errant fight, and fight to eat,
> Their Ostrich stomachs make their swords their meat . . .
> Lord! what a godly thing is want of shirts!
> How a Scotch stomach – and no meat – converts!
> Religion for their seamstress and their cook.
> Unmask them well; their honours and estate,
> As well as conscience, are sophisticate.

This was exact: Parliament had also provided an enormous amount of shirting material to clothe the naked backs of the Scotch soldiery.

'The Scots' Apostacy' makes the point concisely:

> Who reconciled the Covenant's doubtful sense:
> The Commons' argument, or the City's pence?

Actually, Milton's hero, Sir Henry Vane – who had perjured himself to bring Strafford to the block – took in the Scots over the Covenant, when he was sent to negotiate with them. He was no believer in Presbyterianism, any more than Milton was; and he diplomatically inserted a clause which left the imposition of the Covenant to the decision of the English, who dragged their feet in the matter, well knowing that it would never go down, even if swallowed formally for political ends.

Cleveland was in keeping with English feeling in his angry 'Hue and Cry after Sir John Presbyter':

> With hair in characters and lugs in text,
> With a splay mouth and a nose circumflexed ...
> The Negative and Covenanting Oath
> Like two mustachos issuing from his mouth;
> The bush upon his chin like a carved story,
> In a box-knot cut by the Directory ...
> What zealous frenzy did the Senate seize,
> That tare the Rochet to such rags as these?

Zeal was, of course, a key-word in Puritan semantics: it meant self-praise, commendation of themselves, like 'the godly', or 'the Saints' etc. Cleveland wrote a funny 'Dialogue between two Zealots upon the *Etc* in the Oath', the let-up or get-away in its imposition in England.

Cleveland could also be serious. He wrote an Elegy on the murdered Archbishop: no possible proof that Laud had broken the law could ever be made out against him – as the eminent lawyer Selden pointed out; so he was executed by Attainder, i.e. the will of the minority left in Parliament. This was partly to please the unsatisfied Scots: after all, the Archbishop was expendable. Strafford also had been killed by Attainder, not by due process of law. Cleveland summed it all up in a line:

> The State in Strafford fell, the Church in Laud.

And now:

> There is no Church; Religion is grown
> So much of late that she's increased to none,
> Like an hydropic body, full of rheums,
> First swells into a bubble, then consumes.
> The Law is dead, or cast into a trance –
> And a law dough-baked, an Ordinance.

The Ordinances of the revolutionary Parliament were not in any way legal: they were promulgations, edicts, of a revolution. Royalists naturally never regarded them as having authority, and Cleveland made no bones about it, in his 'Elegy upon King Charles the First, murdered publicly by his Subjects':

> Were not my faith buoyed up by sacred blood,
> It might be drowned in this prodigious flood –

The Royalists held by this faith throughout the Interregnum, and it ultimately saw them home –

> This stroke hath cut the only neck of land
> Which between us and this red sea did stand.

However, the Children of Israel did pass through the Red Sea into the Promised Land – as the Royalists did after the failure of the Puritan Revolution and the break-down of its military dictatorship.

Abraham Cowley was another Cambridge poet who, ejected from his Fellowship, came over to Oxford for spiritual sustenance from the like-minded. In his work too we may read his reactions to events, gravely, not satirically. He had greeted Falkland on his 'safe return from the Northern Expedition against the Scots':

> Great is thy charge, O North: be wise and just,
> England commits her Falkland to thy trust;
> Return him safe: Learning would rather choose
> Her Bodley, or her Vatican to lose.
> All things that are but writ or printed there,
> In his unbounded breast engraven are ...
>     And this great prince of knowledge is by fate
> Thrust into the noise and business of a state.

This refers to Falkland's (reluctant) acceptance of office as Secretary of State. Then, to the King:

> Welcome, great Sir, with all the joy that's due
>     To the return of peace and you:
> This happy concord in no blood is writ,
>     None can grudge Heaven full thanks for it.

It had, however, been a shattering defeat for the King and Laud's policy, ominous of the worse that was to come, and preliminary to revolution, which indeed had already won in Scotland.

Next year, 1641, Van Dyke, the portraitist of their threatened world, died:

> Van Dyke is dead; but what bold Muse shall dare
> – Though Poets in that word with Painters share –
> To express her sadness? Poesy must become
> An Art, like Painting here, an Art that's dumb.

A poem on the Bishop of Lincoln's 'enlargement from the Tower' reminds us what a mistake it was for those two prelates, Laud and Williams, to quarrel when there were wolves baying at the door. They had been rivals and were envious of each other. Williams sought to ingratiate himself with Parliament, and to that end was made archbishop of York (he was attacked in a poem by Cleveland for his ambivalent stance): all to no avail.

Cowley saluted the first two books of Davenant's *Gondibert*, 'finished before his voyage to America':

> Methinks heroic poesy till now
> Like some fantastic fairyland did show
> Gods, Devils, Nymphs, Witches and Giants race,
> And all but Man in Man's chief work had place ...
> Instead of those dost Men and Manners plant,
> The things which that rich soil did chiefly want.

From his time at Oxford we have a graceful tribute to the Bodleian: on 'Mr Cowley's book presenting itself to the University Library':

> Hail Learning's Pantheon! Hail the sacred Ark
> Where all the World of Science does embark!

Of scientists the greatest, Harvey, was there at Merton, Bodley's own college. Cowley appreciated that

Every one leads as he is led,
The same bare path they tread ...
Had Harvey to this road confined his wit
His noble Circle of the Blood had been untrodden yet.

Evidently Cowley knew Harvey's losses from the war:

These useful secrets to his pen we owe,
And thousands more 'twas ready to bestow,
Of which a barbarous war's unlearnèd rage
    Has robbed the ruined age ...

O cursèd War! who can forgive thee this?
    Houses and towns may rise again,
        And ten times easier it is     .
To rebuild Paul's than any work of his.

With Samuel Butler we return to the comic muse – and it must have been a factor in getting rid of the humbugs that they were laughed out of court. However, it was not possible to publish *Hudibras* until the Restoration, when it gave the cynical Charles II – such a contrast with his father – much amusement. During the rule of the Saints Butler had been able to observe them at work from close at hand.

As a youth he had served in the household of the Countess of Kent, with whom Selden lived. It must have been an education in itself, and Selden thought highly of the young man for his parts – no wonder Butler's point of view about the Revolution coincided with Selden's, who had begun as a moderate Parliamentarian. Butler studied both music and painting, in which he had some skill, and was a friend of Samuel Cooper, the best miniaturist of the time. Just before the Restoration he published an anonymous pamphlet urging it – it was indeed inevitable, though Milton, always odd man out and never in agreement with anybody, went on, pamphlet after pamphlet, hoping against hope. Milton saw through the humbugs, however, much as Butler did, though he would not have

approved the cynical tone.[1] John Aubrey has a Memorandum
to the point: 'Satirical wits disoblige whom they converse with,
etc; and consequently make to themselves many enemies and
few friends; and this was his manner and case.'[2] However, the
broad-minded Clarendon, no cynic, kept Butler's portrait 'in his
Library, over the chimney'.

He became so famous for *Hudibras*, which went on being
reprinted into the 18th century, that we know him best as
'Hudibras' Butler. In that character he created a kind of bogus
Don Quixote, a symbol for all the nonsense of the time.

> For his *Religion* it was fit
> To match his learning and his wit:
> 'Twas *Presbyterian* true blue.
> For he was of that stubborn Crew
> Of Errant Saints, whom all men grant
> To be the true Church *Militant*:
>
> Such as do build their Faith upon
> The holy text of *Pike* and *Gun*;
> Decide all Controversies by
> Infallible *Artillery*;
> And prove their Doctrine Orthodox
> By Apostolic *Blows* and *Knocks*;

[1] Amusingly enough, the most eminent of Puritans, John Milton, saw their
religious pretences in much the same light as Butler. When I call the Assembly of
Divines an assembly of humbugs, witness Milton to that effect. 'If the state were
in this plight, religion was not in much better. To reform which a certain number
of divines were called – neither chosen by any rule or custom ecclesiastical, nor
eminent for either piety or knowledge above others left out. The most part of
them were such as had preached and cried down, *with great show of zeal*, the
avarice and pluralities of bishops and prelates. Yet these conscientious men
wanted not boldness – to the ignominy and scandal of their pastorlike profession
and especially of their boasted reformation – to seize into their hands, besides
one, sometimes two or more of the best livings, collegiate masterships in the
universities, rich lectures in the City. By which means these great rebukers of
non-residence were not ashamed to be seen so quickly pluralists and non-
residents themselves.' John Milton, *Prose Works*, ed. 1877, V. 238. Instead of so
much academic research into the fatuities these people thought, it would be
more to the point to research into what they got out of it.
[2] Aubrey, I. 135–8.

> Call Fire and Sword and Desolation
> A *Godly-thorough-Reformation*,
> Which always must be carried on,
> And still be doing, never done.

That had been their line, ever since the settlement of religion under Elizabeth I. The Church of England, 'as by law established', had proved itself the best consensus obtainable then, in the circumstances of the time, when no consensus could have been obtained based upon either Left or Right, Puritan or Catholic. And this was proving itself again now, with the failure of the Puritan Revolution, riven by the dissensions of its sects, and never carrying the country with it:

> As if Religion were intended
> For nothing else but to be mended.
> A Sect, whose chief Devotion lies
> In odd perverse Antipathies:
> In falling out with that or this,
> And finding somewhat still amiss ...
> That with more care keep Holy-day
> The wrong, than others the right, way;[1]
> Compound for Sins they are inclined to
> By damning those they have no mind to:
> Still so perverse and opposite
> As if they worshipped God for spite.

For a time Humbug was in the ascendant: it must have been intolerable for people of either cultivation or sense to live under it:

> Whate'er men speak by this *New Light*
> Still they are sure to be i'th'right.
> 'Tis a *Dark-Lantern* of the Spirit
> Which none can see by but those that hear it.

Selden put his finger on this: 'Preaching by the Spirit, as they

---

[1] Some of them disputed whether the Sabbath should not properly be kept on Saturday.

call it, is most esteemed by the Common People, because they cannot abide Art or Learning, which they have not been bred up in.'[1] The envy on the part of the demos went so far that a member of Praise-God Barebone's Parliament, one of the chosen, Elect but not elected, proposed the abolition of universities as useless. Selden pinpointed the exhibitionism of so much sermonising: 'Preaching, for the most part, is the glory of the Preacher, to show himself a fine man. Catechising would do much better' – or, we might add, the impersonal liturgy of the Church. Puritan preaching had not only a language of its own, but a nasal drone to show what a peculiar people they were, God's own. Everybody noticed it – it is said to be represented today in the rather nasal twang of Massachusetts. Not everybody fancied it:

> This Light inspires, and plays upon
> The nose of Saint like Bagpipe drone.

They disapproved of keeping Christmas,

> Quarrel with *Mince-Pies* and disparage
> Their best and dearest friend, Plum-porridge –

Marshall was a good trencherman –

> Fat *Pig* and *Goose* itself oppose,
> And blaspheme *Custard* through the *Nose*.

And what was it like for intelligent people to live under their rule?

> Synods are whelps of th'*Inquisition*,
> A mongrel breed of like pernicion,
> And growing up became the Sires
> Of Scribes, Commissioners, and Triers:[2]
> Whose business is, by cunning slight

[1] *Table Talk, being the Discourses of John Selden* (Temple Classics), 112, 115.
[2] Hugh Peters, Cromwell's Army chaplain, was one of the Triers set up to vet candidates for benefices.

> To cast a figure for men's *Light*:
> To find in lines of beard and face
> The physiognomy of *Grace*,
> And by the sound and *twang of Nose*
> If all be sound within disclose.

In fact, power was all, as both Hobbes and Selden thought – and Milton was to find:

> Sure 'tis an Orthodox opinion
> That *Grace is founded in Dominion*.
> Great *Piety* consists in *Pride*:
> To *rule* is to be *sanctified*:
> To domineer and to control
> Both o'er the Body and the Soul,
> Is the most perfect *Discipline*
> Of Church-rule, and by *right divine*.

When Hobbes diagnosed the causes of the Civil War in his *Behemoth* – and after all his was the most incisive mind in England, not sold on either side – he put Envy and Conceit well ahead. For almost any Puritan, most of all Milton, it could be said:

> For all men live and judge amiss
> Whose *Talents* jump not just with his.

In fact, *Hudibras* sums up the whole course of the Revolution, with its inherent contradictions, and chops and changes, in the hope of holding on to power and making itself permanent: which it could never do.

> Did not our *Worthies* of the *House*
> Before they broke the *Peace*, break *Vows*?
> For having freed us, first, from both
> Th'*Allegiance* and *Supremacy Oath*,
> Did they not, next, compel the *Nation*
> To take, and break, the *Protestation*?
> To *swear*, and after to *recant*

> The *Solemn League and Covenant?*
> To take th'*Engagement*, and disclaim it,
> Enforced by those who first did frame it?
>
> Did they not swear at first, to *fight*
> For the *KING'S* safety, and *His Right?*
> And after marched to find him out,
> And charged him home with *Horse* and *Foot?*
> And yet still had the confidence
> To swear it was in his *defence?*

And so *Hudibras* goes through the turns, and reverses of gear, of the whole bloody experience:

> Did they not *swear* to maintain *Law* ...
> Did they not *swear*, in express words,
> To prop and back the *House of Lords?*
> And after turned out the whole *House-ful*
> Of *Peers* as dangerous and unuseful?
> So *Cromwell*, with deep *Oaths* and *Vows*
> Swore all the *Commons* out o' th' *House.*

It was noted at the time that that action was not at all unpopular: by this time people were sick of Parliament, the name of which had had such magic for the discontented while Charles I dispensed with it.[1] Cromwell, who was a first-class

---

[1] As for Parliament we may recall what the most eminent of Puritans, Milton himself, thought of it. 'Once the superficial zeal and popular fumes that acted their New Magistry were cooled, straight everyone betook himself – setting the commonwealth behind, his private ends before – to do as his own profit or ambition led him. Then was justice delayed, and soon after denied; spite and favour determined all; hence faction, then treachery; everywhere wrong and oppression; foul and horrid deeds committed daily. Some who had been called from shops and warehouses, without other merit, to sit in supreme councils and committees – as their breeding was, fell to huckster the commonwealth. He who would give most or, *under covert of hypocritical zeal*, enjoyed unworthily the rewards of learning and fidelity. Their votes and ordinances, which men looked should have contained the repealing of bad laws, resounded with nothing else but new impositions, taxes, excises; yearly, monthly, weekly. Not to reckon the offices, gifts and preferments bestowed and shared among themselves ... ' *Verb. sap.* John Milton, *The History of Britain, Prose Works*, ed. 1877, V. 236-7. We need only add, what else is to be expected when, in Shakespeare's words, 'blood is their argument'?

[192]

politician as well as soldier, was well up in the arts of
dissimulation: he

> Trolled 'em on, and *swore*, and *swore*,
> Till th'Army turned 'em out of *Door*.
> This tells us plainly what they thought –
> That *Oaths* and *swearing* goes for nought;
> And that by them th'were only meant
> To serve for an *Expedient*.

In a word, it was all politics: a struggle for power: we need not
take seriously what they thought.

# Ideology

We might take Cowley's phrase 'a Ruined Age' for epigraph, for in a word it sums up our theme. The Caroline world of culture in literature, music, painting and the arts received a body-blow from the Puritan Revolution – as pre-1917 Russia, much to the fore in music, painting, literature received almost a death-blow from the Communist Revolution. In 17th-century England the blow was not mortal, for the Revolution was abortive and failed. The governing class, in the struggle for power, had split, mistakenly allowed itself to be divided, its place temporarily taken by the Army, with a man of genius at its head. (One cannot deny genius to Cromwell, or to Lenin or Stalin either.)

But the country could not be ruled without – let alone, against – its natural rulers;[1] and in 1660 they came together to resume power, with the indispensable monarchy and Church restored. Meanwhile the creative springs of English culture had not dried up, but were driven partly underground, partly into exile. When they were freed to resume their course, it was with a difference: the blitheness of morning, romantic attitudes, even romantic melancholy had gone. As Hollar noticed, it was as if the country had been bewitched; it certainly had been soured, and turned not unnaturally to cynicism and moral indifference. The spirit of the age of Charles II was in natural reaction to the rule of the Saints. Samuel Butler, one of the sharpest observers of the time, observed that 'Nothing breeds Atheism like Hypocrisy'.

It is a gift to the historian to be able to see the contrast visibly in the contrasting characters of Charles I and his son Charles II; the one high-minded, with a royal dignity, rather cold and

---

[1]Even Christopher Hill allows the phrase, cf. *The Experience of Defeat*.

withdrawn, his heart in his family and the arts, essentially an aesthete; a man both passive and to appearances impassive, his emotions under control; chaste and pious, what confidence he had being in religion and the Church, where he was both firm and well-read. Otherwise, he was lacking in confidence; both Clarendon and Hobbes were agreed in thinking that he relied too much on others' judgment (particularly his wife's – compare the fatal influence of the last Tsar's wife on him). Hobbes thought that Charles I was too weak a man to grapple the power that was his. His son was a very different man: clever and sociable, affable and kindly, if not much heart; talkative and vulgar, hence always popular; incontinently given over to women – as Grammont said, there was no greater enemy to chastity than the monarch of Great Britain; rather indolent, but a good politician when he gave his mind to it; no illusions whatever, and only a contingent use for religion, if at all. It adds up to the portrait of a cynic, and cynicism was a keynote of the society over which he ruled, and took its colour from him.

There were of course survivors from the earlier Caroline world: in politics, notably Clarendon and Ormonde; in the Church, Archbishop Sheldon, a great administrator, who took up where the martyred Laud left off, though with more realism. He was not a Laudian, but a survivor from the Falkland circle, more broad-minded, though it fell to him to extrude the Dissenters, where Laud had tried to include them in the national Church. (Sheldon must have been glad to see those survivors, trouble-makers, get out.)

Meanwhile, Caroline culture and its promise – it had constantly put forward and promulgated the ideals of learning, the arts and sciences – were broken. The culture, if that is the word for it, that took its place was in marked contrast. To begin with, it was lower-class, and the sects proliferated.

It is compelling to observe how cogently the foremost minds of the age – Hobbes for one, Selden for another – agreed in their diagnosis. Hobbes was hardly a Royalist, and he was no Churchman. He was no admirer of Laud, and thought him a don, whose mind was given to academic squabbles not fit for a minister of state. He had a point here, but Hobbes as good as had no religion. Nor was he a good Royalist; he saw the defects and weaknesses on that side too: he really favoured absolutism of a secular kind. Clarendon deeply disagreed with him over both Church and state.[1] Though I sympathise with Hobbes's poor view of mankind, candour compels me to admit that Clarendon, with his historical view of things and practical experience of politics, had the better of the argument.

Selden was a moderate Parliamentarian, near the centre of events throughout. Where those two are at one it makes a formidable indictment.

A vast amount of unnecessary academic hair-splitting has been devoted to the Puritans, attempting to define nuances between this and that group, till one is led to wonder whether there was such a person as a Puritan at all. Commonsense can recognise one when he sees one. The chief party in making the Revolution are called by contemporaries the Presbyterians; we may follow, simply for convenience. It is easy to distinguish them, as it was at the time, from the second biggest party – the Independents – which grew to power with the Army, with which Cromwell was aligned. Thus the Presbyterians dominated the Rump of Parliament, and affairs under the Commonwealth; as the Independents did, when they outed them in 1653, and ran the country with Cromwell as Protector – the minority of a minority. (As the Jacobins were in France, the Communists in Russia.)

Outed, the Presbyterians went into opposition to Cromwell; when it was too late they reached an agreement with Charles I, with the Treaty of Newport. Though they had vilified the King all through the war, they were opposed to his 'trial' and execution. This enabled them eventually to join with the Royalists to bring about the Restoration.

It is also easy to distinguish between Presbyterians and Independents in what they stood for. The Presbyterians meant to capture Church and state, and to run the Church as a national Church, supported by tithes, but operating full Presbyterian discipline in the parishes; without bishops or

---

[1] cf. Clarendon, *A Brief View and Survey of the Dangerous and Pernicious Errors to Church and State in Mr Hobbes's Book entitled LEVIATHAN.* Oxford, 1676.

Prayer Book, they had their Calvinist Confession of faith on offer, and their Directory of Public Worship – which only themselves were willing to take.[1] The Independents, on the other hand, stood for the independence of their own congregations, not a national Church: we should call it in modern terms, Congregationalism – and it had a successful model in the blissful purity of New England (especially Massachusetts, a godly community 'lifted up, as it were upon an hill', for all, particularly themselves, to admire.)

Beyond these two main bodies swarmed the Sects – they too were 'Saints' – to which the Revolution, and particularly its Bible-mania had given rise. Both Hobbes and Selden pointed out that this was bound to happen when free rein was given to everybody – butcher, baker and candlestick-maker – to interpret Scripture according to his lights. Orthodox Presbyterians were affronted by this development, as intolerant about it as ever the Church had been – with less reason, for their Revolution had given the lunatic fringe its grand opportunity. Again Hobbes and Selden were agreed in putting the blame on the Presbyterians for starting it all.

Both agreed that what they were out for was Power: politics first, religion came second. Hobbes: 'They had the concurrence of a great many gentlemen that did no less desire a popular government in the civil state than these ministers did in the church.'[2] The ministers, with their propaganda and in the pulpits 'continually extolling liberty and inveighing against tyranny, leaving the people to collect of themselves that this tyranny was the present government of the state'. (We may compare, that the tyranny of the Tsars was nothing compared with the tyranny of Lenin and Stalin.) 'Certainly the chief leaders were ambitious ministers and ambitious gentlemen: the

---

[1] In the Preface to this work the authors put forward the claim that the Prayer Book 'hath proved an offence, not only to many of the Godly at home [i.e. themselves], but also to the Reformed churches abroad.' q. G.B. Tatham, *The Puritans in Power*, 221. Their Directory appealed to far fewer, indeed to very few, at home; and the Calvinists abroad were no authority for the English Church.
[2] T. Hobbes, *Behemoth: the History of the Causes of the Civil Wars of England*, 192 foll. *The English Works*, ed. Sir W. Molesworth, vol. VI.

ministers envying the authority of bishops, whom they thought less learned; and the gentlemen envying the Privy Council, whom they thought less wise than themselves.'

Both men thought that the bishops were too hasty; they meant by them the Laudians; here they were right – Laud was an old man in a hurry to do good while he could. When we look at the Church of England today, we see that Laud won, in the long run. Both Hobbes and Selden agreed that the campaign against him in his own day was fuelled by lies. He was not a Papist, he was a firm Anglican (disliked as such by Henrietta Maria, but always upheld by Charles, also a good Anglican). Even the sainted Baxter circulated the dreadful Puritan lie that Charles I had given warrant to Irish Papists to carry out their massacre of 1641. Just as the upright Milton repeated twice the wicked lie that Charles and Buckingham had poisoned old James I (when they were all three only too fond of each other). We are driven to conclude, what Royalists thought, that Puritans had little care for truth.

Preaching meant propaganda from the pulpit; Puritan ministers preached up the overturn of government before it came about, and then preached up the war against the King in the field. Selden made the *mot* that 'if there had been no Lecturers, the Church of England might have stood and flourished at this day'.[1] So Laud was quite right to try and stop them – he could never succeed, they had the support of too many gentry, especially in London, East Anglia and the towns. Hobbes sedately corroborates the satirists as to their manner: 'they so framed their countenance and gesture at their entrance into the pulpit, and their pronunciation both in their prayer and sermon, and used the Scripture phrase (whether understood by the people or not), as that no tragedian in the world could have acted the part of a right godly man better than these did.'

Selden agrees: 'Preaching by the Spirit, as they call it, is most esteemed by the Common People, because they cannot abide Art or Learning.' We have already come across such exhibitionists as Stephen Marshall, Cornelius Burgess, Hugh Peters –

[1] *The Table Talk of John Selden*, ed. cit., passim.

[198]

there were a myriad of them, like gnats: 'Preaching, for the most part, is the glory of the Preacher, to show himself a fine man. Catechising would do much better.' Selden thought that the Presbyterians were better at gulling the people: 'Presbyters have the greatest power of any clergy in the world, and gull the Laity most.' This was what Milton came to see, after a little more experience of what the world was really like. Both Selden and Hobbes agreed that following the Scriptures meant simply following your own fancy; and the sceptical Selden went further to say, '*Scrutamini Scripturas* [Search the Scriptures]. These two Words have undone the world.' Expounding the Scriptures was but human invention: 'If I give any exposition but what is expressed in the text, that is my Invention; if you give another exposition, that is your Invention.' And that is all there was to it.

Selden had a moderate sceptical position, where Hobbes was not a sceptic, and in theory not a moderate (only in disillusioned practice). 'To have no ministers but presbyters, 'tis as if in the temporal state they should have no officers but constables.' Moreover, 'if there be no bishops, there must be something else which has the power of bishops, though it be in many; and then had you not as good keep them?' This was what Cromwell's brother-in-law, the scientifically minded Wilkins, told the Protector at the end of it all – that religion in England could not be run without bishops. At the Restoration he had the sense to accept the unpopular office; and as bishop of Chester set a good example of toleration. 'Holy Mr Baxter' wouldn't take it on when offered the bishopric of Hereford, in ecumenical spirit, at the Restoration.

We should take Richard Baxter as a representative figure in the main stream of Presbyterian orthodoxy: no one more so. He went through the whole experience, talking and writing all the time – chaplain in a Parliamentarian regiment, Cromwell disliked him as much too talkative; he couldn't keep his mouth shut, any more than Marshall and the rest. There are twenty-three volumes of merely his Practical Works, let alone the theology. He is still somewhat alive, with *The Saint's Everlasting Rest*, a Nonconformist classic, which still has its admirers (I am not one). Moreover, his long life, 1615-91, spanned the whole *épopée*, and lets us into its true inwardness: what people and things were really like, not just theorising about them.

Baxter first became famous for repressing the jollities of the ungodly in the streets at Kidderminster. His effective preaching offered an alternative excitement; as Selden says peaceably, 'He that takes pleasure to hear Sermons enjoys himself as much as he that hears Plays.' Here was a new excitement, along with a large increase in the number of preachers – an overlooked factor in the Revolution. Since Elizabethan days there was a much larger number of university graduates among the clergy, trained in academic disputation and disputatiousness – to Hobbes's express disapproval. This also meant a lot of what we should call black-coated, or white-collared, unemployment.[1] Another factor at work: Selden does not miss the point that 'Missing Preferment makes the Presbyters fall foul upon the Bishops'.

Censoriousness was an occupational disease of the Puritans, and when Baxter published the names of the ungodly from his pulpit they replied by erecting a maypole (with its Freudian significance) at his front door. Bridgnorth, where he was curate, he described as 'a dead-hearted, unprofitable people'[2] – were they any better for their town being ruined in the Civil War? At Kidderminster, 'the moral, not to speak of the godly, could be counted on ten fingers'. Coventry[3] simply swarmed with sects, with whom Baxter disputed – this offered crowded, popular entertainment. Only Baxter was right, everybody else out of step; even Cromwell – one of the godly, until he took over power – had 'some misunderstandings of Free Grace himself'. Baxter reflected years later, 'I was then so zealous [the Puritan word for self-glorification] that I thought it was a great sin for such that were able *to defend the country* to be neuters.' We notice the Puritan semantics, and also that it was sinful to be sensible.

They were inspired by the mystical moonshine of the Book of Revelation and the Book of Daniel to expect the imminent

---

[1] cf. Mark Curtis, *Oxford and Cambridge in the Reformation*.
[2] W.M. Lamont, *Richard Baxter and the Millennium*, from which quotations are taken.
[3] This is what the old English phrase 'sent to Coventry' means: an unattractive locale.

Millennium. Even Milton was touched by the revolutionary
excitement of the early 1640s to become something of a
millenarian: what they all got instead was the shock of 1660.
They were all borne up by signs and wonders and providences;
they were convinced that God was with them, simply by success:
'Look at circumstantials,' said Oliver Cromwell: 'they hang so
together.' There was the proof that the Revolution was God's
(sc. their own) doing. When it all crumbled in 1660, was that
also God's doing?[1] It drove Milton in upon himself, to do his best
work in his wish-fulfilment dream of *Paradise Lost*.

The world where the Pope is equated with Anti-Christ,
'where witches fly in the night and women give birth to monsters
[cf. Mrs Hutchinson's companions in New England]; and where
Jesuits peddle lies' (true enough, cf. the Jesuit Parsons)[2] – that is
the world of Richard Baxter, a world of millennial delusions,
and not as he was toned down to suit Victorian sentiment. His
contemporaries would not have recognised him as such an
eirenic figure; one of them dubbed his career as 'The Saint's
Everlasting Contention'. For of course Baxter could agree with
no one, not even himself from one year to another. An earlier
admirer who became disillusioned with Baxter's contradictions
– as in our time people became sick of Bertrand Russell's – noted
that 'while peace and concord figured prominently on the title
page of Baxter's works, the inside pages invariably breathed war
and disharmony'.

'The "undoubted truth" that the Pope was Anti-Christ was
"the principal means of preserving the Body of the people in an
aversion unto Popery".' When Baxter began to have doubts as
to the truth of this proposition also, it led to a breach with the
Cambridge Archangel, Henry More. 'Because Baxter had given
up believing in the Pope as Anti-Christ it did not follow – as
More seemed to think – that he had given up believing in
witches or ghosts', or in the apocalypse. Thereupon three
Protestant Millenarians – one of them the New England

[1] cf. Christopher Hill, 'Justification by success should logically mean condemnation by defeat.' *The Experience of Defeat*, 71.
[2] cf. 'Father Robert Parsons', in my *Eminent Elizabethans*.

Increase Mather – attacked Baxter. This was rather hard on 'holy Mr Baxter', who continued to toe the orthodox Puritan line, at least, on witches. 'Sure it were strange if, in an Age of so much knowledge and confidence, there should be so many score of poor Creatures be put to death as Witches, if it were not clearly manifest that they were such. We have too many examples lately among us to leave any doubt of the truth of this.' The fact that they were put to death is a proof that they *were* witches! After this piece of disgraceful thinking, apart from its inhumanity, we need not attach much importance to the theological nonsense they thought.

Actually Baxter himself disowned his book, *Holy Commonwealth*, to save his skin at the Restoration; and subsequent editors of his works were careful not only to omit what was damaging but by 'judicious *additions* to produce a more coherent and logical one'.[1] Thus the sainted Calamy is revealed as a liar too.

If this is what their spiritual mentors were like, up above, we can learn from their works what their followers were like, lower down. James Nalton, 'the Weeping Prophet', 'wept his way to a premature grave'. Mr Beal, a middle-class auditor of revenue, or tax-man, was a victim of pious melancholy: 'he threw himself out of his garret window, and died immediately'. Baxter kissed his dead body, saying 'he did believe his soul to be as happy as he did desire his own soul to be'. This was disapproved of as approving suicide; and when Joseph Southmead committed suicide, he quoted Baxter in support. Southmead first prayed with his family, then locked himself in a room and shot himself. Baxter himself was a hypochondriac, continually complaining of his health. One recommendation of his *Saint's Everlasting Rest* is that in Heaven, 'There will then be no crying out Oh my Head, Oh my Stomach, Oh my Sides, or Oh my Bowels.' Did any Puritan ever have much of a sense of humour? True, Oliver Cromwell was addicted to horse-play, but his temperament was rather hysterical.

A disillusioned campaigner summed up Baxter's career with some disgust.

[1]Lamont, 79–80; and 33 foll.

Once he was a Chaplain in the Army against the King. Kings did stink in the Nostrils of God, etc. When he writ his Saint's Rest, the wonderful appearance of God in that cause was an argument to prove the Truth of the Scriptures by. After all this, in the reign of Charles II, he turns Non-Resister, calls in his Political Aphorisms. Then he wrote the Book now printed, when a Tory; for he saith that the Person and Authority of the King is inviolable, that he cannot be Accused, Judged, Executed by any having Superior, etc.[1]

We may take this as a concise expression of the transition that took place from Revolution to Reaction.

As for 'Restoration bigotry' – neither Charles II nor Clarendon was a bigot: Baxter and his companions were given the chance of coming in with the Church, to run it on moderate lines. They turned it down, to go out into the dreary corridors of Nonconformity. It was the Restoration Parliament that then persecuted them – understandably enough, considering what the Cavaliers had had to put up with from them.

Religion and politics were closely interwoven in the Puritan Revolution, and we should look at the political side of things. We need not concern ourselves for long with those who gave the Revolution its original propulsion, or, like the grand leader, Pym, left the scene early. With grandees like Lord Saye and Sele or the Earl of Warwick, it looks much like the usual political game of Ins and Outs, and they were certainly not revolutionaries. Lord Saye and Sele wanted office, and he wanted money. Clarendon describes him as 'of a mean and narrow fortune, of great parts and of the highest ambition. . . . He was the oracle of those who were called Puritans in the worst sense, and steered all their counsels and designs.' His home, moated Broughton Castle, was not slighted, for he was on the winning side; when one goes there, up a back staircase is the little Council Room, where 'Old Subtlety' and his companions planned together their moves against the King before the Long

[1] q. Ibid, 91.

Parliament. Charles I tried to buy him off by appointing him to the Privy Council, commissioner of the Treasury, Master of the Court of Wards. When Parliament abolished the last office, Saye and Sele was awarded the handsome compensation of £10,000; according to a friend, he really got £14,000 from the former Treasurer's estate.

Not a revolutionary, 'he had not the least thought of dissolving the monarchy, and less of levelling the ranks and distinctions of men. He was as proud of his quality, and of being distinguished from other men by his title, as any man alive.' Deeply concerned in colonisation in America, he was made a commissioner for the government of the Plantations by Parliament. Another grandee of a Puritan imperialist was the Earl of Warwick, concerned with every aspect of colonial enterprise, in New England, Virginia, the West Indies: he got command of the Navy. Other grandees, Essex, Manchester, Fairfax, got well-paid commands in the Parliament's armies. They were not revolutionaries.

For men of that stripe we should look to the Levellers. Here also we should not think, anachronistically, of them as so extreme as their soubriquet would lead us to think. They were not in favour of equality, an impracticable dream, as Soviet Russia brings home to us. The Levellers were in favour of levelling down only as far as themselves – and they were middle-class men. In the usual human way they were out for themselves, not for those below them; they were all in favour of property, not the property-less, who had no stake in the state. What the middle-class Levellers wanted was a share in power, a voice in government; and to that end, naturally enough, votes, a wider franchise. That seems reasonable enough to modern minds; but their propaganda cry, and what they demanded was always Liberty. What did that mean in practice, in 17th-century circumstances? Army leaders like Cromwell and Ireton – and the Levellers were strong in the lower ranks of the Army – knew well that Liberty for the People meant Anarchy. (We can see the relevance of their fear of anarchy, in the break-down of social order, all round us today.)

On this they were at one with the philosophic Hobbes, whose view was that 'the People understand by liberty nothing but leave to do what they list'.[1] Milton also subscribed to the slogan, though no one fancied less leaving the People to do what they list. Everybody meant by it what suited himself and his own interests; as Selden says, 'We measure from ourselves, and as things are for our use and purpose, so we approve them.' As for people's opinions: 'Opinion is something wherein I go about to give reason why all the World should think as I think.' He adds, 'Affection' - by which he means inflexion, inclination, and at length party-affiliation - 'is a thing wherein I look after the pleasing of myself.'

Pleasing of the lower classes was not the idea of these leaders - just as today we are told by Communist Russia that Equality is a bourgeois deviation. Hobbes says, 'They levied taxes by soldiers, and to soldiers permitted free quarter, and did many other actions which, if the King had done, they would have said had been done against the Liberty and Property of the subject.' To this the question is put: 'What silly things are the common sort of people to be cozened as they were so grossly!' Hobbes's reply is the very cogent one - the People are not the only idiots. 'What sort of people, as to this matter, are not of the common sort! The craftiest knaves of all the Rump [Parliament] were no wiser than the rest whom they cozened.' For they themselves believed the nonsense they told the people, and 'especially the great haranguers, and such as pretended to learning . . . . A great part of them, namely the Presbyterian ministers, throughout the whole war, instigated the people against the King; so did also Independents and other fanatic ministers. The mischief proceeded from the Presbyterian preachers who, by a long-practised histrionic faculty, preached up the Rebellion power-fully.' 'To what end?' 'To the end that the state becoming popular, the Church might be so too, and governed by an Assembly. By consequence, as they thought, seeing politics are subservient to religion [sc. ideology], they might govern, and thereby satisfy their covetous humour with riches, but also their malice with power.'

Selden, from the other side of the fence, agreed with this diagnosis; and really our modern Pareto could not do better.

[1]Hobbes, *Behemoth*, 361-3.

When it was all over, Dryden summed it up in couplets:

> With them joined all th'Haranguers of the Throng
> That thought to get Preferment by the Tongue.
> Where Sanhedrin and priest enslaved the nation
> And justified their Spoils by Inspiration ...
> 'Gainst Form and Order they their Power employ:
> Nothing to Build, and all things to Destroy.

By far the most popular haranguer on the political side was John Lilburne, 'Free-born John', the 'True-born Englishman'. He was responsible for starting the rubbish, which Radical Cobbett took up later, about the Norman Conquest having enslaved free-born Englishmen. They were not historians: Clarendon was. But Lilburne was a prodigious, incessant pamphleteer; like Prynne, there was no stopping him. A born propagandist, he turned the pillory into a pulpit, whither he was followed by adoring crowds. A perpetual malcontent, who would not take even Yes for an answer, he turned against Parliament. Perhaps that was natural enough, for the Rump was not in favour of extending the franchise – oligarchy was what suited them, and they meant to maintain it.

So Parliament sent Free-born John to prison again and again, the Fleet, Newgate, at length the Tower, where Cromwell came to visit his former follower to urge patience and moderation: 'Parliament would speedily proceed with those things that would render the kingdom happy.' Parliament never did, and eventually his patience and moderation ran out; he dismissed the Rump as he had put paid to the Levellers in the Army with a whiff of grape-shot at Burford. Lilburne was able to tell him that the greatest crimes objected to in the King's time were righteous and even glorious compared with Parliament's actions. As Cromwell approached assuming more than monarchical power, Lilburne wrote to him, 'Assure yourself that if ever my hand be upon you, it shall be when you are in your full glory.'[1]

To the Lord Protector, assuming power in Westminster Hall, in purple robe, the Coronation chair brought from the

---

[1] q. P. Gregg, *Free-born John. A Biography of John Lilburne*, 237.

dismantled Abbey for the occasion, Free-born John was more in opposition than ever. There followed further imprisonment, then exile; then return permitted, house-arrest and surveyance. Utterly disillusioned of his early hopes of revolution, the bliss of that dawn having proved a false mirage, he turned to the inner Light and died a Quaker. He was buried in the churchyard of Bedlam.

Meanwhile his family in the North were doing well out of the Revolution – as was the case with another leading Leveller, John Wildman. The views of the Levellers were more clearly and radically expressed by him in the debates within the Army, and with its leaders, Cromwell and Ireton, at Putney and again at Whitehall. There was a danger of mutiny in the Army, and Cromwell was concerned above all to keep it united. The agitators put forward their demands in 'The Agreement of the People': a redistribution of Parliamentary seats according to numbers of population, the people to elect a Parliament every two years; their representatives to be subject to those who elect them. A blue-print for democracy, and of course quite unworkable. Ideologically: freedom of conscience to all; matters of religion 'not at all entrusted by us to any human power'; all laws to be equally binding, charters or property rights notwithstanding; all laws to be 'equal and good', since they were to establish 'our native rights'.[1]

In the ticklish circumstances of 1647, with the war won in the field and yet nothing settled, the Army leaders had at least to meet the Leveller leaders and argue the case with them. Cromwell, the pragmatic, practical man, described the proposals as impracticable, doctrinaire, and worst of all 'tending to anarchy'. Cromwell's son-in-law, Ireton – an able lawyer as well as soldier – argued that manhood suffrage was contrary to 'the fundamental and original civil constitution of this kingdom'. Further, 'no man hath a right to an interest or share in the disposing of the affairs of this kingdom that hath not a permanent fixed interest in the kingdom', i.e. property. A

[1]For all this v. Maurice Ashley, *John Wildman*, esp. cc. iii, iv. We could do with more biographies of interesting, ambivalent figures, such as Marchamont Needham, above all, of Selden and Waller, important and significant subjects.

property-less man – we might say, proletarian – was a menace to stable government, having no fixed interest in stability; the franchise therefore must be a property franchise.

A Colonel of the Puritan Rich family brought the argument home on a personal basis. 'You have five to one in this kingdom that have no present interest.' Some men have ten or twenty servants; if they are equal electors, those who have no 'interest' will choose those who have no interest. Thus the majority may, by law, destroy property; or law may enact that there shall be equality of goods and estates. This was looking forward a long way – it is only in our own anarchic time that it has come about.

The ground of dispute is so familiar, and the debate so trampled over by academic discussion, that it loses intellectual interest. Meanwhile, the really important point goes by default; namely, the great body of people, all are agreed, were 'neuters', hardly concerned in the struggle. Both Hobbes and Selden appreciated that. Hobbes typically says that the people did not understand the issues, 'or the reasons of either party'; and that 'there were very few of the common people that cared much for either of the causes, but would have taken any side for pay or plunder'.[1] The importance of this for us is that it shows that the war came about as the result of the split within the governing class, in their conflict for power, and that gave the opening to revolution.

Cromwell's problem eventually was how to halt it, without losing control of the Army. Always the politician, he proposed a compromise. Cromwell and Ireton refused to give way to what they firmly described as 'anarchy', or at first to have the King tried, as the Army wished. After the second Civil War, unleashed by the King's agreement (too late) with Parliament, they settled for the second, the trial of the 'Man of Blood', the King. That was no settlement either. As for the Levellers, Cromwell settled their hash by shooting a few of the agitators.

Wildman survived. His genius was for survival: he might have answered, like the Frenchman who, asked what he did during the Revolution, said, 'I survived.' He survived plotting against Cromwell, against Charles II and James II, to the Revolution of

---

[1]Hobbes, *op. cit*, 308, 166.

1688, when he was made Postmaster General. Plotting against William III, he managed to clear himself, and was then knighted. Sir John Wildman – the man of the Left became an Establishment figure: we recognise such happy consummations in our own demotic time.

The Leveller agitator, with his emphasis on freedom of conscience – 'in matters of religion that's preferred by us before life' – made a fortune in land speculation from confiscated Royalist estates.[1] So much land was thrown on the market, so many families ruined, that estates went for only ten years' purchase, or less. With his elastic conscience Wildman had a special line in managing 'Papists' interests – to pure Mrs Hutchinson's disgust: 'that cunning person, Major Wildman'. I find these real activities more rewarding than his ideas. He settled himself in an agreeable estate at Shrivenham. His son, having no children, adopted a kinsman, John Chute – or, more appropriately, Shute, one of Founder's Kin at All Souls, first Earl of Barrington, and ancestor of at least one of our College bishops. The Leveller himself, no believer, is buried in the odour of sanctity in the church there; when passing by from Oxford, I have called in before now to pay him my disrespects.

By some curious tendency of the human disposition Left-wing parties spawn groups further to the Left – perhaps from the force of dissatisfaction, conflicting egoisms or disputes about what they suppose themselves to 'think', or more meaningfully, from conflict of interest:

> The Saints engage in fierce contests
> About their carnal interests.

It was understandable therefore that the Levellers, who had no concern for the propertyless, should spawn a group who had: these were the Diggers, who called themselves True Levellers. They have been given an adventitious importance by Leftist

---

[1] cf. Christopher Hill, 'Wildman combined conspiracy with making money by land speculation . . . . It appears that Overton and Wildman at least were double agents, taking money from Thurloe [Cromwell's Secretary of State] as well as from Royalists.' *The Experience of Defeat*, 32, 33.

sympathisers in our time – quite anachronistically, for in their own time they had little or none.

These people were ingenuous, incipient Communists who felt called upon to squat on a few commons or heaths in various places to dig them up and grow food for themselves, since the earth was a common treasury for all, and should not belong to lords of the manor and such. One can sympathise with these poor folk, properly the objects of charity, impoverished by the unnecessary war (as both Hobbes and Selden thought it), crushed by indirect taxation, which had trebled or quadrupled owing to the war. 'No taxes, and all things governed by love', was their cry. *Utinam*! would it might be so, we might echo in our time, when taxation is simple confiscation levied upon those willing to work.

In the spring of 1649 – when a new heaven and a new earth opened up with the execution of a king – a group of hopeful Diggers occupied St George's hill at Walton-on-Thames in Surrey, and began to plant and sow. The movement spread a bit, to Cobham Heath, and one or two places in Puritan counties, Northamptonshire, Buckinghamshire and Bedfordshire. Nowhere was it a success; the Diggers were divided among themselves, they had insufficient resources, and by the winter they were begging for food and financial help. By the spring of 1650 all was over, and they were easily dispersed, ready to give up the attempt.

The ex-Communist historian, Christopher Hill, assures us that 'collective cultivation of the waste by the poor could have had the advantages of large-scale cultivation, planned development, use of fertilizers, etc. It could have fed the expanding English population. ... '[1] This is mere paper-talk, a mare's nest. More than 300 years after, with all the advantages of machinery, tractors etc, collectivisation of agriculture in Soviet Russia is no success – as Mr Hill must know. It is 'the magic of property that turns sand to gold', said the sensible agricultural expert, Arthur Young. Again and again Hill writes of these radical proposals as 'solutions': they were not solutions at all –

[1] C. Hill, *The World Turned Upside Down*, 104.

the very attempts to put them into practice showed how impracticable they were. And an historian especially has reason to know that they could not possibly work in the circumstances, the primitive techniques and conditions, of 350 years ago – they do not make a very persuasive showing even today.

The only interest in the Diggers' movement is a literary one: it threw up an interesting writer in Gerrard Winstanley, a more cogent mind, when all is said, than Leveller Lilburne, who, Hill allows, was 'notoriously volatile' (I should add, a notorious bore). Of course Winstanley began with the usual nonsense about Jesus Christ as the Head Leveller and the Norman Yoke from which we should be freed. More Radical than the political Levellers, who stopped short at votes for the middle-class, i.e. themselves, Winstanley was in favour of the confiscation of the lands of the Crown, aristocracy and the Church. That at least made sense – it was a mundane, terrestrial proposition – even if totally impracticable: 17th-century society could never work on that basis – it hasn't worked at all well even in 20th-century Russia or China.

With the failure of these experiments Winstanley saw that compromise in the pure milk of the word was necessary: a longer process of education and adaptation than he had envisaged would be necessary – just what all Communist countries have found, so that the objective seems destined ever to elude the true believers. It certainly eluded Winstanley, who by 1652, 'disillusioned and exhausted', gave up and is heard no more from, though he lived for another quarter of a century. The moral of his story is that people cannot feed themselves on illusions; he was on better ground in emphasising the necessity for manuring the land in his pamphlets.

These people quarrelled like mad among themselves. We get a piece of factual information from a candid Ranter, one Clarkson, who tells us:

> I made it appear to Gerrard Winstanley there was a self-love and vain-glory nursed in his heart – that, if possible, by digging to have gained people to him, by which his name might become great among the poor Commonalty of the nation. As afterwards appeared a most shameful retreat from George's Hill [NB no

saint] with a spirit of pretended universality: *to become a real tithe-gatherer of property.*[1]

So Winstanley was no better than the rest of the Saints – out for his own ends; and Clarkson puts his finger on another powerful motive with these people, the desire to call attention to their insignificant selves.

Both Millenarians and Fifth Monarchy men, with their Bible-mania, believed in the imminent Coming of Christ. It is not always possible to distinguish them, for there was much shifting of boundaries on the lunatic fringe; and we perceive that absurdity usually increases as we go further down the social scale. One point of distinction is, however, significant. Millenarianism had a general colouring: many people were touched, in the excitement of revolution, by apocalyptic expectations – Milton was for one. (We may compare Alexander Blok's 'The Twelve' – i.e. the Apostles – in 1917 Russia.) Millenarianism was just as rife in Puritan New England. When we read the unreadable writings of such a leading light as Cotton Mather we note his fatuous belief in the imminent Millennium in Massachusetts.[2] As also more disagreeable Puritan features, such as the ferocious hatred of witchcraft, and the usual illusions about supernatural appearances. Strict Fifth Monarchy men believed in force, *making* the Millennium come about. Harrison was a Fifth Monarchy man, who told Republican Ludlow, a mere Millenarian: 'the Saints shall *take* the kingdom.' As a Major-General, he was dangerous; as a Regicide, he was quite unrepentant on the scaffold: all had been done in the fear of the Lord. Another miscreant said that he had followed the preachers' preaching into battle, and would have been convicted of Sin if he had not done so.

What did the Fifth Monarchists believe?

They based themselves on the Book of Daniel, the poetical visions of which – with their literal interpretation of Holy Writ –

---

[1] *A Collection of Ranter Writings from the 17th Century*, ed. N. Smith, 182.
[2] cf. D. Levin, *Cotton Mather*.

they took factually. The four Beasts were taken to mean the empires of Babylon, the Persian, the Greek, and Roman. 'The last Beast had ten Horns, or kings, and a little Horn which destroyed several of the ten. After the destruction of the last Beast, the kingdom was given to the Saints for ever – the Fifth Monarchy.'[1] They were the Saints: the influence of the Calvinistic notion of God's Elect ran through all the sects, a common factor, otherwise they disputed with each other like hell. One ground of dispute among Millenarians was whether Christ would appear in person, or rule by deputy. Were they, as the elect, not called upon to inaugurate the Fifth Monarchy? 'The death of Charles I was a great triumph for the Saints, and they saw it as the beginning of a world-wide revolution in which all kings would be destroyed.'[2]

Milton was touched by the excitement, pointing out 'the *Precedency* which God gave this *Island*, to be the first *Restorer* of buried *Truth*' – Truth, of course, always meaning what the person using the word thought. And indeed, if this is what elect persons thought, perhaps simpler souls may be excused their nonsense, except that it should not have been given expression in the press. A freer press led to an outpouring of this kind of stuff; the press, the streets were filled with it, people prophesying (a lunatic feature of the time), astrologers like William Lilly being consulted and making money out of human credulity.

A foretaste of this kind of thing had been in evidence before 1640: it was multiplied thereafter. Edward Franklin (not, we hope, an ancestor of sensible Ben) proclaimed in church that his brother was God, his son Christ, and one Lady Dyer, the Holy Ghost. A Warwickshire female claimed to be 'the Mother of God and all things living'.[3] The lady who poured tar over the altar at Lichfield saw Archbishop Laud as the Beast from the bottomless pit. John Cotton, of authority in New England, saw the poor old English Church as the kingdom of the Beast, in his absurd *The Pouring out of the Seven Vials*. 'Arise' Evans arose in St Botolph's Bishopsgate and proclaimed that he was Christ: he

[1]B.S. Capp, *The Fifth Monarchy Men*, 23 foll.
[2]Ibid, 53.   [3]Ibid, 33 foll.

was a member of a Fifth Monarchist congregation. 'Several women claimed to be with child by the Holy Ghost' – following in the footsteps of the BVM – 'and that their child would be the Messiah. John Robins, a Ranter, claimed to be God the Father, and found a number of disciples.' A sect at Andover was led by a ropemaker – another Franklin – 'who had deserted his wife to live with Mary Gadbury, who sold pins and laces, and was accused of keeping a brothel'. They moved to Hampshire – obviously the land of Ham, Psalm 105 – where Franklin was able to announce himself as Christ, and about to establish the millennium.

John Rogers, one of the Lecturers poor Laud so much deplored, with reason, saw Charles I as one of the toes of the image in Daniel II, destroyed by Christ. Mary Cary, the Fifth Monarchy prophetess, was able to identify Charles I as the little Horn. Colonel Overton, a prominent military leader and friend of Milton, was a Fifth Monarchy man; his chaplain praised the murder of the King as 'God's work, done in God's way', which, after all, was much what Milton argued. In more mundane terms, it was Cromwell's work, more than anybody's; and when Overton opposed Oliver as Protector, he shut him up. Cromwell was not a Fifth Monarchy man, though several of his officers were, and expected that he would institute it – before the Protectorate came about in actual fact to disappoint them.

Between one area of popular delusion and another is a short step, and so many sects proliferated – like something you see when you turn up a stone – that Hobbes could not remember their names. Beside Baptists and Anabaptists there were Dippers; Adamites were liable to be nudists, as were some of the early Quakers; Muggletonians should perhaps more properly be called Reevites (the relationship between Reeve and Muggleton might be compared to that between the Prophet Smith and Brigham Young). In the 'world turned upside down' there were Seekers and Soul-Sleepers; the Ranters have left a more revealing portrait of themselves in their writings.

Ranters believed that 'Christ would return to earth to rule a kingdom of perfect Saints, and that this would occur in a violent Apocalypse in which all would be reduced to a base material and spiritual level',[1] i.e. their level. QED. We must not go in too much detail into their ideology (we need not call it religion), but observe it merely for its influence upon their conduct. The Ranter, Mary Adams, believed herself with child by the Holy Ghost, and that she would give birth to the true Messiah. Some claimed to be the Risen Christ, like John Robins and William Franklin, who had his Mary Magdalen in Mary Gadbury. One Webbe acquired the living of Langley Burrell in Wiltshire (of the more delightful Victorian memory of Kilvert) – a decent Anglican had been extruded. Here Webbe gathered a community 'which practised sexually licentious rites, under the alleged dictum that "there's no heaven but woman, nor no hell save marriage".' Mrs Attaway, influenced by Milton's doctrine of free divorce, made a getaway from her husband with a fellow-Saint to 'Jerusalem', regarding themselves as free from sin as much as Jesus Christ. Mary Cary was sure that the Resurrection of the Witnesses would occur in 1645, the conversion of the Jews in 1656, and the New Jerusalem come about in 1701.

In my early village days I have come across daft people who thought just like that: 17th-century phenomena are quite familiar down among the people. And so much for the ladies.

Laurence Clarkson is the most revealing of the Ranters, for he is the most autobiographical and ingenuously candid. He began by falling out with a Baptist. Himself was right for he found that the sanctified Baptist had 'lain with his landlady many times. And that he might satisfy his lust, upon slight errands he sent her husband into the country, so that he might lodge with his wife all night. Which being found out so smote his conscience that he shot himself to death in George Fields', i.e. St George's Fields, for Puritans would not soil their lips with saints' names, if they would with their landladies'.

However, Clarkson confessed that he was no better than the Baptist. At Canterbury (shades of poor Archbishop Laud!) he chummed up with

a maid of pretty knowledge, who with my doctrine was affected and I affected to lie with her, so that night prevailed and satisfied

[1] *A Collection of Ranter Writings from the 17th Century*, ed. N. Smith, 9. All quotations come from this illuminating work.

my lust. Afterwards the maid was highly in love with me, and as gladly would I have been shut of her, lest some danger ensued. So, not knowing I had a wife, she was in hopes to marry me and so would have me lodge with her again – which fain I would, but durst not. Then she was afraid I would deceive her, and would travel with me. But by subtlety of reason I persuaded her to have patience while I went into Suffolk – then I would come and marry her. Full glad was I that I was from her delivered. So, having got some £6, I returned to my wife.

Suffolk was good Puritan country. In London Mary Middleton was to hand, and 'Mrs Starr was deeply in love with me' – Clarkson must have had something, besides his preaching, to recommend him to females. 'Mrs Starr and I went up and down the countries [i.e. counties] as man and wife, spending our time in feasting and drinking. So that taverns I called the House of God, and the drawers Messengers, and sack Divinity. Reading in Solomon's writings it must be so.' So much for ideology – another consequence of their Bible-mania. At one meeting Dr Paget's maid 'stripped herself naked and skipped among them; but being in a cook's shop there was no hunger, so that I kept myself to Mrs Starr, pleading the lawfulness of our doings, concluding with Solomon all vanity.'

We might conclude that it was another consequence of the cult of freedom let loose among the people – witness Gerrard Winstanley's word, 'Freedom is the man that will turn the world upside down.' And we may contrast it with the hypocrisy of their Puritan rulers, passing the criminal Act of 1650 making adultery punishable with death. This Act was passed by the Commonwealth Parliament, of which a prominent member was Henry Marten, whom both Charles I and Oliver Cromwell agreed in naming as a notorious whoremonger. All very well for academics in the trend of today to try to explain the inhuman Adultery Act away – what rendered it inoperative was the residual good sense of the country at large, which was never with the Puritans.[1]

[1]cf. Keith Thomas, 'The Puritans and Adultery: the Act of 1650 Reconsidered', in *Puritans and Revolutionaries*, ed. D. Pennington and K. Thomas, 257 foll.

Clarkson is useful for information as to how these people made do. He made money not only by preaching his nonsense but also by publishing his tracts. He had a list of the faithful who sold them for him, while a Leveller publisher brought out Ranter trash. Abiezer Coppe was better known, and more to the fore with such offerings as *Some Sweet Sips of Some Spiritual Wine*. He put out that God would inaugurate apostolic, egalitarian Communism in 1650; he was out by some 300 years – if that is what we *are* witnessing today. Himself was a failure in this world, 'his parents disowned him, his wife and children left him' – I fancy he was mad. (Why republish his nonsense today?)

The most mystical of Ranter writers was one Bauthumley – I suppose Bottomley (though not Horatio).[1] A quarter-master in the Puritan Army, he was cashiered for blasphemy, and his tongue pierced under their military law, not Laud's. He was more interested in Angels than in this world. 'For the Angels I see the world as much mistaken in them, for I really see that man lives in the Angelicall nature, and that Angels are also Spirituall and in man.' And so on endlessly, for it is characteristic of nonsense to be self-generating and thus without end.

A trendy professor of Eng. Lit. at Oxford describes Bauthumley–Bottomley's *The Light and Dark Sides of God* as 'a neglected masterpiece of 17th-century devotional prose'. He rants on, 'Ranter writing is more serious, engaged and impassioned and, from the viewpoint of expression, more adventurous than any of the accredited "literature" that emanated from the Civil War years – than, say, the Cavalier lyrics, which students are still encouraged to think of as one of the war's chief cultural achievements.'

[1]For the benefit of readers today I should explain that Horatio Bottomley was a notorious public figure earlier this century. The proprietor of several popular journals, he cheated his readers, mostly poor folk, poor fools, of hundreds of thousands of pounds. He was a most successful mob orator, with a famous peroration on the Prince of Peace that never failed to bring the house down. Before the meeting he would look round the platform to estimate what the audience would cough up: if £1000, then 'they shall have the Prince of Peace'. He was ultimately jailed by the efforts of the Astors (themselves Christian Scientists).

Where is the professor's sense of *quality*? – always the first thing to go in time of revolution. What about Milton or Marvell, Hobbes or Clarendon; or the Royalist writers cited earlier in this book? – I leave it to the intelligent reader to assess. Yet the professor admits that the Ranters 'were impelled beyond the limits of coherence'. Is incoherence then an estimable quality in literature, let alone to recommend to students?

Such are the trendy fashions of demotic society today; however, an historian appreciates that fashions are transitory, only art survives time.

Ranters shaded into Muggletonians; and such is human idiocy that the last Muggletonian – still committed to the imminent Second Coming of Christ – died only as recently as 1979; with him we are still in touch with the 17th century. Thus the Muggletonians formed a distinct sect, whose preposterous beliefs amused Lytton Strachey, while they have been given serious consideration today by a group of scholars interested in Puritan phenomena.[1] The sect really began with a London tailor, one Reeve, to whom 'God spoke', they say (and do they believe it?) on three successive days in 1652, 'appointing him one of the Two Last Witnesses. In Revelations II God said that he would give power and prophetic gifts to these Witnesses in the last days before the Beast ascended from the bottomless Pit.' The other Witness was Reeve's cousin, Lodowick Muggleton, who outlived Reeve and assumed leadership – though the ingenuous authors consider, with a familiar academic cliché, that Reeve 'has been very much underestimated'.

Where 'Fifth Monarchists looked to the Second Coming of Jesus Christ, Quakers believed that he had already come, the Muggletonians had the indisputable authority of the Two Witnesses'. Revelations II had promised, 'I will give power unto my two witnesses, and they shall prophesy one thousand two hundred and three score days clothed in sackcloth.' These

---

[1] Strachey wrote a comic essay on 'Muggleton' in *Portraits in Miniature*. Three academics treat the subject more seriously than it deserves: Christopher Hill, Barry Reay and William Lamont, *The World of the Muggletonians*, from which all quotations are taken.

witnesses were cousins Reeve and Muggleton, and the powers they claimed marked them off from other sects, though other beliefs they had sufficiently in common. They could at a pinch raise from the dead – and one or two people claimed that they had so risen. They had a very effective power in their prophetic gift of cursing. It is well known that a rat may be 'sent to Coventry', ostracised by the group or herd, and simply give up and die from the experience. Reeve and Muggleton once visited an unbeliever in prison, one Robins, and cursed him so effectively that he yielded up his reason, if that is the word for it, to theirs.

It is probable that their damning and cursing was the most effective weapon in their armoury; it was proof of their authority from God. Muggleton said that cursing did him more good 'than if a man had given him 40 shillings'. 'Muggleton claimed that 'he and Reeve had damned "near upon a thousand" in a ten-year period. He reported spectacular results: dumbnesss, sickness and even death. The Quakers had some explaining to do when two of their number died after they had been cursed by the Prophet.' Reeve died in 1658, leaving the pitch to Muggleton, who had more spiritual gifts ready to hand. He knew more about God than the Apostles had ever known; and, though fear of the Devil 'hath caused many men and women to lose their wits', he Muggleton (like a Muggeridge today) could release them from such fears; 'knowing the Devil, where he is and what he is, he is not afraid of him'. The future Quaker, John Crook,[1] nearly went out of his mind from being persecuted by the Devil following him about in the shape of a big black dog.

Thus Muggleton 'dominated the group, maintaining order either through personal persuasion or pressure (often by letter), or in the last resort by excommunication' – like the leader among the rats. And he could command a faithful following: there was Christopher Hill, a heel-maker – perhaps he was more usefully employed in making heels than in researching into such people's nostrums; a butcher from Cambridge, that hot-bed of Puritanism (the Dictionary defines hot-bed as 'a mass of

---

[1] Not, we hasten to add, the former editor of *The Times Literary Supplement*.

decaying vegetable matter'); a woman schoolteacher and an ironmonger's wife; and a mad Irish gentleman from Cork.

Muggleton's ministrations were reasonably profitable to himself. For five years Reeve had received a 'quarterly Necessity' from a well-wisher – as Clarkson had been kept by weekly subscriptions from his fellows. Apart from regular stipends both Muggleton and Reeve received gifts of food and money, though Muggleton delicately preferred to call them 'love tokens'. 'Gifts varied from several pounds to a few pence, or came in the form of a hat, linen, cider, pippins, cheese, sugar, and even a barrel of pickled limes.' Muggleton got a bit of property from one credulous widow, and nearly £90 – multiply by fifty or sixty – from one legacy. A Scotch Quaker gave him, more circumspectly, 10s 6d; Muggleton gave him a blessing, then a cursing – for it really did not amount to much – but did not return the gift.

One sees that, humans being what they are, nonsense often brings in more cash than sense.

Once more, too, one of these sects will betray a bit of information about his fellows. We learn that Ranter-Muggletonian Clarkson became involved in loan speculation after the Fire of London and died in a debtors' prison. We are instructed by the three witnesses on the subject of Muggletonianism that 'an attractive characteristic of the group is its absence of spiritual élitism', and 'no corseting of divine truths'. Elitism means quality, or the sense of it: is the absence of it ever attractive? And do these authors regard the nonsense of the sect as 'divine truths'?

John Reeve's starting point, 'the divine call which he received, is for most of us today difficult to accept'. I regard this as disingenuous. 'What then was the doctrine communicated to John Reeve? It was not very illuminating. God said, "Look into thy own body, there shalt thou see the Kingdom of Heaven and the Kingdom of Hell." ' Several times these authors recite the formula 'God spoke', 'God announced to John Reeve' – as if they believed it themselves. Why do they not say outright, and honestly, that it was rubbish? And sometimes harmful rubbish: even the editor of the Ranters' Writings admits that their language is full of violence and carnage – not good for people. It is better that such lunatics should be suppressed, and the Restoration proceeded to suppress them; certainly Soviet Russia (*pace* Christopher Hill) would shut them up.

Muggleton told the Quakers, 'God is well pleased in the damnation of those that I have cursed.' He had by the time of the Restoration 'damned 103 persons, nearly half of whom were Quakers. He blessed 46 [only] to eternity' – no doubt his following.

Everybody had it in for the Quakers – and that is difficult to understand today with so ultra-respectable and relatively[1] harmless a body. To understand it we have to go back to the beginnings – the historical approach is the only way. To put it shortly, they were the most obvious and visible trouble-makers in the localities wherever they appeared. They made disturbances in church by interrupting the services; and again in the streets, where some of them did strip themselves naked, even if George Fox did not, though credited with doing so in the market-place at Lichfield, crying 'Woe unto the wicked city of Lichfield!' They were a greater nuisance than anyone to the local J.P.s; for when had up in court for making a disturbance they rejected the jurisdiction of the court, refused to take an oath or to take their hats off. Edward Billing, a Cornish Quaker who was part-founder of New Jersey (also an unreliable speculator) was summoned before a court in Westminster Hall. He swore that, if compelled thither, it would be in sackcloth and ashes. When summoned, he ripped down his breeches with a string to reveal that he was indeed clothed in sackcloth; when his steeple hat was removed from his head there fell a cloud of dust and ashes which he had crammed into it. Really, how daft these people were!

---

[1] I say 'relatively' for the adherence to an absolute 'peace at any price' principle is not a possible political stance, when confronted with the Hitlers of this world, or his (and the Kaiser's) Germany. As C.R. Attlee lays down, reasonably and rationally, absolute pacifism is an individual position, not a practical political one – as many Quakers have realised, and resisted Hitler's Germany 1939-1945, as their seniors resisted the Kaiser's, in 1914-1918.

Foremost among the early Quakers was James Nayler, George Fox's senior by some seven years. His preaching and appearance attracted the crowds. He had been a quarter-master in Lambert's horse, and fought at Dunbar. An officer who heard him shortly after said, 'I was struck with more terror by the preaching of James Nayler than I was at the battle of Dunbar'.[1] He was a handsome man, with a remarkable resemblance to the popular portraits of Christ, which he carefully cultivated, long hair parted in the middle, fancy beard, etc. This was too much for the palpitating hearts of the womenfolk, who were willing to worship him, and rather too much for Nayler himself, whose head was turned by it.

Touring the West Country, he made an entry into Bristol based on Christ's entry into Jerusalem: men bare-headed preceding him, women on either side leading the horse on which he was mounted (it should have been an ass), singing 'Hosanna, Hosanna', and crying 'Holy, Holy, Holy, Lord God of Israel'. The women knelt to him; the authorities were alarmed by the crowds that followed him. He was arrested and sent up to London, where he very narrowly escaped the death-penalty for blasphemy from Cromwell's Parliament. Instead, this humane assembly ordered him to be whipped for hours through Westminster and the City, pilloried, then his tongue pierced with a hot iron, and the letter B branded on his forehead.

The poor man was left in such a mangled state that there was an intermission before he was pilloried. There a Quaker merchant placed a placard over his head, 'This is the King of the Jews.' The victim 'put out his tongue very willingly, but shrinked a little when the iron came upon his forehead'. His Quaker follower stroked his hair, kissed his hand and 'strove to suck the fire out of his forehead'. He was then taken back to Bristol for further whipping on horseback, tied face to tail; then back to London for imprisonment in Bridewell. 'He came out sobered and penitent', and returned to Bristol to make public confession of his offence – though at his examination before the luminaries of Cromwell's Parliament (which had no legal

---

[1]For Nayler, v. the account in *Dict. Nat. Biog.*

jurisdiction) he pleaded that he did not know his offence. The Speaker told him that he would know it from his punishment.

He was a Yorkshireman, with wife and children at Wakefield, whom he had deserted years before for the excitements of the Puritan Revolution, serving in the Parliamentary Army, preaching and touring, writing tracts, cooperating then quarrelling with his junior in the cause, George Fox, with whom he did not see eye to eye. Exhausted and ill, he was making his way back to the North when he fell by the wayside, where he was robbed by footpads. Found and succoured by local Quakers, he shortly died, aged about forty-three.

The leading Quaker controversialist was Edward Burrough – and they were in continual controversy with everybody. Burrough was against 'Free Willers, Fifth Monarchists, Ranters, Seekers and Waiters, Levellers and Presbyterians'.[1] Only himself was right – this was true of all of them. 'He also expended much energy in criticising Richard Baxter and John Bunnion' (or Bunyan), neither of whom could stand Quakers. How right Laud had been to try and stop the mouths of all these fools, impossible as the task had been!

Burrough admired Cromwell, however, for his iconoclasm. 'Alas for him! who was once a great instrument in the hand of the Lord to break down many idolatrous images. And did not once his children, officers and his brave soldiers and Army pull down all the images and crosses and suchlike Popish stuff wherever they met it?' The early Quakers were by no means the peace-loving folk of later legend. Howgill, the devoted correspondent of holy Margaret Fell, wrote in 1655, 'Spare none, neither old nor young; kill, cut off, destroy, bathe your sword in the blood of Amalek and all the Egyptians and Philistines, and all the uncircumcised.' Bible-mania again. Burrough himself wrote, 'All that would not that Christ should reign, slay them before him . . . . The Saints shall rule with a rod of iron.'

The earlier George Fox was by no means the man of peace he was subsequently made out to be. Like Burrough he several

---

[1]Christopher Hill, *The Experience of Defeat*, 143-4; from which all quotations come.

times urged Cromwell to undertake a military crusade in Europe. When Cromwell had already led the country into an imperialist war with Spain, hoping to snatch the West Indies (it was a fiasco), the saintly Fox told the Protector that 'if he had minded the work of the Lord as He began with thee at first, the Hollander had been thy subject and tributary, Germany had given up to have done thy will, and the Spaniard had quivered like a dry leaf. The King of France should have bowed his neck under thee, the Pope should have withered as in winter, the Turk in all his fatness should have smoked.' The Puritan Protector should 'let thy soldiers go forth, that thou may rock the nations as a cradle'.[1]

What more jingoistic sentiments can one imagine, from so unlikely a source? Can one imagine Charles I or Laud expressing such sentiments? But this was the unadulterated spirit of Puritanism. Even after Cromwell's death Fox wrote a paper 'for the inferior officers and soldiers to read, urging them to conquer Spain: "If ever you soldiers and true officers come again into the power of God, which hath been lost, never set up your standard till you come to Rome." ' Still in the months before the Restoration Fox was breathing fire against Spain: 'as you have killed with the sword, so shall you perish by the sword. Now shall the Lamb and the Saints have the victory.'

We see that George Fox was a more forceful character than usually thought. Of course he was a remarkable man, *sans peur et sans reproche*; he seems to have had no interest in sex, regarding procreation as 'beneath me'. This was appropriate for one who considered himself as the Son of God. He was an apocalyptic, believing that he lived 'in the last times. The day doth appear that God will rule in his Saints above the heathen. Now is the Son of God come.' Though the fact has been slobbered over in later Quaker historiography, and written out of Fox's writings, he did regard himself as the Son of God. Christ gives power to those who receive the Light (Fox's of course) 'to become the Sons of God; and this would bring them into unity with the Son and the Father.' Thus 'Christ is risen' (in 1653), 'Christ is come' – here is a difference from all the other sects still expecting him.

[1] q. Ibid. 157–8.

However, 'the Quakers survived, prospered and rewrote their history – as Muggleton rewrote the history of the sect which he took over'.

How did they do it?

Essentially, after the collapse of all the lunatic hopes and expectations we have been studying, by sensibly accepting the fact. Fox, who had a reserve of common sense underneath his beliefs and a marked capacity for organisation (like Wesley), imposed strict discipline upon his community, excommunication for departures from it; and the over-riding principle of non-resistance, the 'peace principle'. All this worked, as it did in a more preposterous form with Muggleton and the Muggletonians.

We learn that 're-writing the history meant demoting James Nayler, once regarded as at least Fox's equal – as Muggleton to a lesser extent demoted John Reeve in re-writing Muggletonian history' – or Baxter, we may add, in re-writing himself up. 'Fox appears to have exercised a *de facto* censorship', wise man. And the re-writing continues today in his sect: 'many interesting omissions are noted in the 1925 edition of the *Short Journal*, including miraculous healings, Fox claiming to be the son of God, Fox as Moses, Fox's Millenarian expectations and his Cromwellian sympathies, the loan of a meeting-house to soldiers. Fox's *Book of Miracles* was suppressed; William Penn and Thomas Ellwood do not refer to miracles to which Fox himself attached considerable significance.'

This was regular enough with these Puritans, as we saw with Baxter. 'Muggleton doctored Reeve's works, and Toland pursued a similar policy when he edited Ludlow's *Memoirs* for publication', after the Revolution of 1688. He omitted much of the Millenarian stuff Ludlow had believed in as much as the others.

Enough is enough. We recall the words of that sensible, very rational man, Clement Attlee, when confronted by the heirs of Stalin – Malenkov, Mikoyan, Molotov and the rest in Moscow, but *sotto voce*, 'Sick of the lot of them.'

# VIII

## The Ruined Age

The Caroline culture we portrayed earlier may be said to have
been decapitated with the King; and we have seen that what
came to the fore in its place stood in some contrast. Historians do
not go in for might-have-beens; on the other hand, we must not
regard what happens in history as inevitable, though much may
be unavoidable. Both sides were taken aback by what
happened. Parliament had the game in its hands in 1641, the
King reduced to agreeing with its demands. Hobbes thought
that at that point there need have been no war; others agreed,
'the cause too good to be fought for'. Then the Left-wing pushed
beyond reason to invade the undoubted sphere of the Crown's
prerogative, and to attack the Church. This raised up a party to
support King and Church, when Parliament never expected
that he would be able to raise an army in their defence. Wars
break out when each side misjudges the other; and the conflict
gave the opportunity for the scum to rise to the surface, all the
odious phenomena of revolution we have also been studying.

It was thus with the French Revolution, that pattern of
modern revolution. In 1789 and up to 1791 there was a
remarkable degree of good will in the country in effecting
overdue reforms, lightening feudal burdens on the exploited
peasantry, etc. Then the Left-wing pushed further to attack the
just rights of the Church, with the Civil Constitution of the
clergy, and divided the nation from top to bottom. There
followed the usual revolutionary horrors: the September
Massacres, the guillotining of King and Queen and many of the
best people in France, even poets like André Chénier and the
great scientist Lavoisier; popular savagery, like the 'noyades' at
Nantes, the drowning of boatloads in the Loire. The revolutionaries then ate each other up. In our time we have observed
similar phenomena in Russia and China, on a much vaster scale

in accordance with the low level of demotic society. Even in 17th-century England and Scotland quite a number of Puritan revolutionaries ate each other up. Who are we to regret them?

Things might have worked out more reasonably, and yet ... One cannot avoid the feeling that some kind of explosion was in the air, from the way that unquenchable Puritan fervour had been building up, against the established order in Church and state, for the past three generations. The issue does not need to be argued, with tedious academicism, for events showed that the established order of monarchy and the Anglican Church represented the only consensus upon which England could be run, let alone governed. The Puritan Revolution, by its abject failure, proved that.

The really difficult point worth considering is whether it had been necessary.

Sometimes in history grievous events *are* necessary. It is obvious to any thoughtful observer of modern Germany's history that the terrible chastening the Germans received in their Second War - recorded in art in Strauss's tragic *Metamorphosen* - was necessary to bring them to their senses. Stalin thought to excuse his appalling misdeeds by claiming that they were 'necessary' - I do not accept that, certainly not on that scale.

In the English Revolution - one should say Puritan Revolution, as Gardiner did, for it included Scotland, which indeed began it - it was the split within the governing class that gave the unquenchable revolutionaries their chance. *They meant to have their way*, against everybody else, against the great majority of the nation, who didn't want them and didn't like them.[1] One can see that in the Puritans who left the country to have their way in New England - no use for anybody else, no arts to speak of, subjugation of people to their bleak discipline, with the characteristic phenomena of Bible - and witchcraft - mania.

[1]Christopher Hill and Co., authors of *The World of the Muggletonians*, urge upon us the value of studying the reactions of ordinary people. But these fanatics were not ordinary people, they were the minorities of a minority. Ordinary people enjoyed themselves (or not), went to church, and shut up.

In England things were moving to some sort of confrontation - could it have been contained? The out-dated personal government of Charles I was not strong enough, and certainly not efficient enough, to contain it; the first breath of crisis, the rude air from Scotland, blew the gaff. By 1640 the monarchy could not govern without support from Parliament, the representative organ of the governing class, let alone against it. Some measure of agreement was indispensable, and moderates like Clarendon thought it possible. We can only conclude that the moderate, middle way is always best. The odious experience of the Revolution taught everybody a lesson, i.e. everybody capable of learning (James II was not); and that was what came about in 1660. Should the experience have been necessary? Well, humans are what they are; as the philosopher-bishop Butler wrote in the next century, the more rational 18th-century: 'Things are what they are, and their consequences will be what they will be: why should we *seek* to be deceived?'

Caroline culture in the arts for the most part went underground, or went abroad - to return, with a different inflexion, naturally much affected by French influence, with the Restoration. We may look at the vestiges that remained at home.

In architecture, nothing to show. Inigo Jones's talented nephew, John Webb, was completely frustrated in his career for, naturally, no public buildings were built. We have only a few designs from him, notably for Greenwich Palace, one wing of which was built at the Restoration, the rest by Wren later in the century. Sir Roger Pratt, a distinguished amateur-architect, was out of England till 1649 and thereafter 'lived as a private gentleman'. He built beautiful Coleshill, which I am fortunate enough to have known: recognisably influenced by Inigo Jones, splendid double stone-staircase, with Renaissance roundels occupied by Caroline busts. Destroyed in our time by a fire, through a careless workman - a characteristic feature of the age (what do *they* care?) - leaving a naked blow-lamp aflame. Now nothing there but a vacant space, the splendid piers by the road (painted by Piper) leading to vacancy.

Meanwhile Christopher Wren, 'that miracle of a youth', growing up at Wadham College, was the product of an ultra-

Royalist family; his father, Dean of Windsor, imprisoned, while his uncle, the Laudian bishop of Ely, was in the Tower throughout the Interregnum. Cromwell, who longed for settlement, would have released him, but Laud's faithful disciple would accept nothing at Cromwell's hands. Thurloe, Cromwell's Secretary of State, decided, 'Settlement I fear is not in some men's minds, nor ever will be.' Settlement – it needs no argument – was never possible on *their* basis.[1]

Distinguished works of Caroline art were the Mortlake tapestries, in which Charles I had taken a personal interest as in all worthwhile artistic matters. Dissatisfied with merely copying previous designs, he had called in the artist Clein to execute new ones. The most splendid set were wrought for the King; bought by the Spanish ambassador at the Commonwealth's wretched sales, they ultimately fetched up in Paris. 'The Royal set, even in its present faded condition, gives perhaps a truer impression of the magnificence which Charles I loved than any surviving works of the period, except for the grandest of Van Dyke's portraits and the Rubens ceiling at Whitehall.'[2]

'The quality of the work produced at Mortlake and the prestige it enjoyed – it was perhaps the best tapestry of its time in Europe – is proved by the competition by connoisseurs for the pieces belonging to the King when his goods were sold after his execution. Cardinal Mazarin was a particularly eager buyer, and acquired before his death at least eleven Mortlake sets.' But the factory was dying, without the King's patronage and support; by the Restoration it was down to only twenty-five workmen, and within a couple of decades it was dead.

Painting, an inextinguishable art, continued on a much smaller, less public scale, confined almost wholly to portraits, and at best miniatures. Samuel Cooper, best of the miniaturists, had genius; but that was small beer compared with Rubens and Van Dyke, or even the *Sturm und Drang* of Dobson. As Lord General, and then *de facto* head of the state, Cromwell had to be painted; Cooper rendered the finest portrait of the great man,

---

[1]q. *The Interregnum: The Quest for Settlement, 1646–1660.* Ed. G.E. Aylmer, 1.
[2]M. Whinney and O. Millar, *English Art, 1625–1714*, 127 foll.

painted with penetrating sense of character, and an appropriate honesty, as against the idealised romanticism of Van Dyke. Painters learned what they could from his technique, but the grandeur and the magic had gone.

Robert Walker, 'the favourite painter of the Parliamentarian party', was in truth a pedestrian painter.[1] 'In Walker's portraits of the Parliamentarians their heads are attached to bodies lifted straight from Van Dyke .... His dry and impersonal use of paint and his lack of any feeling for colour were perhaps well suited to his sitters' – very appropriate we might agree. 'The portraits of Cromwell and of Colonel Hutchinson and his wife are convincing studies of the Puritan temperament.' They are 'equally typical of Walker's limp lay-figures against pedestrian backgrounds. The portrait of the Colonel is so bad as to verge on caricature' – good enough for a Regicide anyway.

Other practitioners were inferior even to Walker; but one of them, Edward Bower, is memorable for the pathetic interest of his portrait of the King at his 'trial'. 'Bower made drawings in Westminster Hall on that tragic occasion; the portraits are documents of great value and their *gaucherie* enhances their pathos.'[2] The King's insuperable dignity, the withdrawn regality, the sadness all come through. Many copies were made for loyal houses all over the country – we have one at faithful Sheldon's All Souls; they must have played their part in the cult of the martyred King, along with the *Eikonbasilike*, which gave thousands some idea of what he had been like, as against the lies of Milton.[3]

These things looked forward to the great reversal that would certainly take place – as Clarendon never doubted that it would. Things were preparing themselves for renewal. The young Lely had arrived, to copy Van Dyke. He painted a portrait of the King with his three young children, presumably when they were allowed to visit him in confinement at Hampton Court – a reminiscence of Van Dyke's group of the children, a work which Lely had acquired with other works at the Commonwealth's sales. By 1654 he was judged already 'the best artist in England',

[1]Ibid, 77.    [2]Ibid, 80.
[3]cf. my *Milton the Puritan*, 133 foll.

but it would be the Restoration that would give him his grand opportunity, to portray the whole Court of Charles II.

Meanwhile the real Caroline world was in exile, abroad, or no less so at home. Abroad, the Court continued, with Charles as Prince then King at St Germains, his mother installed at the Louvre. There was a government in being, an embryo ministry, around the secretaries of state, Clarendon and Sir Edward Nicolas, with a complement of Court officials, chaplains etc. It is all well documented, but we have an intimate close-up through the eyes of John Evelyn in his Diaries.[1] He was a representative Royalist gentleman, in touch with many sides of life, social and scholarly, both scientific and religious; intelligent, highly observant, a normal well-balanced family man.

He spent some years of the Interregnum abroad, and in Paris he had plenty of company – any number of peers and Royalist gentry; among poets and intellectuals Waller and Hobbes; among painters Michael Wright, who was to have a future after the Restoration. Above all were the Anglican clergy, for Evelyn was exceptionally pious; regular Prayer Book services, communions and sermons by Dean Cosin, Dr Earle, Dr Morley and others to become bishops in the restored Church. Evelyn's father-in-law, Sir Richard Browne, was the Court's diplomatic representative to the French Court; and throughout the nineteen years of his service as such he provided a chapel where the Church service and ritual were unfailingly observed and attended. In all that time of tribulation there were very few converts to Rome, in spite of the efforts of the proselytising Queen Mother – and that put paid to the Puritan lies that Laudianism was Papistry in disguise.

When Evelyn returned to England in 1652 he toured round to see the state of the country. On Whitsunday at Rye, 'I went to church, heard one of their Canters, who dismissed the assembly rudely and without any blessing. I was displeased when I came home that I was present at it, having hitherto kept my ears incontaminate from their new-fangled service.' At Reading,

---

[1] cf. *The Diary of John Evelyn*, ed. E.S. de Beer, esp. vols II and III, from which quotations are taken.

'saw my Lord Craven's house at Caversham now in ruins, his goodly woods felling by the Rebels'. At Oxford, 'the glass windows of the cathedral, famous in my time, much abused'. Sir John Glanville's mansion at Broad Hinton burned by the Royalists to prevent it being garrisoned, himself now living in the gatehouse. At Worcester 'we found the cathedral extremely ruined by the late wars'.

He confirms what we know had happened at Lincoln. Soldiers 'went in with axes and hammers, and shut themselves in till they had torn off some barges full of metal . . . brasses which were on the gravestones, so as few inscriptions were left. The malicious soldiers had, beside the sacred places and churches, exceedingly ruined this city.' In London 'I went to see York House and gardens belonging to the former great Buckingham, but now much ruined through neglect.' 'His Majesty's house at Eltham, both palace and chapel in miserable ruins, the noble woods and park destroyed by Rich the Rebel' – this was Colonel Nathaniel Rich, a Fifth Monarchy fanatic. Evelyn found Colchester 'swarming in sectaries' – it had long been a hot-bed of Puritanism.

In December 1656 Evelyn attended a last sermon at St Gregory's in London, 'after which Cromwell's Proclamation was to take place that none of the Church of England should dare either to preach, administer sacraments, teach school etc on pain of imprisonment or exile. So this was the mournfullest day that in my life I had seen, or the Church of England herself since the Reformation.' Inoperable to the fullest extent, and exceptions were made; Cromwell's own daughter was married to Lord Fauconberg by the Prayer Book rite – was this hypocrisy, or did they think it otherwise inoperative?

Evelyn had brought over a Frenchman to the Church, and got an Irish bishop to ordain him, both deacon and priest on one day; 'I paying the fees to his lordship, who was very poor and in want, to that necessity were our clergy reduced.' There was some danger of the succession of bishops dying out in the long Interregnum, what with consecrations and ordinations being proscribed. 'August 3, 1656: to London to receive the Blessed Sacrament, and was the first time that ever the Church of England was reduced to a chamber and conventicle, so sharp was the persecution. The parish churches filled with sectaries of all sorts, blasphemous and ignorant mechanics usurping the pulpits everywhere.'

In Puritan Suffolk this upper-class gentleman of education and taste, a connoisseur and scholar, made his first acquaintance with Quakers. 'At Ipswich I had the curiosity to visit some Quakers there in prison, a new fanatic sect of dangerous principles. They show no respect to any man, magistrate or other, and seem a melancholy proud sort of people, and exceedingly ignorant. One of these was said to have fasted 20 days; but another, endeavouring to do the like, perished the 10th, when he would have eaten but could not.'

The observance of Christmas Day, and the feasts and Saints' days of the Church was everywhere prohibited. On Christmas Day 1657 Evelyn went to the private service in the chapel of Exeter House, conducted by the distinguished preacher, Dr Gunning, subsequently to become Bishop of Ely.

> Sermon ended, as he was giving us the holy Sacrament, the chapel was surrounded by soldiers: all the communicants and assembly surprised and kept prisoners by them, some in the house, others carried away. In the afternoon came Colonel Whalley, Goffe and others from Whitehall to examine us one by one; some they committed to the Marshal, some to prison. When they examined me why, contrary to an Ordinance made that none should any longer observe the superstitious time of the *Nativity* (so esteemed by them), I durst offend, and particularly be at Common Prayers, which was but the Mass in English, and particularly pray for Charles Stuart, for which we had no Scripture – I told them we did not pray for Charles Stuart, but for all Christian kings, princes and governors.... These wretched miscreants held their muskets against us as we came up to receive the Sacred Elements, as if they would have shot us at the altar; but yet suffering us to finish the Office of Communion, as perhaps not in their instructions.

This takes us right into the heart of things as they really were, as late as Cromwell's last year. It is all very well to give him credit for being 'tolerant', as historians are wont to do. He was more tolerant than stiff-necked Presbyterians, tolerant of his own Independents and some other Puritan deviationists; but to proscribe Anglicans and Roman Catholics was to proscribe the majority of the nation. The miscreants Whalley and Goffe were two Regicides, who were lucky to escape to New England, where they were concealed and cherished by their fellow brethren in Christ.

Their day was coming to an end: we can read the collapse of their régime as witnessed by Evelyn. April 1659, 'the new Protector Richard slighted, several pretenders and parties strive for the government: all Anarchy and confusion, Lord have mercy on us.' May: 'the nation was now in extreme Confusion and unsettled, between the Armies and the Sectaries; and the poor Church of England breathing as it were her last, so sad a face of things had overspread us.' By October, 'we had now no Government in the nation, all in Confusion; no Magistrate either owned or pretended but the Soldiers, and they not agreed.'

Evelyn himself took a hand, and tried to persuade his old school-fellow, Colonel Morley, Governor of the Tower, to bring back the King; but he was afraid to risk his neck. Evelyn risked his by publishing his bold *Apology* for the King, in November 1659, when it was still 'capital to speak or write in favour of him. It was twice printed, so universally it took.' And a great deal more sense it made than the doctrinaire discussions of the Rota, the bees in Harington's bonnet, or the desperate pamphlets of Milton. The return of the King, and the old Constitution, was the obvious and only way out, in the collapse of order, the self-evident bankruptcy of the Puritan Revolution. We now know that General Monck, loyal man, had already made up his mind to that effect before he marched South, to bring it about with singularly little fuss and no more bloodshed.[1] That showed.

Evelyn had letters from the Queen Mother to present at Whitehall, though he could not at once get through for the 'infinite concourse of people. It was inexpressible the greediness of all sorts, men, women and children, to see his Majesty and kiss his hands, in so much as he had scarce leisure to eat for some

[1] cf. Maurice Ashley, *General Monck*.

days, coming as they did from all parts of the nation.' Whitehall was put in order again, for the reception of a king, apparently by Webb; Windsor Castle, i.e. the Royal apartments there, the eastern quadrangle and private chapel, were repaired and reconstructed on a handsome scale by Hugh May.

A month after the King's return, Evelyn noted, 'Goods that had been pillaged from Whitehall during the Rebellion, now daily brought in and restored upon Proclamation – as plate, hangings, pictures, etc.' Christmas Day at Westminster Abbey that year was very different; 'I received the Blessed Sacrament, the Dean [Dr Earle back from Paris] officiating. The Service was also in the old cathedral music.' Pepys had already noted the restoration of the organ, and the crowd flocking to hear it. At New Year Evelyn went to see a Beaumont and Fletcher play, at a new theatre in Lincoln's Inn Fields.

We see that everything was back.

Shortly the carcases of the three revolutionary leaders responsible for Charles I's death were exhumed (it is like the relegation of Stalin from the holy place beside Lenin in the Red Square), 'dragged out of their superb tombs in Westminster among the kings to Tyburn, and hanged on the gallows . . . . Thousands of people, who had seen them in all their pride and pompous insults, being spectators: "Fear God and honour the King, but meddle not with them who are given to change." '

The King set out to meet the Queen Mother and bring her back to Somerset House, which needed a vast amount of restoration to make it once more habitable for a queen. In April 1661 came the Coronation in all full traditional glory, though the plate and regalia had had to be made anew. And the Scotch Covenant was publicly burnt by the common hangman in various public places in the City where it had been received.

Literature too came into its own, though with a different voice, with again (and understandably) French influence coming to the fore after the Restoration. The notorious defender of Puritan enormities – now blind, though lucky to have escaped execution – was driven in upon himself to write an epic of the Paradise that was Lost. It needed a mighty genius to 'justify the ways of God to men' after the crumbling of all their hopes and expectations, and no less the exposure of how foolish they had been to entertain them. (Hobbes and Clarendon, Selden and Butler, all in their different ways had been more sensible in their views of human nature – above all, no illusions, *surtout point de zèle.*) And the heroic spirit that accomplished this great work wrote his own autobiography into *Samson Agonistes.*[1]

It is perhaps not paradoxical that the greatest poet of the age (after the collapse) and the greatest man of action should have been Puritans; for it was the experience of the Revolution that raised them to extraordinary heights. (Where would Lenin have been but for the collapse of Tsarist Russia and the Revolution of 1917?) It is a fascinating might-have-been to think what Milton might have become, if he had not been infected by Puritanism when young, at both school and university. Suppose if he had been at Oxford like his father, the scholarly musician from Christ Church? Puritanism was not in keeping with the inner side of Milton's nature, the sensuous, feminine make-up of the beautiful youth, the ambivalent love of Charles Diodati, the unmistakable emotion, to anyone of perception in such things, of the *Epitaphium Damonis.* But Milton, intellectually the most arrogant of men of genius, would not have it; he *made* himself a Puritan: hence the harshness, the sense of strain, the insistence on the inferiority of women – so unlike the Cavalier poets.

His collection of his earlier poems in 1645 received little attention; it was his prose that made him notorious, especially the tracts arguing for freer divorce. The most upright and moral of men was traduced by his own fellow Puritans as a polygamist: that should have taught him what humans are – and it did contribute largely to his disillusionment with the Presbyterians. Milton too learned what hypocrites they were, and wrote them down as such.

Royalist writers put paid to Puritan pretences, not only the hypocrisy they found so sickening but to its religious nonsense, Calvinism, the Westminster Assembly of Divines, Predestin-

---

[1]The professor of Eng. Lit., who was so enamoured of Ranter Writings, cannot even see the obvious autobiographical inspiration of *Samson Agonistes*, and with entire lack of chronological sense or literary judgment places it before *Paradise Lost*, when it obviously comes at the end of Milton's life. cf. *The Poems of John Milton*, ed. John Carey and A. Fowler.

ation and all. The very word 'nonsense' occurs again and again in Cowley's early satire, *The Puritan and the Papist*.

> Religion is a Circle: men contend
> And run the round in dispute without end.

To the Saints:

> your Non-sense well enough might pass,
> They'd never see that in th'Divine Looking-glass ...
> Nay, White,[1] who sits in the Infallible Chair
> And most Infallibly speaks Non-sense there ...
> You must have *Places*, and the Kingdom sway.

Just what Hobbes and Selden said, and Cowley wrote again what Hollar noticed when he returned to the saddened country: people were

> Like men bewitched, they know not how, nor why.

Cowley was a far more popular poet than Milton, more widely read and admired. (The cult of Milton came later, and was in part due to his continuing Nonconformist readership – another reason why Dr Johnson had it in for him.) Cowley was a most intelligent and precocious young man, already publishing when a schoolboy at Westminster. People who are mesmerised by sentimental, heterosexual love-poetry – of which the anthologies give us far too much, neglecting more intellectually rewarding matters – overlook Cowley's prose, his Essays, or his remarkable *Discourse concerning the Government of Oliver Cromwell*.[2] It traverses his whole character and career, in prose and verse, and gives one a most discerning portrait as intelligent Royalists saw him at the time – not mere abuse, but appreciating the greatness of the man, the astonishing pinnacle to which events raised him, and which he (alone) had the force to control.

[1] John White, the patriarch of Dorchester, member of the Assembly of Divines, active in the Puritan colonisation of Massachusetts.
[2] Abraham Cowley, *Essays, Plays and Sundry Verses*, ed. A.R. Waller, 342 foll.

Cowley begins – like Clarendon's History – with England as it was before the war:

> When all the riches of the globe beside
> 　Flowed into thee with every tide;
> When all that nature did thy soil deny
> 　The growth was of thy fruitful industry;
> When all the proud and dreadful sea,
> And all his tributary streams
> A constant tribute paid to thee,
> When all the liquid world was one extended Thames.

Ship Money had rebuilt the Navy: 'Why take arms against taxes of scarce £200,000 a year, and to raise them himself to above £2,000,000? To quarrel for the loss of three or four Ears, and strike off three or four hundred Heads?' Later, with Cromwell's imperialist wars, taxation reached unheard-of heights: ''tis madness in a nation to pay £3 millions a year for the maintaining of their servitude under Tyrants, when they might live for free for nothing under their Princes.' In the end it was the refusal of the civilian population, in especial of the City of London, to support the financial burden of the Army any longer that brought the military dictatorship to an end – for that was what the Parliamentary Revolution had come to. (As the French Revolution ended in Napoleon, and the hopes of the Russian Revolution ... in nuclear militarism.)

Cowley saw that Cromwell was lucky in the time of his demise, for the country was turning against the heavy burden. 'He seemed evidently to be near the end of his deceitful glories; his own Army grew at last as weary of him as the rest of the people. And I never passed of late before his Palace ... without reading upon the gate of it, *Mene, Mene, Tekel, Upharsin.*' At the end Cromwell seems to have lost faith, the certainty that merely continual success had given him – as Lenin in his last years was worried at the way his Revolution was working out. 'No usurpation, under what name or pretext so ever, can be kept up without open force; nor force without the continuance of those oppressions upon the people, which will at last tire out their patience, though it be great even to stupidity.' The last word is in place too.

Cromwell had indeed had extraordinary luck, Charles I all the ill-luck; and luck is an element necessary to historic greatness. 'No man ever bore the honour of so many victories at the rate of fewer wounds or dangers of his own body. And though his valour might perhaps have given him a just pretention to one of the first charges in an army, it could not certainly be a sufficient ground for a title to the command of three Nations.' How had he done it? 'That he did all this by Witchcraft?'

That was what the simple-minded were apt to suppose. Cromwell, like Hitler, certainly had magnetism; Andrew Marvell speaks of the 'piercing sweetness' of his eyes – and Hitler had mesmeric eyes. Cowley appreciates that Cromwell had 'extraordinary diligence', where Charles I found politics a bore. Cromwell's 'infinite dissimulation' is then diagnosed, the turns and twists in policy, the contradictions, the reversals of previous positions he had taken up. The humble instrument of Parliament, for ever protesting his loyalty to it in his letters to the Speaker, eventually put his foot through it; the Commonwealth's general brought the Commonwealth to an end.

This month he assembles a Parliament and professes himself with humble tears to be only their Servant and Minister; the next month he swears By the Living God that he will turn them out of doors; and he does so in his princely way of threatening . . . What shall we call this? . . . there is no name can come up to it.

It was bold unquestionably for a man, in defiance of all human and divine laws – and with so little probability of a long impunity – so publicly and so outrageously to murder his Master. It was bold with so much insolence and affront to expel and disperse all the chief partners of his guilt and creators of his power.[1] It was bold to violate so openly and scornfully all Acts and Constitutions of a nation; it was bold to assume the authority of calling, and bolder yet of breaking, so many Parliaments . . . . It was bold above all boldnesses to usurp this tyranny to himself, and

[1] cf. Stalin's disposal of nine out of eleven members of Lenin's Politburo.

impudent above all impudences to endeavour to transmit it to his posterity.

This recital cannot be denied: it was what had happened. But *how* had it all come about? Cowley does not deny Cromwell's astonishing achievement.

> Do but consider seriously and impartially with yourself what admirable parts of wit [i.e. intelligence] and prudence, what indefatigable diligence and invincible courage must of necessity have concurred in the person of that man who, from so contemptible beginnings and through so many thousand difficulties, was able not only to make himself the greatest and most absolute Monarch of this nation, but to add to it the entire conquest of Ireland and Scotland ... and to crown all this with illustrious and heroical undertakings and successes upon all foreign enemies.

Royalists were apt to put Cromwell's success down to his extraordinary talent for dissimulation, which he called up at will with himself, all the more effective for taking in others. No doubt it was partly unconscious self-deceit, so strong in Puritans: no man goes so far as he who knows not whither he is going. An observer of his last attempts to come to terms with the King – on Cromwell's, the Army's terms, of course – concluded that by that time he saw himself as the Second Person in the kingdom, if not residually the First.

What is obvious is that Cromwell was not only a first-class soldier, but a first-class politician. He was therefore a pragmatist, who made the most of every opportunity with which events presented him. Just as the run of success with which Hitler had built up his power: re-militarisation of the Rhineland, the Saar, annexation of Austria, then Czecho-Slovakia ... Cromwell took his unbroken successes, as Puritans did, as 'providences', signs that 'God' was with them. On this basis, 'God' ultimately was not in 1660.

It was the Puritanism in the great man that was so distasteful, and offended persons of discrimination that contrasted the regal dignity of the tragic King. 'I must confess that by these arts, how grossly soever managed – as by Hypocritical praying and silly preaching, by unmanly tears and whinings, by falsehoods and perjuries, he had at first the good fortune to attain his ends.' Some of the Protector's little ways were not such as to appeal to those used to the dignity of Charles I's Court. 'Today you should see him ranting so wildly that nobody durst come near him, the morrow flinging of cushions, and playing at snowballs with his servants.' Antics such as these would not have put off his chaplain, Hugh Peters; while the posturings and wrestling with the Lord, the preachings and prayers, kept him in the odour of sanctity with the Sects – good politics:

> What croaking Sects and Vermin has it sent
> The restless nation to torment?

Samuel Butler gave the returned Charles II, the 'merry monarch', and his court much amusement with his *Hudibras*, which had marked success and continued to be read well into the 18th century. Butler had been very close to his subject, for one of the few things this rather morose and reserved man tells us about himself is that in Hudibras and Ralph he had a West Country Puritan knight and his servant, with their endless religious argy-bargy, under observation. *Hudibras* is a classic, but Butler's Satires and his prose Characters offer no less close a record of the distasteful features of the Puritan ascendancy.

Butler had a coarse nose for every kind of hypocrisy, deceit and self-delusion; and pays his respects to 'An Hypocritical Nonconformist' in both verse and prose; evidently such subjects gave him a kick, as they did Swift later. 'He cries down the Common-Prayer, because there is no ostentation of gifts to be used in the reading of it, and labour in vain that brings him in no return of interest and vain-glory from the rabble: who have always been observed to be satisfied with nothing but what they do not understand.'[1] This is precisely the point that Selden makes, whom Butler must have known; for at one time he served the Countess of Kent, to whom Selden may have been secretly married.

[1] Samuel Butler: *Characters and Passages from Note-Books*, ed. A.R. Waller, from which quotations are taken.

Butler has a low view of the genus Politician: he 'is a speculative statesman, student in the liberal art of free government, that did all his exercises in the late times of cursed memory at the *Rota*.' That was the club of doctrinaires that met under the inspiration of Harrington to discuss the useless nostrums for government which the Restoration put an end to. Butler practically equates a politician with 'A Leader of a Faction: he is a great haranguer, talks himself into authority and, like a parrot, climbs with his beak . . . . He gathers his party as *Fanatics* do a Church.' 'A Fifth Monarchy man is one that is not contented to be a Privy Councillor of the kingdom of Heaven, but would fain be a Minister of State of this world. He fancies a *Fifth Monarchy* as the quintessence of all governments, abstracted from all Matter and consisting wholly of Revelations, Visions, and Mysteries.'

As for Truth:

> Things determined by most voices
> Are not the greatest truths, but noises . . .
> To fight for Truth is but the sole dominion
> Of every Idiot's humour or opinion.[1]

Selden again – but indeed it is only common sense.

> There's nothing so absurd or vain,
> Or barbarous, or inhumane,
> But if it lay the least pretence
> To Piety and Godliness,
> Or tender-hearted Consciènce,
> And Zeal for *Gospel-Truth* profess,
> Does sacred instantly commence.
> And all that dare but question it, are strait
> Pronounced the Uncircumcised and Reprobate.[2]

This was what intelligent people had had to put up with – intolerable enough from inferiors at any time, it was unbearable

---

[1]Samuel Butler: *Satires and Miscellaneous Poetry and Prose*, ed. R. Lamar, 184.
[2]Ibid, 85.

when they got up into the pulpits and had the say-so. Their betters were now getting their own back.

'Saint Paul was thought by Festus to be mad with too much learning, but the Fanatics of our times are mad with too little. He chooses himself one of the Elect, and packs a Committee of his own Party to judge the twelve tribes of Israel .... He calls his own supposed abilities Gifts – he owes all his Gifts to his ignorance.' As for an early Quaker, he is dangerous, 'a scoundrel Saint, of an Order without Founder, Vow or Rule; for he will not swear, nor be tied to anything but his own humour. He is the link-boy of the Sectaries, and talks much of his Light, but puts it under a Bushel, for nobody can see it but himself. He believes he takes up the Cross in being cross to all mankind. You may perceive he has a crack in his skull by the flat twang of his nose, and the great care he takes to keep his hat on, lest his sickly brains should take cold at it. They abhor the Church of England, but conform exactly with those primitive Fathers of their church, in which they observed the very same ceremony of quaking and gaping now practised by our modern Enthusiasts at their Exorcisms, rather than exercises of devotion.'

And the Puritan world was full of witches:

> There's forty female witches sent to jail
> Condemned and executed for one male.

It is curious that the most striking and popular contrast between the Caroline world and that of the Puritan Commonwealth and Protectorate should receive no comment from historians of the period. All the more so since it concerns witchcraft, a subject which has attracted attention almost *ad nauseam* of late. Why have they missed the point? Perhaps for one reason that Agatha Christie was well aware of: people usually miss the significance of the obvious.[1] The point is more than obvious, it is striking: there were very few witchcraft prosecutions under Charles I and

---

[1] A point she made in regard to my findings regarding Shakespeare; e.g. that Mr W.H. was the publisher, T. Thorp's man, not Shakespeare's at all; the unanswerable identification of the Dark Lady, etc.

Laud, but the persecution rose to a ferocious height during Puritan rule. Surely there is some connexion here.

We do not need to go into the disgusting phenomena of the subject, the physical oddities or deformities of the poor crones who were fancied, often fancied themselves, as witches. We knew a good deal about that sort of thing in Cornish village life early this century. The *D.N.B.* tells us that 'the special mark of a witch was a third pap or teat on the body: this was searched for with little regard for decency. The accused were placed cross-legged, and bound if necessary, in the middle of a room, with a hole in the door for their "imps" to enter by. They were kept for 24 hours, sometimes for over two days without sleep or food. The next measure was to walk them about till their feet were blistered. Thus confessions were produced. ... ' If the inquisition failed, 'the victim was thrown into a pool; the possession of a teat prevented the body from sinking, hence those who swam were hanged.'

We do not need to argue such a matter, we want only the figures. It is perfectly true that belief in witchcraft was fairly general; ordinary humans will believe anything – the point is what they do, whether they kill for the nonsense they believe. That is how societies are to be judged. The detailed figures and graphs available show that the county of Essex was responsible for a larger number of witches condemned than any normal county, in the Elizabethan and Jacobean period.[1] During the personal government of Charles I, from 1628-37, the number of prosecutions sank remarkably to a mere 10; but from 1638-47, during the Commonwealth, the number rose to 45. In Kent the number during the first period is a mere 2; in the second period, Puritans in the ascendant, it rose to 37. In Sussex under Charles I's personal government – none. Surely there is a significant correlation here: very few witchcraft prosecutions under the King, large numbers under the Commonwealth.

These local figures are corroborated by such as are obtainable for the Assize Circuits: for 1628-37, 10; but for 1638-47, 50; for 1648-57, 60. These figures are far from complete; but the trend they show is unmistakable, and what we know from all other

[1] *Witch Hunting and Witch Trials*, ed. C.L'E. Ewen. Graphs and figures, 101-110.

evidence. The Puritan ascendancy coincided with a cruel increase in the persecution of poor old women as witches, few men.

In 1644 Matthew Hopkins, of the godly county of Suffolk, began his three-year career as 'Witch-Finder General'.[1] His experience began with seven or eight of them who lived near him at Manningtree; they met together with others every six weeks to commune with the Devil on a Friday night. He claimed that he procured the condemnation of twenty-nine women in a batch; 'four were brought twenty-five miles to be hanged for sending a Devil, like a bear, to kill him in his garden.'[2] One cannot trust Hopkins's figures, they need checking; he claimed that sixty were hanged in Essex in one year, and others at Norwich. The 18th-century investigator, Hutchinson, specifies 16 hangings at Yarmouth in 1644, 15 in Essex and 1 at Cambridge in 1645, nearly 40 at Bury St Edmunds in 1645-6, and many in Huntingdonshire in 1646. Hopkins extended his operations over four Puritan counties, Essex, Suffolk, Norfolk, Huntingdonshire, which he found rewarding soil, with the aid of a known Puritan, John Stern, and a woman searcher.

> Not only were such measures sanctioned by local authorities, but a special commission of oyer and terminer was granted for the trial of witches at Bury St Edmunds, Suffolk, in 1645. Serjeant John Godbolt was the judge. Samuel Fairclough, who was on the commission, preached two sermons on witchcraft at the opening of the assize. Edmund Calamy the elder was also on the commission. A clergyman who had preached against the 'discovery' was forced to recant by the commission.

He had the authority of Baxter, the humbug, against him.

Judge Godbolt was another Suffolk man, no doubt godly, for he was promoted to the bench by the vote of the Commonwealth Parliament. Samuel Fairclough enjoyed the patronage of the rich Barnardistons, leading Puritan gentry of Suffolk, who encouraged opposition to Laud's reforms in the Church; and

[1]For his career v. *Dict. Nat. Biog.*
[2]Names and sentences of these poor creatures are given by Ewen, 107-8.

Fairclough had acted in accordance. Edmund Calamy, of that saintly Nonconformist family, had also given trouble, as a 'lecturer' in both Suffolk and Essex, then in London. He was one of the Smectymnuus authors who attacked Bishop Hall's moderate claims for episcopacy. A member of the Westminster Assembly, he was very intolerant of the Independents. At the Restoration he was offered the see of Lichfield and Coventry, in good ecumenical spirit: his wife made him refuse it. He preferred to be one of the 'Ejected': no loss.

We learn that, at the hands of this godly commission, 'the number of victims was very large'. In justice we must remember that not all those accused were hanged; if they confessed – and it was a regular ploy to drive them to confession by ill treatment – then they were liable to be hanged. We must remember too that these were Puritan counties. Down in un-Puritan Cornwall the persecution of Anne Jeffries was very unpopular and created a scandal. 'Confined in Bodmin gaol in 1645 she was starved by order of a Justice of the Peace, who kept her in his own house "a prisoner, and that without victuals".'¹ That J.P. happened to be the Puritan John Tregeagle, the foster-brother and steward of the Parliamentarian leader, the second Lord Robartes. I recall too that the judge at the infamous session in Essex, where Matthew Hopkins procured so many victims, was the Earl of Warwick, of that Parliamentarian family which descended from the Catholic Lord Chancellor Rich, who perjured himself to bring Sir Thomas More to the scaffold.

Mr Keith Thomas tells us that from the 1620s 'the number of trials on the Home Circuit fell off sharply, to rise spectacularly during the Hopkins period, and then to dwindle to a mere trickle for the rest of the century .... The most acute period was 1645-7, when the campaign led by Matthew Hopkins and his associates resulted in the execution of several hundred witches in Essex, Suffolk, Norfolk and neighbouring counties.'² I think that this is correct, for the figures show that the persecution

¹Ewen, 65-6. 'Withholdment of food as a means of persuasion also was ordered by authority.'
²Keith Thomas, *Religion and the Decline of Magic*, 457.

continued after Hopkins's disappearance in 1647. Mr Thomas concludes, with mild meiosis, 'it is a fair guess that his career would not have been permitted in the Laudian period'.[1] Why not? – The answer is pretty clear: because Laud and Charles I were not Puritans. It is true that James I was a believer in witches; but he was theologically a Calvinist, with all that that implied in personal acquaintance with the Devil, such as all Puritans enjoyed. In modern terms, they had a complex about the Devil. Charles I and Laud were not Calvinists, they were anti-Calvinist, based on the moderate Anglican theology of Richard Hooker. Mr Thomas bothers himself needlessly with the question of how to explain the witchcraft-mania. 'For reasons which have never been explained, Essex was particularly subject to such persecutions.'[2] But so was Suffolk. These were specially Puritan counties, and the rise of persecutors of witches in Puritan East Anglia needs no explanation.

Nor does the fact that the civilised Anglican rule of Charles I and Laud coincided with no such persecution require any explanation.

Once more Samuel Butler has got the right of it in *Hudibras*:

> Has not this present Parliament
> A Leger to the Devil sent,
> Fully empowered to treat about
> Finding revolted *Witches* out?
> And has not he within a year
> Hanged three score of 'em in one shire?
> Some only for not being drowned,
> And some for sitting above ground,
> Whole days and nights, upon their breeches
> And feeling pain, were hanged for *Witches*.
> And some for putting knavish tricks
> Upon green-geese and turkey chicks,
> Or pigs, that suddenly deceased
> Of griefs unnatural, as he guessed:
> Who after proved himself a *Witch*,
> And made a rod for his own breech.

[1] Ibid, 500.    [2] Ibid, 451.

There was something in that; for, charged with being a witch himself, he *swam* and, it was said, was hanged for one as he had brought so many others, almost all women, to hanging.

But what a horrid thing the Puritan world was, when all is said, mentality and all!

Naturally the Restoration produced a reaction against all this – after the rule of the Saints, the frivolity and licence of Charles II's Court, with its French overtones. In the literary sphere we see the somewhat sour cynicism of Samuel Butler – what wonder? Marvell wrote no more romantic lyrics, but turned to satire too, satire, in his case, of the Court and its policies. There is a world of difference between the exquisite beauty of Milton's earlier poetry and the hardened heroism of the later. And satire reached its highest art with Dryden. Theological disputation continued (as always), but relegated to a secondary place. More important was to explore the real world of nature with the scientists; in the Royal Society Charles II and Prince Rupert – returned to live in his apartments in the Round Tower at Windsor – took a personal interest. The new King, after his appalling experiences, did not believe in much, with a residual, contingent hope in Catholicism, though he had the sense to keep it secret. (The brilliant and very rational Halifax guessed the secret.)

Painting flourished once more, if not to the height of Van Dyke. Music returned to Court and in the cathedrals and churches, a number of the old musicians who had survived the bleak years reinstated in their former offices. Architecture, with the grand opportunities of an expanding society opening up, reached nobler heights than ever before, with the genius of Wren to meet the demand. It is significant that his first big commission came from the Church – the Sheldonian Theatre at Oxford. Sheldon had kept the light of Anglicanism glowing all through the dark days, and with his organising ability had aided the extruded clergy – as Juxon and others did – and kept contacts going for the day of the return. After Juxon, who had been on the scaffold with the King at Whitehall and, broken, had accompanied the body to Windsor, Sheldon now occupied Laud's throne, with equal ability and more tact. It must be added that, after the trials they had been through, tested in the fire, the Restoration bishops were a distinguished lot.

The Restoration represented a reaction also in a less favourable sense. The Elizabethan age up to the threshold of the Puritan Revolution had witnessed a notable educational expansion in the founding of grammar schools all over the country – now no more, or hardly at all. I dare say that the governing class, now re-united, had had enough of their products. The universities had been much too lively, sizzling with academic disputes – which Hobbes constantly inveighed against. He thought that their disputatiousness, their addiction to classical authors with their republican cult of liberty, etc had formed an important element in the intellectual ferment that had overturned society. We note the beginnings of educational reaction and decline. The universities become more restricted to being seminaries for the staffing of the restored Church – itself more restricted, sending out the trouble-makers to their own hole-and-corner conventicles. Schools begin their long decline – to reach their nadir at the beginning of the nineteenth century.

In the parishes all over the country the gentry ruled once more, and without question; squire, with his ally (often dependent), the parson, ruled the roost – no more nonsense from butcher and baker and candlestick-maker. The motto of the Restoration may be said to have been, Never Again! The governing class had learned its severe lesson too.

On the secure basis of monarchy, Parliament, Church – founded firmly on squire and parson everywhere in the country, society held confidently together right up to the social revolution, the anarchy and breakdown of our own time. On that satisfactory foundation, sociologically speaking, England went forward to create a commercial Empire across the seas, a great place in the world.

Christopher Hill concludes his *Experience of Defeat* with the words: 'Now that England's historical destiny has whimpered to its end [is he perhaps pleased that it should be so?], we may perhaps see that the defeated had points to make which got forgotten in the two-and-a-half centuries of imperial success.' Had they? What were they? He continues, 'We would no doubt define an equal commonwealth differently; but it might seem a more attractive ideal than being the top of nations.'

We may well ask, is the world the better for what has taken its place? for the withdrawal in India? or everywhere in Africa? We must admit now that what it stood for was altogether more civilised; what has taken its place altogether more barbarous.

Fortunately there is the United States – an extrapolation chiefly from the British Isles – with other English-speaking countries, daughters of that Empire, to take its place in the appalling world of today.

# Appendix
## on 'The Puritan Revolution'

A recent essay by Dr John Morrill, 'The Religious Context of the English Civil War' (*Transactions of the Royal Historical Society*, 1984), brings admirable order into the unnecessarily confused academic discussion of the causes of the war. He corroborates the view of its great historian, S. R. Gardiner, that it was the religious issue that made the war, that it was a *Puritan* revolution, the Puritans the revolutionaries.

He corroborates Clarendon too on the internal peace in the years before: 'what is remarkable about early Stuart England is the absence of political violence: virtually no treason trials, no rebellions, a decreasing and localised incidence of riot, no brigandage.' Such a contrast with appalling conditions on the Continent: in a notorious phrase of today people 'never had it so good'.

Then what accounts, he asks, 'for the pressure for war in 1642?'

It was not the political issue; there was no desire to overthrow the monarchy, merely to clip the excrescences of monarchical power – Ship Money, the prerogative courts, forest laws and such unpopular pressures. In Parliament, 'in contrast to the debates on religion, the rhetoric of the constitutional debates was conservative, restorative'. And in the country in general there was no confrontation with the Crown, as at Westminster: that was 'entirely absent in the provinces'.

What was revolutionary was the determination of the Puritan minority, quite unrepresentative of the country at large: 'the Elizabethan settlement was to be dismantled and reconstituted' on their basis. Time had proved that the Elizabethan religious settlement, the Anglican Church, represented the best consensus, as between Left and Right, Puritans or Catholics, practicable in the circumstances. The experience of the Puritan Revolution proved that this remained true: there was no holding England together on the Puritan basis – Scotland had a different settlement (which the English detested). The aim of the radicals was 'not simply of ecclesiastical reconstruction, but of building a godly commonwealth' – *their* 'godly commonwealth'. We have seen throughout this book that their 'vision' was not only inherently deplorable, but turned out to be nonsense, as the event proved.

However, like revolutionary minorities, they were venomously determined. In contrast with the comparative moderation shown in regard to political objectives was the vicious attack on the Church: at once '13 bishops impeached in 1640, and the overlapping group of 12 impeached in December 1641 .... In those early weeks when 20 clerics were hounded, only two civil officers were investigated.' There were illegal interferences with individual clergymen and in the parishes, with parish uses, 'followed by widespread iconoclasm, by swarms of conventicles and by anti-Catholic mobs winked at and countenanced'.

It is true that these fanatics believed that there was a Popish Plot, and we may readily agree that the conduct of Henrietta Maria was injudicious in proselytising – though the King was a firm Anglican, and Archbishop Laud, whom she disliked, had persuaded more converts away from Rome than anyone. The 'Popish Plot' mentality was pure Puritan hysteria – like MacCarthyism or the Watergate hullabaloo in USA.

The Puritan attack on the consensus of the Church had been going on for three generations – propaganda, preachings, unlicensed Lectures; organisation, conventicles, semantics – they alone were the 'godly', the persecuted 'Saints'. Actually, Dr Morrill tells us, 'the scale of religious persecution under Laud was in fact quite limited; there were fewer deprivations and suspensions in the 1630s than in most other decades since the Reformation'. Laud had little justice done him in his day, and scant justice in history ever since.

Laud's innovations were reforms: he was a reformer. The Church had been gravely impoverished by the Reformation – even Christopher Hill shows that in his best book, *The Economic Condition of the Church*. The lands of the monasteries had all by now come down to the laity, mainly aristocracy and gentry; but they had also, by lay-impropriations, got hold of rectorial tithes all over the country (one motive of the Puritan-minded was to acquire more). Meanwhile, many of the clergy were impoverished, the churches neglected, often semi-ruinous, their interiors showing scars of 'reformation'; chancels open to animals, communion tables repositories for cloaks, hats, whatever.

Laud embarked on an heroic effort to restore and repair what he could: improve poor livings – as the Laudian Scudamores did – though only a few would restore tithes; repair the churches – as a good many were under his impulse; rail in the sanctuary and altars properly – as everywhere today; beautify the churches with stained glass, organs, etc. The Puritans hated it all. Intellectually and spiritually Laud was a much better Christian than they were. Take the cruel nonsense of Predestination which they were addicted to, consigning everybody to perdition except the Elect, i.e. themselves. Laud was able to reply to the ambitious, self-seeking Puritan politician, Lord Saye and Sele, 'almost all of them say that God from all eternity reprobates by far the greater part of mankind to eternal fire. Which opinion my very soul abominates.'

He was, we see, a humane and civilised man. All through, his efforts at reform were not only obstructed and misrepresented, but he was subjected to an incessant campaign of lies – as the Parliamentarian, Selden, admits – and personal vilification. The Puritans made him the most detested man in England; 'the sty of all pestilential filth', Sir Harbottle Grimston's phrase for him was one of the milder terms of the opprobrious abuse heaped upon him. He never replied, so far as I know; indeed, when recalcitrant ministers accepted the proper terms of their vocation, the Prayer Book – which Puritans vilified (today many Nonconformists use it) – Laud generously gave them prefer-ment. If not, not – quite fair.

Dr Morrill tells us that at once in 1640 Parliament was 'subjected to a pulpit oratory and to a petitioning campaign that called not for the restoration of the pre-Laudian order [which was in itself traditional, Laud an Elizabethan by birth and upbringing], but for the abolition of the entire ecclesiastical order and its reconstitution along pure Biblical lines'. They took no account of the fact that more than half of the counties petitioned on behalf of the Church they knew. The Puritans never represented the country; they were a minority bent on their unappetising revolution. Self-righteous Calamy was at least candid: they meant to 'reform the Reformation'.

Laud was the conservative reformer; Charles I was in entire agreement with him and urged him on in his good work. It is wonderful how much the poor archbishop achieved against such organised and vicious opposition – but it is his work that ultimately survived and prevailed.

[253]

Dr Morrill tells us that the constitutional points of disagreement were swamped by the religious issue, four times as many pamphlets devoted to the impeachment of the bishops as to the political issue of the Five obstreperous M.P.s. 'No self-doubt can be found among those who pushed forward towards godly reformation in 1642, as iconoclasts, as the protectors of illegal gathered churches, as campaigners for Presbyterianism', which the country never wanted and never took to, when imposed on it by the godly.

Naturally the Puritans, blinded by their fanaticism and self-conceit, could not understand the depth of the King's attachment to the Church. Dr Morrill speaks of their revolutionary claims to control both militia and executive as merely 'pragmatic responses to a King increasingly seen as deranged and incapable of governing, no longer a tyrant but a man incapable of discharging his trust'. This is just Puritan inability to understand anybody else's point of view; when the Scotch Presbyterian, Henderson, found the King more than capable of defending his religious position intellectually, it gave the humbug a virtual breakdown.

Charles I was far from 'deranged' or incapable of governing; it is true that he was rather impassive, and probably dragging his feet, hoping to out-wait the crisis, until people came to their senses. By 'discharging his trust', they wanted the King to underwrite their intolerable and intolerant (to him, understandably nasty) Puritanism. A cultivated and civilised man, he never had any intention of ruling as a Puritan king. How could he?

# Index

Abbot, George, archbishop, 10, 12
Adams, Mary, Ranter, 215
Aix-en-Provence, 37
Andover, 214
Antwerp, 105
Arundel, Thomas Howard, earl of, 92, 93, 97, 98, 105–6, 110
Arundel castle, 83, 152
Ashby-de-la-Zouch castle, 81
Astley, Sir Jacob, 32
Attaway, Mrs, Ranter, 215
Aubrey, John, 70, 71, 80, 84, 153, 159, 160, 188
Auckland castle, 8, 72, 120

Baillie, Robert, Scotch Presbyterian, 16, 17, 181
Banbury, 59
Bancroft, Richard, archbishop, 10, 11–12, 88, 94
Barnard, John, music collector, 124
Basing House, Hampshire, 73–5, 92
Bath, 159; – abbey, 44
Bauthumley, J., Ranter, 217
Baxter, Richard, 199–203, 223, 225
Baynton, Sir Edward, 85, 159
Beal, Mr, Puritan suicide, 202
Bedfordshire, 61
Beeston, Christopher, actor, 138
Bernini, G.L., 90, 108–9
Billing, Edward, Quaker, 221
Blackfriars theatre, 117, 125, 135, 138, 143, 144, 145, 148–9
Bolsover, Derbyshire, 83–4
Borders, war on, 5, 133, 141, 146, 154, 170, 185

Bower, Edward, painter, 230
Brampton Bryan castle, 42
Brasses, 60–61
Brereton, Sir William, Parliamentary commander, 77
Bridgnorth, 77, 200
Bridgwater, 76
Bristol, 64, 222
Britten, Benjamin, 131
Broghill, Roger Boyle, Lord, 156
Brome, Richard, dramatist, 139, 144–5
Broughton castle, 203
Browne, John, copyist, 116; –, Sir Richard, ambassador, 231
Buckden, Huntingdonshire, 12
Buckingham, George Villiers, duke of, 17, 90, 97, 102–5, 111, 133
Buckinghamshire, 58–9
Burgess, Cornelius, Puritan propagandist, 14–15, 31
Burghley, William Cecil, Lord, 68; – House, 68
Burrough, Edward, Quaker, 223
Bunyan, John, 223
Butler, Joseph, bishop, 228; –; Samuel, 158, 180, 187–93, 194, 241–3, 247, 248
Byron, John, Lord, 77, 82

Calamy, Edmund, preacher, 180, 245–6
Calvin, J., 2
Cambridge, 44–9, 104–5, 148, 180–1, 185, 201, 219
Canterbury, 215–6; – cathedral, 36–8, 118

[255]

Carew, Thomas, poet, 132, 145, 155, 164-5
Carleton, Sir Dudley, 94
Carlisle cathedral, 8-9; -, Lucy Hay, Lady, 141, 155
Carlyle, Thomas, 3
Cartmel priory, Lancashire, 30
Cartwright, William, poet, 147-8, 153, 163, 169
Castlemaine, Barbara Villiers, Lady, 70
Cavendish, Sir Charles, 84
Chapel Royal, 116, 118, 120, 123, 125, 126, 127
Charles I, 5, 12, 14, 18-19, 28, 41, 51, 61, 67, 70, 80, 89, 120, 133, 143, 147, 152, 166, 173, 175, 178, 183, 196, 213, 239, 247, 253; - and the arts, 90-3, 97-102, 108-14, 144, 165, 170; -, character of, 194-5; - and masques, 134-7; - and music, 119, 123; - and theatre, 140-1
Charles II, 67, 80, 99, 112, 161, 167, 172, 178, 187, 235; -, character of, 195, 248
Chester, 3, 77-8, 95, 199
Cheynell, Francis, fanatical divine, 83, 158
Chichester cathedral, 35-6, 118
Chillingworth, William, 83, 152
Churchill family, 82
Clarendon, Edward Hyde, Lord, 3-4, 32, 33, 87-9, 160, 161, 196, 251
Clarkson, Laurence, Ranter, 211-2, 215-7, 220
Clergy, extruded, 62-5
Cleveland, John, poet, 168, 180, 181, 183-5
Colchester, 78-9, 232
Cooper, Samuel, miniaturist, 187, 229-30
Coperario (John Cooper), composer, 118, 119, 127
Coppe, Abiezer, Ranter, 217
Corbet, Richard, bishop, 57-8, 59
Corfe castle, 81

Cornwall, 49-50, 60, 61, 71, 79, 120, 246
Cosin, John, bishop, 7-8, 22, 45, 64-5, 80
Cosyn, Benjamin, composer, 132
Cotton, Charles, poet, 172-3, 179; -, John, preacher, 213
Cowley, Abraham, poet, 185-7, 237-41
Cranborne manor, Dorset, 82
Critz, Emmanuel de, artist, 99, 109; -, John de, painter, 97
Cromwell, Oliver, 3, 24, 25, 47, 66, 67, 74-5, 80, 100, 115, 142, 168, 173, 175-9, 196, 200, 201, 202, 207, 208, 214, 224, 229-30, 232, 233-4; -, character of, 257-61; -, Richard, 234
Crook, John, Quaker, 219
Crowland abbey, 19-20, 58
Croydon palace, 72
Culmer, Richard, fanatic, 36-8

Dallam, Robert, organ-builder, 12, 43, 48
Davenant, John, bishop, 56; -, Sir William, poet, 139, 140-3, 164, 165
Davies, Lady Eleanor, nuisance, 27, 213
Denbigh castle, 78
Denham, Sir John, 143-4
Derby, James Stanley, earl of, 83, 172-3
Dering, Richard, composer, 116
Devizes, 83
Devonshire, 59, 82
D'Ewes, Sir Simonds, 149
Dieussart, F., sculptor, 110-1
Digby, Sir Kenelm, 96
Diggers, the, 209-12
Dobson, William, painter, 97, 229
Donne, John, 6-7
Dorset, 62
Dort, Synod of, 23, 56, 160
Dowsing, William, iconoclast, 45-9
Drake, Eleanor, Lady, 82; -, Sir Francis, 113

Dryden, John, 18, 248
Dugdale, Sir William, antiquarian, 4, 83
Duppa, Brian, bishop, 34, 62
Dürer, A., 105-6
Durham cathedral, 7-8, 72

East Anglia, 24, 53, 84, 247
Eccleshall castle, 72-3
Edgehill, 2-3, 17
Education, Restoration reaction in, 249
Eleanor crosses, 13-14
Eliot, Sir John, 111
Eliot, T.S., 52
Elizabeth I, 12, 68-9, 89, 101, 111, 113, 114, 126, 177, 189
Elizabethan architecture, 68; - drama, 117; - music, 117
Elizabeth, the 'Winter Queen', 111, 123
Eltham palace, 232
Ely cathedral, 24-5
Essex, 17, 23-4, 244, 245
Essex, Robert Devereux, earl of, 29, 59, 71
Evans, 'Arise', fanatic, 213
Evelyn, John, 78, 101, 231-5
Exeter cathedral, 32-3, 56

Fairclough, Samuel, persecutor of witches, 245-6
Fairfax, Thomas, Lord, 45, 179
Faithorne, William, the elder, engraver, 74-5
Falkland, Lucius Cary, Lord, 87, 88, 152, 157, 159, 185
Fanelli, F., sculptor, 110
Fanshawe, Sir Richard, ambassador, 166
Faringdon, 59
Farnham castle, 72
Ferrabosco, Alfonso, II, composer, 118, 127
Ferrar, Nicholas, 51
Fifth Monarchy men, 212-3, 242
Fox, George, Quaker, 221, 222, 223-5

Franklin, Edward, fanatic, 213

Gardiner, S.R., historian, 3, 227
Gascoigne, William, scientist, 152-3
Gell, Sir John, Parliamentarian commander, 28
Gentileschi, Orazio, 104
Gerbier, Sir Balthasar, art agent, 103
Germany, 227
Gibbons, Orlando, composer, 118
Glapthorne, Henry, dramatist, 170
Globe theatre, 117, 138
Gloucester cathedral, 30-1
Godolphin, Sidney, poet, 152, 159
Goldsmith's Company, 113
Gonzaga collection of paintings, 94, 102-3, 125
Greenwich palace, 69, 92, 109
Grenville, Sir Bevil, 169
Grindal, Edmund, archbishop, 12
Grotius, Hugo, 22
Gunton, Symon, antiquarian, 19-22

Hacket, John, bishop, 28
Hales, John, divine, 157, 159-60
Hall, Joseph, bishop, 22-3
Hampden, John, trouble-maker, 137, 175
Hampshire, 214
Hampton Court, 66, 100, 110, 115, 148, 170, 230
Harley, Sir Robert, iconoclast, 29, 30, 42
Harvey, Sir William, scientist, 2-3, 153, 187
Haselrig, Sir Arthur, Parliamentarian, 72
Hatton, Sir Christopher, 68-9
Haydock, Richard, artist, 45
Henderson, Alexander, Scotch divine, 17, 41, 254
Henrietta Maria, Queen, 66, 89, 92, 96, 113, 134, 135-6, 139, 147-8, 152, 165, 174, 231, 235, 252
Henry VIII, 6, 19, 112
Herbert, George, poet, 54-5, 127

Hereford cathedral, 29-30; -shire,
76, 199
Herrick, Robert, poet, 56-8, 161-3
Hertfordshire, 58
Heywood, Thomas, dramatist, 138
Hilton, John, composer, 129, 132
Hitler, Adolf, 1, 240
Hobbes, Thomas, 3, 110, 137, 142,
152, 191, 195-6, 197, 198, 199,
204-5, 208, 226, 249
Holdenby House, 18-19, 68-9
Holkham, Norfolk, 93
Hollar, Wenceslas, artist, 3, 36, 74,
194, 237
Honthorst, G. van, painter, 104
Hopkins, Matthew, 'Witch-finder
General', 245-8
Huntingdonshire, 60, 245
Hutchinson, Anne, 24; -, John,
regicide, 80-1, 96, 98-9, 107; -,
Lucy, 67, 85, 138, 209

Iconoclasm, 4, 5-61, 223
Imperialism, Puritan, 142-3, 177,
204, 224
Independents (Congregationalists),
197, 205
Ipswich, 53, 233
Ireton, Henry, Cromwellian general,
207-8

James I, 69, 102, 133, 148, 198, 247
Jeffries Anne, persecuted, 246
Jenkins, John, composer, 116, 128-9,
131-2
Jews, 177
Johnson, Robert, composer, 141
Johnson, Samuel, Dr., 28, 237
Johnson, Thomas, botanist, 152
Jones, Inigo, 9-10, 35, 74, 91-3, 104,
118, 132, 138, 151
Jonson, Ben, 84, 118, 132, 138, 144,
154-5, 163, 165
Jordan, Thomas, actor, 168
Juxon, William, archbishop, 27, 38,
71, 161, 248

Kenilworth castle, 70
Kent, 170, 244; Kentish Petition, 171
Kidderminster, 200
Killigrew, Thomas, 143
Kilpeck castle, 76
King, Henry, bishop and poet, 79,
166
King's Men, the, acting Company,
138, 140, 143, 148

Lambeth Palace, 11, 64, 71-2, 88
Lancashire, 83
Lanier, Nicholas, 94, 99, 100, 125-6,
141; - family, 94, 100-1, 125
Lathom House, 83
Lawes, Henry, composer, 3, 80, 123,
127, 129-31, 132, 142, 174-5; -,
William, composer, 3, 115, 117,
127-30, 133
Leeds, 50
Leicester, Robert Dudley, earl of, 70
Lely, Sir Peter, painter, 99, 170,
230-1
Le Sueur, Hubert, sculptor, 43, 109,
110
Lichfield, 221; - cathedral, 22, 27-8
Lilburne, John, Leveller, 206-7
Lilly, William, astrologer, 213
Lincoln, 72; - cathedral, 22, 27-8
Lisle, Sir George, 78-9; -, Robert
Sidney, Lord, 99
Little Gidding, 51-2
Locke, Matthew, composer, 142
London, 198, 232-3; Cheapside Cross,
13; City Guild of Musicians, 124-5;
St Paul's cathedral, 9, 13-14, 27,
175; -, Tower of, 3, 12, 50, 141,
206, 229, 234
Lostwithiel, 71
Louvre palace, 90; - gallery, 98, 100
Love, Christopher, trouble-maker, 14
Lucas, Sir Charles, Royalist
commander, 78-9
Ludlow castle, 80; -, Edmund,
regicide, 82, 235

Malmesbury, 59-60

Marshall, Stephen, preacher, 17–18, 180, 182, 190
Marston Moor, 24, 152, 183
Marten, Sir Henry, regicide, 80, 216
Marvell, Andrew, 166, 248
Mary I, 35; – Queen of Scots, 20, 78, 80
Maryland, 141
Masques, 118, 127, 129, 138, 139, 153
Massachusetts, 24, 161, 190, 212, 237
Mather, Cotton, 212; –, Increase, 202
Mazarin, Cardinal, 90–98, 229
Mildmay, Sir Anthony, 101–2
Millenarians, 212–3
Milton, John, 10, 16, 47–8, 54, 80, 127, 131, 136, 163, 176–7, 183, 187, 198, 199, 201, 205, 212, 213, 230, 234, 235–6, 248; – on Westminster Assembly of Divines, 188; – on Parliament, 192
Miniatures, 106–7
Minster, Kent, 38
Monck, George, General, 234
Montgomery castle, 80
More, Henry, philosopher, 201
Morley, George, bishop, 72, 231; –, Herbert, Governor of the Tower, 234
Muggleton, Lodowick, fanatic, 218–21; Muggletonians, 214, 218–21, 225

Nalton, James, 'the Weeping Prophet', 202
Navy, Royal, 175
Nayler, James, Quaker, 222–3
Newark castle, 80
Newcastle, William Cavendish, duke of, 80, 84, 140
New England, 197, 204, 227, 234
New York, 114
Nonsuch palace, 69–70
North, Roger, on music, 125, 132
Northamptonshire, 85
Norwich cathedral, 22–3
Nottingham castle, 80; – shire, 77, 84, 85

Noy, William, attorney-general, 137
Nuneham Courtenay, 93

Oatlands palace, 70
Organs, church, 7, 9, 17, 29, 31, 36, 37, 39, 43, 46, 48, 51, 61, 115, 119, 120–1
Orme, Sir Humphrey, 21
Osborne, Dorothy, 18
Overton, Richard, Leveller, 209; –, Robert, Fifth Monarchy man, 214
Oxford, 10, 20, 29, 44–5, 49, 95, 97, 102, 108, 109, 115, 141, 143, 153, 173, 180, 186, 217, 228, 232, 248; All Souls, 160, 209, 230; Christ Church, 39–40, 127, 147, 148; St John's, 11, 27

Paris, 90, 229, 231
Parker, Matthew, archbishop, 12, 71–2
Parliament, the Long, 12, 13, 14, 24, 25, 30, 33, 68, 88, 103, 112, 141, 148–50, 168–9, 171, 173, 181, 183, 184, 205, 208, 216, 226, 239; Cromwell's 'Parliaments', 178, 190; –, Restoration, 203
Paulet family, 73, 75
Peake, Sir Robert, print seller, 74
Pennsylvania, 49
Peterborough cathedral, 19–22, 61
Peters, Hugh, preacher, 16, 66, 73, 76, 82, 190
Petre, William, Lord, 64
Philip IV, 90, 98, 103–4
Plate, royal, 112–4
Pontefract castle, 70–1
Popham, Alexander, Parliamentarian colonel, 31
Porter, Endymion, connoisseur, 103, 140, 165
Portland, Richard Weston, earl of, 35, 95
Prado gallery, Madrid, 98
Pratt, Sir Roger, architect, 228
Prayer Book, 16, 61–2, 127, 141, 171, 181, 197, 231, 232

Presbyterians, 196-7, 199-203, 205, 236
Prideaux, John, bishop, 121
Prynne, William, 3, 10, 11, 46, 133, 134-6, 139
Puddletown, Dorset, 52
Puritan Music, 122-4
Pym, John, 16, 141, 142, 147, 149, 152, 183

Quakers, 218, 219, 220, 221-5, 233
Quarles, Francis, poet, 153, 163-4
Queen's Men, the, acting Company, 143, 144

Raglan castle, 76
Raleigh, Walter, dean, 65
Randolph, Thomas, poet, 153
Ranters, 211, 214-8
Reading, 231-2
Reeve, John, Muggletonian, 214, 218-20, 225
Reformation, in England, the, 6, 107, 108
Regalia, 15-16, 112
Remy (Remigius Van Leemput), painter, 101
Restoration, the, 28, 38, 72-3, 76, 86, 99, 109, 115, 122, 143, 179, 187, 199, 203, 221, 231, 234-5, 248-9
Revolution, Chinese, 1, 2, 226; -, French, 1, 12, 196, 208, 226; -, Russian, 1, 2, 18, 39, 88, 194, 212, 226, 236
Rich, Nathaniel, Fifth Monarchy man, 208, 232
Richmond palace, 69
Robins, John, Ranter, 214
Rochester cathedral, 36
Rogers, John, Ranter, 214
Rose castle, Cumberland, 8
Rouse, Francis, Puritan, 16, 123
Rubens, P.P., 90, 93-4, 102, 104
Rupert, Prince, 111, 248

Russia, 1-2, 39, 136, 179, 197, 210, 221, 225
Rye, 231

Sabbatarianism, 137
St Andrew's cathedral, 5-6
St David's cathedral, 31, 120
St Ives, Cornwall, 61
St James's palace, 92, 95, 109-10
St John, Oliver, Parliamentarian, 21
Salisbury, 55; - cathedral, 33-4, 120, 126-7
Sanderson, Robert, bishop, 72
Sandys, George, poet, 123, 130
Saye and Sele, William Fiennes, Lord, 27, 161, 203-4, 253
Sayebrook, Conn., 27
Scarborough castle, 80
Scone abbey, Scotland, 6
Scot, Thomas, regicide, 71
Scotland, 120, 178, 227, 251; -, Reformation in, 5-6
Scots, the, 7, 16-17, 89, 141, 176, 178, 183
Scudamore, John, Lord, 29, 30
Sculpture, 90, 104, 107, 108
Selden, John, scholar, 4, 82, 93-4, 167, 181, 187, 189-90, 196, 197, 198, 241
Shakespeare, William, 6, 60, 100, 117, 138, 141, 146, 163
Sheffield castle, 80
Sheldon, Gilbert, archbishop, 39, 45, 195, 248
Sherborne castle, 83
Sherfield, Henry, iconoclast, 55
Ship Money, 136-7, 175
Shirley, James, dramatist, 139-40, 167-8; -, Sir Robert, church builder, 50
Shrewsbury castle, 80
Smectymnuus, 180-1
Somerset, 61, 85; - House, 41, 66-7, 92, 100, 110-11
Somner, William, antiquary, 37
Southwell minster, 44
Spain, 90, 102, 103, 166, 224

Sports, Book of, 137, 180
Spurstow, William, preacher, 180–1
Stafford castle, 81
Stalin, J., 1, 179–80, 227, 235
Staunton Harold, Leics., 50
Sterne, Richard, archbishop, 64
Stone, Nicholas, sculptor, 95, 102, 108, 118
Stowe-Nine-Churches, Northants, 108
Strafford, Thomas Wentworth, earl of, 10, 12, 141, 149, 168, 184
Strode, William, poet, 55–6, 148
Stuart, Lord Bernard, 95
Stubbes, Philip, trouble-maker, 126
Stud, Royal, 60
Suckling, Sir John, poet, 141, 145–7, 153, 154–6, 157–9
Sudeley castle, 83
Suffolk, 52–4, 216, 232, 248
Sussex, 60, 83, 244
Swift, Thomas, Royalist cleric, 78
Symonds, Richard, antiquarian, 58–9, 76, 101

Tapestries, 37, 100, 102; –, Mortlake, 229
Taylor, Jeremy, 160–1
Taynton church, Glos., 50
Theobalds House, Herts., 68
Thorney abbey, Cambs., 30
Thornborough, John, bishop, 28, 29, 120
Thurloe, John, 229
Titian, 90, 91, 95, 98, 102, 103
Tomkins, Thomas, composer, 119–22; – family, 120–2, 128
Tonkin, Thomas, antiquary, 49–50
Townsend, Aurelian, poet, 129, 153
Tradescant, John, collector, 104
Tregeagle, John, Parliamentarian J.P., 246
Truro cathedral, 8

United States, 177, 250

Van Dyke, Sir Anthony, 11, 91, 93–6, 108, 174, 186
Vane, Sir Henry, 10, 183
Velasquez, D., 90, 98
Venn, John, regicide, 14
Vianen, C. van, jeweller, 112

Walker, Robert, painter, 230
Waller, Edmund, poet, 143, 173–9; –, Sir William, Parliamentary general, 30
Wardour castle, Wilts., 81–2
Warwick, Robert Rich, earl of, 17, 203, 204
Washington, D.C., 95, 99
Webb, John, architect, 142, 144, 228
Webbe, Thomas, Ranter, 215
Weelkes, Thomas, composer, 118
Wells, 65; – cathedral, 15, 31
Wentworth Woodhouse, 93
Westminster, 61, 62, 180, 206; – Abbey, 13, 15–17, 112, 132, 181, 235; – Assembly of Divines, 16, 180–2
Whalley, Edmund, regicide, 233, 234
White, John, colonial promoter, 237
Whitehall palace, 42, 66, 92, 100, 102, 134, 235
Whitelocke, Bulstrode, lawyer, 82, 116
Whitgift, John, archbishop, 72
Wigmore castle, 42
Wildman, Sir John, Leveller, 207, 208–9
Wilkins, John, bishop, 23, 199
Williams, John, archbishop, 51, 186
Wiltshire, 85, 93, 215
Wilton house, 93, 127
Winchester, 72; – castle, 73; – cathedral, 34–5, 61, 95, 107
Windsor, 160; – castle, 14, 42–3, 66, 112–3, 235, 248
Wingfield manor, Derbys., 78
Winstanley, Gerrard, Digger, 211–2, 216
Witches, Puritan mania about, 163, 202–3, 243–8

Wither, George, poet, 15, 43, 101, 143
Worcester, Edward Somerset,
    marquis of, 76; – battle of, 172;
    – cathedral, 28–9, 120, 121, 232;
    – shire, 85
Wren, Sir Christopher, 3, 15, 27, 91,
    151, 228; –, Matthew, bishop, 3,
    43, 229

Yarmouth, 24
Yaxley church, Suffolk, 21
Young, Thomas, preacher, 180
York, 9; – cathedral, 9; – House,
    London, 102, 103, 104, 105, 232